1 MONTH OF
FREE
READING

at
www.ForgottenBooks.com

By purchasing this book you are eligible for one month membership to ForgottenBooks.com, giving you unlimited access to our entire collection of over 1,000,000 titles via our web site and mobile apps.

To claim your free month visit:
www.forgottenbooks.com/free49384

ISBN 978-0-483-82712-7
PIBN 10049384

AUTOBIOGRAPHY

OF

CHARLES FORCE DEEMS

D.D., LL.D.

PASTOR OF THE CHURCH OF THE STRANGERS, NEW YORK CITY
AND PRESIDENT OF THE AMERICAN INSTITUTE
OF CHRISTIAN PHILOSOPHY

AND

MEMOIR

BY HIS SONS

REV. EDWARD M. DEEMS, A.M., PH.D.

AND

FRANCIS M. DEEMS, M.D., PH.D.

NEW YORK   CHICAGO   TORONTO

Fleming H. Revell Company

Publishers of Evangelical Literature

AUTOBIOGRAPHY

OF

CHARLES FORCE DEEMS

D.D., LL.D.

PASTOR OF THE CHURCH OF THE STRANGERS, NEW YORK CITY
AND PRESIDENT OF THE AMERICAN INSTITUTE
OF CHRISTIAN PHILOSOPHY

AND

MEMOIR

BY HIS SONS

REV. EDWARD M. DEEMS, A.M., PH.D.

AND

FRANCIS M. DEEMS, M.D., PH.D.

NEW YORK   CHICAGO   TORONTO

Fleming H. Revell Company

Publishers of Evangelical Literature

THE NEW YORK TYPE-SETTING COMPANY
THE CAXTON PRESS

IN FILIAL LOVE THIS BOOK IS DEDICATED TO

OUR MOTHER

WHOSE UNSELFISH DEVOTION, TENDER SYMPATHY, AND HELP-
FUL ENCOURAGEMENT STIMULATED AND SUSTAINED
OUR FATHER IN ALL HIS ASPIRATIONS
AND ACHIEVEMENTS

PREFACE

IN preparing this volume, the editors have been impelled by filial love, indeed, but more especially by the conviction that Dr. Deems was a unique character, who lived through the larger part of the greatest century of the ages and did original work for society. We have been influenced also by the conviction that when the reader sees how Dr. Deems rose to a sublime life by perseverance, industry, and faith in God, he too will be encouraged to make his life sublime.

If the autobiographical notes appear at times too complacent, let all blame attach to the editors and not to Dr. Deems, for he wrote for his family only. In our work we have omitted his sermons and many letters and articles written for the press, because of the abundance of such materials, there being enough for another volume. Nevertheless, whenever we could tell the story of his life in his own language we have done so, thus striving to let him speak for himself.

Being his sons, we have attempted no elaborate estimate of Dr. Deems's character and work, but have either quoted from the estimates of others or left this matter to the judgment of the reader. We take this opportunity to thank all who have sent us letters or other material, thereby aiding us in our work.

We now send forth this book on its mission of love, trusting that it may enable our father, though dead, yet to speak.

EDWARD M. DEEMS.
HORNELLSVILLE, N. Y.
FRANCIS M. DEEMS.
NEW YORK CITY.

7

CONTENTS

9

PART II. MEMOIR

ILLUSTRATIONS

A Little Letter in Rhyme

Dear friend,

   The world is wide
      In time and tide
      And — God is guide;
Then do not hurry

That man is blest
      Who does his best,
      And — leaves the rest;
Then do not worry.

      Yours faithfully
Charles F. Deems

PART I

AUTOBIOGRAPHY

CHAPTER I

CHILDHOOD, 1820–30

M Y children desire some autobiographical sketches. As permitted I will write them; the writing may do me good, and what is written may entertain my family. But most sincerely I do not believe that there will be a hundred people in the world who will have the least curiosity about my life fifty years after my death.

I am told that I was born in the city of Baltimore, Md., on Monday morning, December 4, 1820. The house in which this event, so important to myself, occurred is still (1886) standing on Lower Water Street, near what is called the "Marsh Market." Baltimore was at that time a little city as compared with its present dimensions. My very earliest recollections were bounded by the market of which I have spoken and Light Street.

One of the first things of which I have any recollection is that of being in love, of which I shall have more to say farther on in these notes. My second recollection is of attending a circus. My nurse was a colored girl of athletic strength but peculiar gait, the latter owing to a dislocation of her left thigh. This circumstance did not seem at all to diminish either her strength or her celerity, while it did afford me a capital saddle-place. Her splendid name was Lucretia, which the family dreadfully abbreviated into "Creesh." She was entirely de-

17

voted to me, and, I believe, loved me intensely, unselfishly, and constantly. Her name for me was "Bebe," which, I suppose, was a softening of babe, a name too hard to be given to her little darling. Creesh was accustomed to snatch me up and toss me upon her hip, which I learned to mount with the agility of a monkey, and then she would go tramping through the streets to any kind of gathering, show, meeting, or other collection of people which interested her. She had a negro's delight in spectacular performances, and cultivated an acquaintance with all the showmen that visited the city. She seemed to have a free entrée to all circuses but one. I recollect that upon that occasion, when she sailed up to the door like an ostrich with her little Arab at her side, she was refused admittance without pay. She indignantly sailed away. "Me pay? You not let this chile go in that circus? No, sir; I would not go in a circus so mean that would not let me go in without pay!" And she flew back home to tell the family of the indignity which had been put upon Bebe and her. She did it with a fiery eloquence that brought the whole family into roars of laughter. My aunt Juliet, with tears of fun running down her cheeks, said, "Do hush, Creesh; you are as good as a circus yourself." But before this she and I had visited these shows, and once or twice I had been put upon the ponies to ride. I recollect that on one occasion, when I was making my round, the life was nearly frightened out of me by a loose monkey jumping on the pony behind me and striving to clasp me around the waist.

The family, of which Lucretia formed no inconsiderable part, was small. It consisted of my father, my mother, and her half-sister, who was with my mother from her earliest married life. My father, George W. Deems, was of a Dutch family, that came from Holland and settled in Maryland somewhere between Baltimore and Reisterstown. The original name, De Heems, eventually was shortened into Deems.

I have heard my father tell that his grandmother had spanked him soundly for speaking English, so perseveringly did she hold on to her Dutch. I never saw my grandparents on either side. I know nothing of my father's family above him, except that they were farmers and his mother was a Cole. If there be any great ancestral line I know nothing of it, and, having had an honest, excellent, and revered father and, as far as I know, plain, honest, and decent Dutch grandparents, I do not care to go any farther back. I might go farther and fare worse.

My mother's maiden name was Mary Roberts. She was the daughter of the Rev. Zachary Roberts, a Methodist minister, who lived on the Eastern Shore of Maryland, and who was, I am told, a cousin of the late Robert Roberts, one of the bishops of the Methodist Episcopal Church. My mother's grandfather, James Roberts, was a farmer.

When my father and mother were married, August 22, 1811, they were young and poor, but giddy and gay. My mother was especially devoted to dancing. She was a woman of great natural endowments, which largely overcame her want of culture. In the early part of this century girls in her condition of life had little schooling. But whatever she undertook she did thoroughly, and by employing what time she could command from her domestic duties in the reading of books she became exceedingly well informed and acquired a literary taste. She devoted herself to religion with that earnestness which distinguished her in every department of her activity. I have heard my father say that it shocked him greatly when my mother became religious. He thought it would cut them off from all the pleasures of their lives. He became very unhappy. But one day as he passed her door he heard his wife in earnest prayer to God, pleading as for the very life of her husband. It convinced him that true religion but deepened and heightened and purified the affection of a wife for her husband, and the thrilling tones of my mother's prayer so followed him that he determined to become religions; he began to attend church. One night, during a revival in a Methodist church in Exeter Street, Baltimore, he had a profound sense of his need of a Saviour, but, being surrounded by his companions in pleasure, he had not the courage to go forward to the "altar," as it was called, when the invitation was given to the penitents to present themselves. When one of the ministers came to him as he sat in his seat, betraying his agitation in his manner, and invited him to go and kneel with the other penitents, he made the excuse that he had promised himself he never would become religious in that way, and that to go forward now would be to tell a lie. The good old minister replied: "My young friend, count that promise among your other sins, and go forward now and have the forgiveness of all." The suddenness of the reply brought him to his feet, and he bowed with the other suppliants. But while engaged in prayer he heard a voice next to him which he seemed to recognize, and, looking up, beheld the very man whose presence in the assembly had kept my father from earlier doing his duty; but when he had come to the point of discharging that duty his friend immediately followed.

One of the first things my father and mother did after his conversion was to erect a family altar, and from that time until his death my father carefully held domestic services, which no business was allowed to interrupt. All visitors were invited to join in them, and at that home altar I have heard many of the most notable Methodist ministers and laymen offer prayer.

In addition to my father and mother there was, as I have already stated, an aunt, Miss Juliet Roberts, my mother's half-sister, who came very early into the family, being younger than my mother. She remained while we kept together, and at the breaking up of the family went with me to Carlisle when

I went to college. She was a devoted Christian maiden, and while I write these reminiscences (1886) she is still living in Baltimore, and spent last winter with me in New York, her plain little Methodist bonnet and general drab and Quaker appearance attracting attention to the exquisite, neat little lady wherever she went. My parents had had a daughter born to them. They named her Josephine, from my mother's admiration of the wife of Napoleon Bonaparte. She died in infancy.

After an interval of nearly eight years I made my appearance. As children came so slowly in our family, my parents loaded me down with names. They called me Charles Alexander Force. I do not know what friend bore my first name; it was some one with whom my parents were intimate. The Alexander was for a Mr. Alexander Gaddess, who dealt in marbles and monuments. He was an excellent man, at whose house I recollect to have taken tea frequently with my parents in my childhood. I visited him on the same spot when I was fifty years old. The other name came from the Rev. Manning Force, a Methodist minister, at one time exceedingly popular in Baltimore and Philadelphia. He was an extraordinarily large man. His manners were very pleasing, and that acquired him a reputation he could never have gained by his pulpit talents. He is said to have had two sermons, upon which he played variations. The divisions of one were "The World," "The Flesh," and "The Devil," and the divisions of the other, "The Father," "The Son," and "The Spirit." That may have been a joke perpetrated by one of his clerical brethren who could not make women and children love him as we all loved "Uncle Force."

On this matter of naming children I have held forth elsewhere. Parents do not stop to think of the effect which a name may have. The earliest display of shrewdness upon my part which I can now recollect was in the change of my name. I did not come to be a large boy before I found that my initials spelled c-a-f, and I knew that if I entered school with those initials it would not be a week before some other boy would perceive the effect of the collocation of the letters, and that then there would begin a persecution to terminate only with my life. So as soon as I learned to write I signed my name, "C. M. F." I never told my parents the secret reason of the change, and never have spoken or written of it before the writing of these lines. I justified myself to the family by saying that Alexander was too big a name for a little boy, and, besides, that I thought "Uncle Force" would rather I should have his whole name. Their affection for him made this really quite an argument, and so I bore the name through college. A few years after I dropped the "M.," and so have passed through public life with three initials instead of four, and a hundred times have wished they were only two.

I have only three recollections connected with my first residence. That of the circus I have already narrated. I am not sure whether it preceded another event, namely, my falling in love. I was an exceedingly young man, wearing a little frock, because I had not attained to the dignity of pantaloons. She was a very lovely little lady, but, as almost always happens in the case of first love, she was several years older than her admirer. Her name was Sarah Ridgeway, and her father lived opposite our home. There was a garden attached to her house, and I used to persuade her to come out and sit there and talk with me.

More than a half of a century has intervened between those little garden scenes and the time that I am writing, but I recollect as distinctly as if it were yesterday how I sat by her side, how she held my little hand in hers and talked to me, and how my little heart filled almost to bursting with adoration of her charms, and how, because I could not yet speak plainly,

I called her "Lallie." More powerful passions have swayed me since, and I have gained a more manly, profound, exalted affection for her who has been my fellow-traveler through more than half of life's journey; but never did I have a sweeter, tenderer, truer sentiment than my infantile affection for "Lallie" Ridgeway.

A third recollection comes to me. It was the beginning of my literary pursuits. As touching letters I was a slow and stupid child. At one time it was feared that I never could learn the English alphabet. When that was finally mastered, it was several years before I could at all spell, and then there was a long lapse of time between that and my discovery of the possibility of reading. Both these events are as plain to my memory as if they had been two epileptic fits. My father, my mother, and my aunt Juliet in turn showed me letters of all kinds and colors in books and newspapers and placards. At last it was determined to send me to a little school, taught by an excellent lady, whose name was Oldham and who resided in a little house on Upper Water Street, near Light Street. She was very kind, and I worked hard. At last I learned to spell a number of words of one syllable. I kept the precious secret to myself for weeks. At last I ascended to dissyllables.

These steps in education were taken in Comly's spelling-book. How fresh in memory is my own copy! When I learned to spell "baker," "cider," etc., I could hold my secret no longer. My faithful Creesh was accustomed to take me to school and carry me home. One day when my enthusiastic pedagogue came for me, as we passed out of the gate I said, "Creesh, I can spell!"

Her reply was, "Bebe, hush! you know you must not tell stories!" Poor thing! although she possessed no literary acquirements, she used to stand by in an agony of interest while the family attempted to teach me my letters. I can recollect to this day her look of mingled love and despair when she saw how unavailing were the efforts of my father and mother and aunt Juliet to initiate "the sweetest child that ever was born " into the secrets of literature. No wonder that after such sights at home Creesh felt doubtful of such a huge statement as that "I could spell in two syllables." She exclaimed, "Bebe, you can't learn!"

"Yes, I can, though," said I; "you try me." She incon. tinently sat down on the curbstone and took me in her lap. I opened the spelling-book and turned to the place. On the left-hand page was the picture of a whale, on the right-hand rose the column of dissyllables; I put my left finger on the first and began to spell. Now the fun of the whole scene was that Creesh didn't know a capital " B " from a moss-rose, and she was the examiner of my literary acquirements. But Creesh had acute ears; if it sounded all right she passed it; so when I commenced "b-a-k-e-r," "c-i-d-e-r," at each letter her great eyes grew greater. She felt that that was really spelling "baker" and "cider," and the two words were very familar to Creesh. She used to go often to the baker's, and not infrequently she imbibed cider as a favorite beverage. I was about half-way through the third word when my black ostrich caught me up and, flinging me upon her hip, tore down the street like some. thing wild. Now it so happened that the entire family were assembled around a roll of carpet which was to be laid. Creesh burst in. She was accustomed to call the white members of the family by the names I called them. She went through the row like a flash. "Fazzer! muzzer! aunt Julet! Bebe kin spell!"

"Hush, Creesh!" said my aunt Juliet, who was often very impatient. "Here you are with one of your yarns again."

"I 'clare to gracious, he *kin* spell! You t'inks dis chile a fool, but he ain't none!"

My mother, who was concerned about the laying of her carpet, carefully interposed, "Hush, Creesh, be quiet!"

"But, muzzer, I ain't gwine to be quiet! Bebe kin spell, and you all fixin' the carpet when Bebe kin spell, and you ain't hearin' him!"

My father said, "Son, have you learned to spell?"

"Yes, sir!"

"Well, now let us hear you begin."

So I was placed upon the roll of carpet, and the family immediately grouped around me.

I have stood a good many tests since that, but few things ever tried my nerves so much. I was afraid that in my excitement I should fail. That would put Creesh in trouble and spoil my reputation for veracity, and, behind it all, I had a feeling that if I failed now I never would be able again to spell in dissyllables. But I commanded myself enough to go down the entire "baker" and "cider" column. The gratification of my family was intense. My father has since that held a volume of my writings in his hands, but I do not think that I ever gave him greater delight. Before the admiring eyes of my fond mother and aunt there stretched vistas of great literary acquirements for the beloved boy, and I can hardly keep the tears back as I now recall the face of poor Creesh. Her eyes stretched till the whites were startling to behold; her mouth opened almost from ear to ear, and the delight of her soul was so great that it seemed as though she would grow frantic. After the home triumph she caught me up and sailed round the whole neighborhood, exhibiting me at every house as the Bebe who could "spell in two syllables."

While I was still quite young my parents moved to Upper Water Street. It was a pleasant residence. I have very few memories of what happened there, but there are a few things important. I remember that I still sucked my thumb, and the family had great difficulty in breaking me of the habit. I remember my chagrin, after I had been thought to have stopped, at my mother looking out from the window and seeing me as I

sat in the door, having for the moment resumed my old comfort. Her upbraiding me for want of firmness in resisting the
temptation stung me to the very quick.

I recollect also that it was at this residence that, when some
money had been given me, I failed to resist the temptation to
make a purchase of something good to eat on a Sunday afternoon. The scorpion lashes of my conscience for this act I
shall never forget. Mingled with them also was the shame of
having been detected, and by my mother. Her good opinion
was my heaven; she stood to me a representative of the purity
as well as the providence of God. My mental suffering, and
the correction which she administered, effectually cured me of
all Sunday purchases, and from that day to this I have never
bought anything on Sunday except what seemed to be necessary medicines.

I have another remembrance of this residence. There was
high political excitement. Andrew Jackson and John Quincy
Adams were candidates for the Presidency. I was a strong
Adams boy, just because I had heard ugly campaign stories
about General Jackson. I could not read. I was too small
to attend any meeting. My recollection is confined to certain
noises made in the streets at night.

I also distinctly recollect that the watchmen of the city used
to cry the hour. Sometimes I would be awakened and a great
awe would come upon me as I heard the watchman cry, "It
is—ho!—three o'clock, Sunday morning! All's well!" That
seemed to be a municipal regulation so that the wakefulness of
the watchmen of the city might be secured, for if a watchman
failed to make his cry any household on his beat could report him.

The most beautiful remembrance I have of this residence
is a visit of John Summerfield to my mother. In 1860 I embodied that remembrance in a letter to my dear friend, the
Rev. Dr. Sprague, for his "Annals of the American Pulpit."
As I cannot repeat it any better, I insert the letter here:

"MY DEAR SIR: Among the very first of my recollections of men, and certainly of Methodist ministers, is of John Summerfield. Amid all subsequent studies, travels, labors, joys, and sorrows there has followed me the serene image of his winning manners and his extraordinary face—a face so full of strange beauty and a suppressed pain. None of the extant portraits I have been able to examine presents that remarkable face as it has dwelt in my memory. One is so much softer and more girlish, and another is, especially about the mouth, so much coarser, than the original. The expression of a tugging pain, which he seemed to be perpetually holding down by the main force of his will, as a man would hold a wolf which he was barely able to master, kept my childish heart in awe before the feeble, strong man. And yet something about him so drew my heart that all toys and sports would be left at his approach, that I would find myself unconsciously at his side. It seemed so strange that a man whose name was in all mouths, and whose wondrous utterances in the pulpit, although beyond my comprehension, I could not fail to see producing great effects upon the grown people around me and exerting a magnetism over my heart, could be playful; and yet, when a blister was drawing on his chest, I have known him to sit at the fireside of my father's house and for a quarter of an hour at a time, with raillery and badinage, exert himself to arouse me to a controversy and to provoke me to give 'as good as he sent.' But he always had the upper hand, for though, when sometimes stung, I was willing to reply perhaps impertinently, I could never look into his eyes, which had a peculiar and not always angelic expression, without dropping the weapons of my childish repartee.

"It was my blessed mother who drew him to our house, and who has since rejoined him in the city of our God. Her peculiar, sympathetic nature created a strong tie between them, and her determined will and strong faith made her such a female friend as Summerfield always needed and always appreciated. She was like an older sister to Summerfield, and, I believe, made strong prayers for him daily and almost hourly. For a time, while in Baltimore, he had his lodgings with Dr. Baker, I think, on the corner of Charles and Lexington streets. On one occasion I accompanied my mother to see him, after he had been confined several days. Not being allowed to go into the sick-chamber, I was left to amuse myself with a number of toys in the sitting-room below. It seemed a long time before my mother returned, and I can now distinctly recall her expression of sorrow for the sufferings of her friend, and the elevated, saintly joy which the interview seemed to have afforded her. Thus upon young and old he exerted the power of his pure spirit. I heard him preach in what the children of my acquaintance were accustomed to call 'The Round Church,' on the corner of Sheaf and Lombard streets. On this occasion his strength failed before the completion of his discourse, and he dropped his handkerchief as a signal for the uprising of the orphan children, whose cause he was pleading. The remembrance of his words and tones, his gracefulness, his exhaustion, his lovingness, all united with the silent standing up of the children to create a most thrilling sensation.*

"The last time I can recollect having seen him in public was at the preaching of a sermon in Dr. Breckenridge's church, in Eastern Baltimore Street. A large body of military was present. I recall not a word of the discourse, and only have in my remembrance the contrast between the helmeted and

* Upon reflection, I think I may have confounded two things. I heard the sermon, and I also heard Summerfield preach in that church, which belonged, I believe, to the Baptist denomination; but whether I heard that sermon in that church I do not so well remember.

uniformed soldiery and the serene, placid, pure young preacher, who stood up amid them, setting the story of the cross to the music of his intonations, and telling it with the ardor of his elevated and holy enthusiasm; and I remember how deeply I felt his irrepressible devotion to the ministry, by a remark of my mother as we were threading our way out through the crowd: 'Dear fellow, three blister-plasters on him, and he talking so like an angel!'

"The most vivid picture before me is Summerfield's last visit to my father's house. After an earnest conversation with my mother about matters of religion and the church, which I could not understand, he turned to me, and commenced, in his playful way, to get up a battle. 'And, Charlie, what is your middle name?' 'Why, Uncle Summerfield, I told you long ago, and you ought to remember.' 'Oh, I am such a forgetful fellow, please tell me again.' And I told him again. 'Frosty! Frosty! What a cold name for a warm boy!' 'Not Frosty, Uncle Summerfield, not Frosty; you know as well as I do that it is not Frosty.' 'Do tell me again! Sister Deems, am I growing old and deaf?' And so for a long time we had it, and I never could determine whether he really did misunderstand me, or was merely making game of me. At last he dropped it all, and calling me to him, told me that he was going away, perhaps never to return, and that he wished to pray with my mother and me before we parted. We knelt, my mother at her own chair, and I beside Mr. Summerfield's. His intonations and emphasis were always peculiar to my ear, and especially on this occasion. I paid little attention to the prayer until it became personal to the family. He prayed for my father, and then with what tender, loving tones for my mother, that, whereas to him, a stranger in a strange land, she had been such a comfort, so her boy might, everywhere in life, find friends to sustain and console him. And then he interlaced his fingers, and bringing his hand like a band over my head, he prayed most impressively and especially for me, that God would call me to the work of the ministry. Up from under these hands I peeped, child as I was, to see how he looked, and down into my heart there sank a picture whose lines are as sharp and whose coloring as fresh this day as they were the day it took its place in the gallery of my memory. Just in that picture, and with that look, I have preserved Summerfield to myself. It was a look of awe, of gratitude, of exaltation, and of tenderness. He seemed so full of the thought of the solemnity of talking with God, and the pain of parting from a cherished friend, of gratitude to God for putting him into the ministry of Jesus, and an appreciation of the grandeur of that work, and a feeling of tenderness to all who had loved him therein, and a sense of the responsibility of invoking a blessing even upon a boy! The face was lovely and great and luminous.

" He arose, and with humid eyes left us, never to return. And my mother sat and wept. And I was thoughtful. I did not like that prayer, dear Dr. Sprague. I did not say in my heart, ' Amen;' for I did not want to preach the gospel with blister-plasters on my back and breast. And in after years, when the question of the ministry came home to my conscience, I had great disturbance lest my call might be only from Summerfield and not also from my God.

" I have written these paragraphs to present an account of the impression this blessed young minister of Jesus made upon women and children, that being, in my humble judgment, the best criterion known to men of the real character of their fellows.

" I am, my dear sir, most sincerely yours,

" C. F. DEEMS."

CHAPTER II

From some personal recollections, dated May 10, 1839, written just before leaving college, the following extracts are made.

IN May of 1830 my mother and myself paid a visit to Philadelphia, to the family of the Rev. Manning Force, from whom I received my middle name. Being only nine years of age, of course I remember but little of the city, and need only record the recollection I have of the Rev. Dr. Sargeant and his kind family. The doctor has since deceased. He was struck with paralysis while preaching. While in Philadelphia my mother felt the first symptoms of the disease which terminated in her death. What that disease was I have never been able to learn.

On my return from Philadelphia I was placed in the school of the Rev. V. R. Osborn. I can never forget the love which I entertained for this gentleman; mild and benignant, he won my esteem, and inspired in me an affection for himself and his family which will last forever. He was in Baltimore some time before he brought on his family from New England, and he treated me as kindly as though I had been his son. This familiarity with our family attached him to us all, and I looked upon him more as a relative than a schoolmaster.

[A break in the autobiographical notes occurs at this point, but the substance of the incident whose close is narrated in the next paragraph we give from our recollection of Dr.

Deems's account of it. It appears that in a hall in Baltimore there was held a public competition, by boys from the schools of the city, for a gold medal to be awarded to the youth who should deliver the best declamation. Among other competitors appeared Charles Deems, of Mr. Osborn's school. When his name was called, with great inward trepidation he stepped forward and delivered his declamation with all the energy and oratorical effect that he could command.—Ed.]

With the closing words, "A patriot Tell, a Bruce of Bannockburn," I sank back to my seat perfectly exhausted. The judges communed for a few minutes, when the president of the board announced that, with but one single opposing vote, I was declared victor. The loud expression of congratulation which greeted the announcement was the sweetest music that has ever fallen on my ear. From the hall I hastened to the embrace of my mother, who was detained by sickness, and the excitement of the afternoon confined me to my bed. My medal bears date "June 5, 1832, aged 11 years and 6 months." A certificate dated July 4, 1832, signed "V. R. Osborn, principal," and "E. G. Welles, professor of rhetoric and history," attests that the "honorable board" gave me preference at the second trial also.

During the following fall my time was occupied with my studies and writing. I was quite a hard student. I would generally be up with my father before daybreak, closely applied to my books. My parents indeed seemed to fear that this intense application was injuring my health. The first item which I have journalized was my first speech delivered at a little Sunday-school two or three miles from the city, at a place called Hart's factory. This was the commencement of my career in original speaking, and was of course very simple, even with the assistance of my father's experience.

I have the memorandum of a little incident which I will record, although not of any peculiar interest but by the association it calls up. It is my father's preaching in one of the graveyards of the city on the Sabbath evening of May 5, 1833. I remember the beautiful afternoon, the solemn service, the affected assembly. In that graveyard was a beautiful spot where had been interred an infant, and I have often gazed on its fresh grass and secluded situation and wished that I might be permitted to lie there. Melancholy was one of my first companions.

On the 11th of the following June I delivered an address at Elk Ridge, Md., on the subject of " Temperance "; on the 14th of the following July I spoke at Whatcoat Chapel on "The Advantages of Sunday-schools"; and on the 28th of the same month I delivered an address before the Juvenile Temperance Society, in Wesley Chapel. (Memorandum.— Father presented me with the watch which I have at present, August 7, 1833.)

About this time I heard the Rev. John N. Maffit preach for the first time. Eloquence has ever thrilled me with most peculiar feelings, and for nights I listened with rapt attention to his discourses. I find passages in my journal, and particularly anecdotes, which he was so peculiarly felicitious in relating, which were written before the excitement his sermons produced had entirely subsided. There is a witchery and eloquence for which I am not able to account, and yet he holds his congregations almost perfectly entranced.

In September of 1833 my father and I made a temperance excursion to Elkton, Md. I notice this incident as marking a happy period of my life. I was here called before the public on several occasions, and formed during my visit a Juvenile Temperance Society. (My whole soul was devoted to the temperance cause about that time, and it is even now a cause in which my affections are enlisted. I ever after looked upon this society with the eyes of peculiar regard. What has since been its fate I am unable to tell.)

In October, 1833, the missionaries Wright and Spaulding left America for Liberia in Africa. During their stay in Baltimore I became acquainted with them, and became peculiarly attached to the first-named gentleman. Indeed, when I entered the parlor, where I had an introduction to him, he singled me from a large company which had come to pay their respects to these devoted men, and taking me in his lap, he held me to his bosom as a near relative. He gave me his address on paper, which sacred relic I still preserve, and insisted on our corresponding. On board the steamboat, when it was about to leave the city to carry them to the vessel, he took me in his arms and wept over me as over a beloved brother; indeed, so greatly were we moved that a gentleman standing near inquired of my father if we were not brothers. Alas, the eloquent, the zealous, the devoted Wright sleeps beside his beautiful wife in the hot soil of Africa! I pray Heaven that if it is consistent with divine providence I may be permitted to stand by the grave of my beloved and lamented Wright, and preach "the unsearchable riches of Christ."

About this period my father gave up his business by selling off his stock in trade to a man by the name of ——. My father's being kept out of his just dues at this time has been probably the whole cause of my passing through college with such contracted means, and the many heartburnings and miseries which poverty will ever bring upon a student. Oh, if there is a situation truly to be deplored, it is that of an enthusiastic youth burning with desire for knowledge and yet under the galling restraint of a limited supply of means! From my first recollections I can recall the remembrance of the intense interest which I took in my father's business, and the great pain which the perplexity of his concerns caused me. A slight incident will illustrate them: I was once returning from the dentist's with my mother, weeping bitterly for the pain caused by the extraction of two teeth. To soothe me as much as possible she proposed to stop in a book-store where my father had an account and purchase me a toy book. I would not consent to this, for I remembered that I had heard my father sigh on the previous evening when making a calculation of the amount of his notes which would be due that week. As young as I was, I would not permit mother to add the smallest amount to the weight which rested already upon my father.

In October of this year I again visited Elkton to stir up my little temperance society and to cultivate the friendship which I had formed for several families in that place. Toward the close of 1833 I commenced to correspond with the " Temperance Herald," a publication of some interest when first started, but which has now dwindled into an insignificant sheet. This was my first appearance in public print. The articles arrested the attention of the editor of the " Mechanic's Banner," a literary paper, who requested me to let him have some few articles. I wrote for him a series of little papers under the title of the " Pretended Beggar," and, indeed, gave him occasional articles until he left the city.

Sabbath, February 9, 1834, I delivered a speech at Reisterstown, Md., on the subject of Sabbath-schools.

In May of this year the first pieces of poetry I ever published made their appearance in the " Mechanic's Banner." Previously to this my reading in poetry had not extended beyond the hymn-book of the Methodist Episcopal Church and a few stray pieces of newspaper rhyme.

About this time I find in my journal that I became very much attached to Virgil's Æneid, and to this day I prefer it to all the classics with which I have become acquainted. His Bucolics are also favorites of mine. Never having read his Georgics, I cannot tell how I should be pleased with them; not much, however, I presume, and the agricultural terms cannot well be appreciated. I have read some books of the Æneid over several times.

The first volume of poetry I remember to have read was Moore's "Lalla Rookh," in my freshman year.*

The year 1834 was an eventful year for me. Its earliest days looked in upon the room in which my mother was fight‑ing a long battle with death. There has never been a day since in which I could not call up most vividly the circum‑stances attending the last hour. We had been a small family from my first recollection, just four of us: father and mother, her half-sister,—whom I always called "Aunt Juliet,"—and myself. My training had devolved upon my mother and my aunt. I have always felt the evil of being an only child. I am frequently humiliated by a sudden sense of a selfishness which would have been corrected if I had been reared with brothers and sisters younger or older than myself. And then I also suffered from that other trouble which besets an only child, the trouble of being exceedingly much raised; the hav‑ing two women with scarcely anything else to do but to devote themselves to this one individual boy. The being the only son of two mothers, one an invalid and the other an old maid, was a most trying position.

My mother was a woman of strong character; she ruled wherever she went, and had unusual natural abilities, with the very slight school culture of that day. She was a woman of prodigious faith and great gifts in prayer. I have heard her pray till strong men bowed their faces to the very carpet on the floor. The remembrance of her prayers is such that I can never speak of them without feeling that tingling in my blood which one feels while hearing thrilling eloquence; and it has been fifty-two years since that voice was stilled. Her inva‑lidism extended over a long period; indeed, I am told that she never was well after the hour of my birth. Her disease caused so much pain that the physicians administered great quantities of laudanum. It became so costly that when I was eleven

* End of extracts from recollections, dated May 10, 1839.

years of age I was taught how to make the laudanum, and would buy the spirits and the opium in quantities. I recall now the very appearance of the knife with which I was accustomed to cut the opium into small pieces before putting it into the bottle of spirits. I do not believe that I have tasted opium for half a century; but some of it would stick to my fingers, and I frequently took it off with my teeth. I look back to that experience with wonder that I totally escaped addiction to either alcohol or opium. The effect of this drug upon my dear sick mother was necessarily to obscure her fine intellect and strong natural spirits, so that very frequently she was under a cloud, very frequently irritable, very frequently feeling as if her trust in God were gone, and she could read no portion of her title to a mansion in the skies. Then at other times her pain was frightful. I have had my hand crushed in hers, and my arm held tightly, so tightly as to exhibit the marks of my mother's fingers. But my devotion to her never ceased, and it has been a comfort to all my after life that the assurance has never failed me of my being a comfort to her up to the last moment of her mortal life. She who in former years had been such a buoyant, triumphant Christian had, during the latter years, been in heaviness through temptation that at the last moment she should lack dying grace. But God was better to her than all her fears. When the last came I was not a Christian, and this was a real sorrow to her; but she died believing that her only son would live to be a useful Christian man, and expressed that belief in the most decided tones. She had always been fond of Pope's poetry, and her last intelligible articulations were made in striving to repeat Pope's version of the Roman emperor's little poem. She spoke it gaspingly:

> " Vital spark of heavenly flame,
> Quit, oh, quit this mortal frame;
> Trembling, hoping, lingering, flying—
> Oh the pain, the bliss, of dying!

> " Cease, fond nature, cease thy strife,
> And let me languish into life!"

Then for some time there was silence; she had almost exceeded her strength. My recollection is that she missed the next verse in the well-known poem, but evidently her mind was going over the sentence. She began again, gasping at each word:

> " The world recedes, it disappears,
> Heaven — heaven — heaven — "

She could not get farther, she looked into our eyes. My aunt added the next line:

> " Opens on our eyes."

My mother smiled, nodded her head, and closed the eyes into which we had been gazing, to open the eyes of her spirit on the vision of God.

The year 1834 was also remarkable in my history as the date of the beginning of my church-membership, the breaking up of our little family, and my departure for college. I had always been a serious boy, and really desired to be religious. The death of my mother brought a crisis in my experience; I desired to live with her forever. I had promised to meet her in heaven. I was not a vicious boy; very few external violations of the moral law had marked my short history, and yet I felt that there was need of some act of consecration which should separate me from the world, and that for my own spiritual purification and growth there was needed something to be received into my heart. This led me to listen carefully to religious conversations, to seek to hear practical preaching, and to find out what that "change of heart" meant of which I heard the Methodist brethren speak so much. If my mother had been living, as she was a few years before, in the fullness of her powers, and I had opened my heart to her, how she might have led me! As it was, I remembered many of her teachings, and think that I was very much affected by her spirit, but I did not know how to come out " on the Lord's side."

My father and my aunt, as I afterward learned, were deeply solicitous for my condition, and became more anxious as I became more reserved; and I became more reserved as my religious exercises deepened in my soul. I have since learned how natural this is, and know how to appreciate the delicacy of the soul of a young person who shrinks from talking about that which concerns his innermost being and which really is indescribable.

But through the spring I had fixed upon an approaching camp-meeting which was to be held in the summer, about fourteen miles from the city, on what was called the Reisterstown road. When the time of preparation had arrived the question of our going came up in our little circle, and my father observed that he did not think he would go; he could see no good of it. This startled me; it seemed to be taking away my day of grace. I made a quick expression of desire that we should go, and he said to me, "Son, you have had so many religious opportunities that I am afraid to go to camp-meeting with you, for if you pass through those exercises unconverted, you will come out harder than you are now." I said, "O father, do go!" and I suppose there must have been more in the expression of my face than in my words, as I learned the next day that we were to attend camp-meeting, and afterward learned from my father that he saw in my countenance that something unusual was passing in my mind.

The camp-meeting of that day was very different from things that bear that name in this. There were no two- and three-story cottages with bay-windows and balconies, with carpeted floors, pictured walls, and swinging cages of birds. Every tent was really a tent—canvas put up on poles. Before the encampment there were no signs of it, and, but for the fires and the clearings for the "stand," as it was called, and the arbor, there were no signs after the encampment departed. Two or three city churches would unite, and their officers would take charge of the whole affair. Companies went out on wagons, with their tents, their bedding, and their cooking utensils.

On one such occasion we started up the turnpike. We passed quite near the place where my father was reared. That neighborhood had its ghost-stories, as every neighborhood has. My father had told me several, to all of which there was a rational explanation. But there was one which none of us could ever explain; it was as follows:

Within a few rods of the turnpike a gentleman had, in the days of my father's boyhood, undertaken to build a dwelling. Before it was finished, the inner walls, however, being plastered, my father and some other urchins saw a light in the house one night, and went to its open door, where they beheld an old hag, who was considered a sort of witch in the neighborhood, sitting and warming herself beside a very large fire made of shavings, blocks, and other light pieces of wood. The flame roared up the chimney, and the old crone was holding her hands toward its genial warmth. When the boys came near the door and saluted her she rose with a stick to drive them off. Her rising was enough, for they fled with terror. Next morning, when the sun was shining and the workmen had returned, the boys came back and examined the fireplace. It was absolutely clean, the bricks and the mortar which joined them being fresh and free from any mark of fire. This was a great puzzle to the boys, and no explanation of it ever was reached, but the house was always uninhabitable. A number of families had tried to live in it and had failed; after a night or two they were flung from their beds. The owner had never been able to occupy it himself nor to keep a tenant, and, after a few efforts, the house came to have such a bad fame that it could neither be sold nor given away. All this I had heard years before.

We were approaching the house in the gloaming, and I determined to try the strength of my nerves; so I jumped from the wagon, let it pass the house a little distance, and then entered. It was an old-looking house now, for the weather had beaten through it. There was light enough to see. I boldly walked to the middle of the room, out of which stairs ascended to the second story. At the turn of the stairs I laid my hand upon the open floor above, and thought I would simply draw myself up and look in. All at once all the ghost-stories that I had ever heard in my life rushed upon my mind. I heard the dying sounds of the retreating wheels as they passed away. It flashed upon me that some mischievous or wicked persons might use the bad fame of the house to carry out their improper designs upon travelers, and that so unnerved me that I dropped to the floor and ran after the wagon.

I have never had any belief in ghosts, and have always gone into weird places, sometimes visiting graveyards at midnight just to see if I could do it. And yet I do believe from that early experience and subsequent experiments, whatever may be the state of a man's logical understanding toward the whole subject of ghosts, in the bravest of boys and of men there is something in what they have heard which so affects the imagination as in some measure to unnerve them.

The camp-meeting was held on what the Baltimore Methodists of that day were accustomed to call "Clark's Old Ground." In the personal recollections (1839) already referred to, I find the following record of my experience:

On the bright and beautiful morning of August 18th—can I ever forget the scene?—I accompanied a young friend to an adjoining hill. I there erected an altar of stone, and, bowing down, I resolved never to rise until God should speak peace to my soul. My cries for mercy drew several persons to the spot. I wrestled for a long time. I had laid down a particular plan in which I wished to receive the blessing, but when

I gave myself up entirely to God, then he listened to my prayer, and answered it to the joy and comfort of my soul. It did not come, as I had supposed, like the rushing of a mighty wind, but it was a still, small voice, whispering, " Peace." I knew not how long I was on my knees, but was so earnestly engaged as not to know that I was surrounded by strangers. When I arose the fields seemed greener, the air sweeter, and the heaven itself brighter, and my soul was filled with love.

CHAPTER III

M Y mother's death had made a great break in our circle. My father had been a local preacher in the Methodist Episcopal Church, and would have entered what is called the itinerancy but for my mother's health. When she was gone I was still left with my aunt, the half-sister who had reared me, and who was devoted to me then as she is now (1886), and who could not be separated from me. For months my father was in doubt as to what course to pursue. I was not quite ready for college. His losses in business and the expenses of my mother's sickness necessitated the consideration of economy. It was just at this juncture that Dickinson College, in Carlisle, Pa., passed over from the hands of the Presbyterians to the hands of the church in which my father was a minister. The Methodists reorganized the college with great vigor. At that time there was in the city of Baltimore a man of extraordinary physical and intellectual endowments, the Rev. Stephen George Roszell, who had great influence over my father. He came to see us. He insisted upon my going to Dickinson College, and met the difficulty of my lack of preparation by the statement that a most excellent preparatory school was to be organized in connection with that college. He increased the inducements by offering to take my father and myself to Carlisle in his own carriage.

43

It was determined that we should go to the college to hear the new president's inaugural. To me the ride was one of very great interest. Before the existence of railroads one saw the country so much better in carriages and on foot. This time we rode; but in one of my college vacations afterward, when I wanted to revisit my native city, my funds were so low that I walked the distance to within twelve miles of Baltimore, out to which point a railway had been made. So from Baltimore, on that old Reisterstown road, up to Carlisle in the beautiful Cumberland Valley, I once knew the whole road.

In the summer of 1834 my father took me to Carlisle and entered me in the preparatory school of Dickinson College. This institution, as I have already stated, had just passed from the hands of the Presbyterians into the control of the Methodist Church. It was intended to do for the Methodists of the Middle States what Wesleyan University was accomplishing for New England. The Baltimore and Philadelphia conferences of the Methodist Church had it especially in charge, and they entered upon the work of rehabilitation with great zeal and managed it with marked ability. Perhaps no college in America ever started with a more able faculty. The Rev. Dr. John Price Durbin, who had had experience in the colleges of Kentucky, was called to the presidency. He was an extraordinary man in many particulars. As a pulpit orator he had attracted the attention of the nation while traveling for the other colleges with which he had been connected. In person he was slight. His face was not handsome, nevertheless it was peculiarly attractive. The life of it was in an eye of remarkable expression. When calm it was sweetly benevolent, but when excited it seemed really to flash. His sermons very frequently dwelt on speculative themes. In the beginning of their delivery there was such a drawl that when he went to strange places persons who knew nothing of the fame of the preacher would frequently leave the church in disgust while he was reading the morning lessons or the hymns or making the opening prayer. He would drag on sometimes for fifteen or twenty minutes, making preliminary statements, searching the mind for some startling thought. The expression of his countenance in the beginning was that of a man intently interested in what he had in hand, as if preparing to do something startling with it. Suddenly, without premonition, lifting himself to his height, he would flash the climacteric sentence on his audience. A shock from an electric battery could not have produced more marked effect. Sometimes the whole audience would be startled into a movement forward.

I remember that in one of his sermons he administered such a shock that, sitting in the gallery of the church, I was compelled to run into the street to avoid outright screaming. After my graduation, when he had quit the college, I went to his church in Philadelphia on one of the hottest days of summer—and no place on earth that I have ever visited can become hotter than Philadelphia. The house was packed. Nearly every one slept, except while standing to sing, and many of the congregation were too much overcome to do that. It was one of those dull, hot days when it seems impossible to keep awake. It was one of the four times in my life in which I had slept during divine service. Even under those circumstances, several times during the discourse Dr. Durbin roused his audience by the peculiar intonations of his voice and administered that peculiar thrill. I could see the audience in the thrill, and then, when it was over, relapse into slumber.

Dr. Durbin not only was very attractive in the pulpit, but he had excellent governing powers. He won the respect of the students, administered discipline wisely and well, and kept the conditions between the faculty and the body of students comfortable. He had four remarkable men associated with him.

On our way from Baltimore to Carlisle we stopped to pay

our respects to the Rev. Bishop Emory, who lived on the road about sixteen miles from Baltimore. While my father was conversing with him I was sent outdoors to play with the children, one of whom was a sweet little girl, who afterward grew to be an admirable woman and died the wife of my friend and classmate, the Rev. Dr. George R. Crooks. When it was time for my father to resume the journey, a tall young man of blond complexion and wearing glasses recalled us to the house. It was the bishop's son, Robert Emory, who had been called to the chair of ancient languages in the college. His father had been book-agent of the Methodist Church, and Robert had been graduated with distinction in Columbia College in the city of New York. He was not a brilliant man, but he had rare equipoise of mind and an elevated, manly nature, a thorough training, and all the ways of a gentleman. He not only discharged his duties as a teacher with piety and success, but devoted much of his time to personal intercourse with his students and attention to their religious condition.

To the chair of mathematics there had been called a brilliant young man, recently graduated from the University of Pennsylvania, John McClintock, afterward distinguished by the contributions he made to religious literature, especially as editor-in-chief, up to the time of his death, of McClintock and Strong's Encyclopedia.

The professor of moral philosophy was Merritt Caldwell, a layman, who had come from Bowdoin College, in Maine. He was a quiet, distinguished, scholarly man. To promote economy among the students each young man was assigned to a professor who had charge of his financial affairs. Professor Caldwell received the amounts my father sent him and acted as my bursar.

A fifth man was in that young faculty, a layman, Professor William H. Allen, who had charge of the department of natural science. His was a rich mind. His lectures were peculiarly charming, and his store of thought and illustration appeared to be exhaustless. After leaving Dickinson College he became president of Girard College and of the American Bible Society.

How these five men did work, and what enthusiasm they kindled among the students! They were so different, so individual, so earnest, making themselves so acquainted with the peculiarities of the dispositions and circumstances of all the students, that their influence now seems to me wonderful. Only one is now (1887) living, Dr. Allen, president of Girard College, who has just resigned the presidency of the American Bible Society on account of advancing years.

In charge of the preparatory school was a Mr. Dobbs. He left soon after I entered college, and the last I heard of him he was in the ministry of the Protestant Episcopal Church. I spent one year in the preparatory school, and boarded in town with a family named Keeney. My father had made arrangements that my aunt, Miss Roberts, should accompany me. Her devotion to me was so great that she could not endure to be separated from me. Thus it came to pass that I had the protection of this most affectionate and pious woman. She is living while I write this, forty-two years after quitting college, and this very morning I hear from a near relative in Baltimore that she is pining to see her "old boy." Having her oversight and affectionate caresses was a blessed thing for me.

I was admitted to the freshman class in the summer of 1835, a class which graduated seventeen strong. Of that number five entered the ministry, three in the Presbyterian Church and two in the Methodist. Of the men in my class few have become distinguished.

Daniel E. M. Bates died chancellor of the State of Delaware. He was a gentle, excellent, high-minded boy, and became a noble and useful man.

James D. Biddle, a relative of Nicholas Biddle, well known as the president of the Bank of the United States when General Jackson made his famous movement on it, was a very agreeable and gentlemanly student.

William F. Roe was an excellent scholar, and afterward became professor in Shelby College, in Kentucky.

Lemuel Todd was in after years a general in the army of the United States during the Civil War, and afterward represented his district in Congress.

In the class next after ours was Spencer Fullerton Baird, who afterward became distinguished for his scientific attainments and for the position which he held at the head of the Smithsonian Institution. While in college he showed his great fondness for studies in natural history, spending much of his time in the fields and streams around Carlisle, noting the habits of animals.

George R. Crooks was a member of our class, but by reason of ill health fell back and was graduated with the class of 1840. He was a laborious student. His thickness of hearing was very much in his way. I recollect distinctly how, when he recited in the ancient languages, he was accustomed to go and stand beside the professor while making his translation. He afterward became quite distinguished in the Methodist Episcopal Church, was a professor in Dickinson College, and assisted Dr. McClintock in his great cyclopedia. For years he was the editor of the " Methodist," published in New York, and subsequently professor in Drew Theological Seminary.

George David Cummins entered the freshman class when ours became junior. He became the well-known founder of the Reformed Episcopal Church.

My first room was in the old building, a long room over the chapel. At that time interest in the two literary societies was very intense, the members of the Belles-Lettres and the Union Philosophical societies severally exerting themselves to secure members. I joined the latter and took very great interest in all its affairs to the close of my career.

My habits of study were ruinous. No one then seemed to have any care for the health of students. A man or boy, as the case might be, was allowed to go forward without warning in regard to his health. Frequently I studied until twelve o'clock at night and rose next morning at four. No boy, at my time of life, should have been allowed to do such a thing as that. Afterward I modified it, studying until eleven, then walking up and down the campus, my mind occupied in musings, in brown studies, or in excited thoughts about the future. In my freshman year I know there were periods in which I went from Sunday night when I returned from church, until Sunday morning when I went to church, without going out of college. Of course such things told on my health.

The pulpit in Carlisle was an educational influence. The two Methodist preachers who were stationed in the town during my term were the Rev. George G. Cookman and the Rev. Thomas A. Thornton. Both these gentlemen had been stationed in Baltimore and were friends of my father. Under the former I had become a member of the church before going to college. His name is one that is likely to live in the annals of Methodism. An Englishman by birth, he had not been in this country many months before he made a national reputation by a most extraordinary speech before the American Bible Society. From that day to the day of his death he drew crowds. He was a slender man, trim, well made, about the medium height, very alert in his actions, with a ringing voice and a gray eye full of life. He afterward became chaplain of the Senate of the United States. He started on a return voyage to his native land in the unfortunate " President," which has never been heard from since her departure from the American port. His sermons were neither profound nor polished, but they were full of life, and very vivifying to the hearer.

Dr. Thornton was a Virginian, a gentleman of pleasing manners, an interesting though not a great nor stirring preacher. Young Professor McClintock came to the college a preacher, and the young Professor Emory was licensed to preach while I was still in college. Outside the Methodist Church the other pulpits were ably manned. The Episcopal clergyman, who boarded in the house next to the one in which I spent a whole year of my college life, was a preacher of very considerable intellect and much culture, and had a rich rhetorical style. He was very social and markedly convivial. A very different man was Dr. McGill, in the Seceder Presbyterian Church, who now (1887) in his old age is a professor at Princeton. He was tall, angular, and highly intellectual. His matter was beaten oil before it was brought into the sanctuary. It was an intellectual treat to hear him preach.

In the First Presbyterian Church was the Rev. Dr. Duffield, who in after years labored and died in Detroit. His congregation embraced many of the élite of the town, and he himself was a gentleman as well as a scholar, and his scholarship, although high, did not dry up his powers of preaching. His wife was a New Yorker connected with the Bethunes and the Grahams. His sons became my intimate friends, and I was especially attached, and am to this day, to Divie Bethune Duffield, who is practising law in Detroit. The Duffields were most kind to me, and I frequently spent my Saturdays at their beautiful home on the edge of the town of Carlisle. I believe that the influence of that family upon my Christian character was very marked and very useful.

With such preachers as these to fill up our Sunday hours and cultivate the spiritual side of our characters, we who were then students at Dickinson College had very great privileges.

Twice while I was an undergraduate I seemed to be near the end of my life. Many of us were accustomed on Saturday afternoon to go to the Canadaquonet Creek for bathing.

It gave us a walk of two or three miles, besides the pleasure of the bath. Here one Saturday I had the experience of drowning. I had been in the creek some time and was probably weakened. One of the older collegians, coming down to plunge in, proposed to me to swim across. I consented if he would hold one of my hands and let us strike out together. He caught my hand and we started. He thought that I was just pretending that I needed the help of his hand, supposing me to be a very good swimmer. In the middle of the creek he loosened his hold, shot under my breast, and threw me back in the water. I could not recover myself sufficiently to know which shore was the nearer. In my confusion I became alarmed, my alarm took away what little strength I still had, and I began to sink. A student on the bank saw my condition, and called out; that student's name was Francis A. Baggs. He afterward became a Methodist clergyman in Virginia. A young man from Newark, N. J., a powerful fellow, who had been to sea, took in the state of affairs, plunged into the stream, caught me by my arm and leg, and flung me into shoal water, and then, with the assistance of other students, flung me out. I had gone through the horror of the struggle and had come into a condition of perfect peace and perfect comfort, the kind of comfort a tired boy feels on a warm spring day when he comes from a race and lies down to sleep—the feeling that precedes the loss of consciousness. At that moment, too, I seemed to remember every event of my outward life, every thought of my mind, every emotion of my heart; my whole life, in separate, condensed panorama, rose up before my view. I had never read anything in mental philosophy, and this seemed very strange to me, but very awful.

Subsequently I found that it is common experience. To this day I never refer to it without a feeling of solemnity. It seems so strange that my mind could see at once ten thousand things that had come into a life of fourteen years. Apparently it was at once, although they must have come up into the memory successively, but with such rapidity as to appear to be seen all synchronously. This event sobered me, and, I think, gave a tinge to my feelings through my whole college career.

My rank in scholarship was never very high in college; I sought no prizes. As I intended to study and practise law, I took from the curriculum only what I supposed would be helpful to me in future law studies. I devoted myself mainly to *belles-lettres*, to compositions, and to preparation for debates. I did not put a proper estimate upon the training which was given by the regular college course. This error I perceived later in life. Now I believe that in the undergraduate course a man should give himself up wholly to Latin, Greek, and mathematics; and, if I had the shaping of all our college work, I would exclude every study except those three. No boy should enter college until he had a thorough preparation for the higher study of the Greek and Latin tongues and the masterpieces in those languages. I should put other studies afterward, in a postgraduate or university course, beginning with the English language and literature. I should never put an English grammar in the hands of a boy until he had pretty well mastered the Latin and Greek grammars. The university or postgraduate course I should have to include studies in law, medicine, and the Bible.

Of course preparatory to law would be the English language and literature, rhetoric, and dialectics; and connected with medicine would be all the departments of physical science. A boy at fifteen should be thoroughly prepared to enter the college; three years should then be devoted to the college course, two years to the postgraduate preparatory course for one of the professions; then two years in a legal, medical, or biblical school would complete the theoretical education of the young man and prepare him to enter the practical school of the profession of law, medicine, or the ministry.

But the college course of the classical languages and mathematics gives the mental discipline needed by every man who is to take high rank as agriculturist, mechanic, or manufacturer; for this discipline is needed by such men as much as it is needed by those men who intend to pursue one of the learned professions. It should not have anything in it optional, and no man should be admitted into one of the learned professions who had not taken his degree out of some well-established college giving thorough training in Latin, Greek, and mathematics. But I had no friend to give me advice, and so floated along, picking up what I could and looking at everything in the light of the use it might be to me at the bar.

I believe all my teachers liked me. I am sure that Professor Emory and President Durbin were fond of me. Within a few days Dr. Durbin's son-in-law, Mr. Harper, of Harper & Brothers, publishers, told me that the dear old doctor, up to the day of his death, would frequently speak of me, and always mention me with pride as one of his stars. Generally my intercourse with the students, so far as I know, was pleasant. I was never called before the faculty, never reprimanded. This is a very stupid record of a college career. I am at a great disadvantage at a reunion of the "old boys." They all have some narrative to tell, but if I stick to the truth I cannot repeat a single exploit.

[In the paper dated May 10, 1839, from which Dr. Deems drew most of the above facts concerning his college life, we find near and at the end the interesting extracts which follow this parenthesis.—ED.]

In a few weeks my collegiate course will be finished. O Carlisle! can I ever forget you? Shall I cease to remember the haunts· of five of the most important years of my life?

The hand of time can never erase from the tablet of memory the images it has graven there. I shall cherish the remembrance of pleasant walks and kind friends, and I can never forget hours of misery and a few bitter foes. Oh, how often in after life will I call up to my mind's eye the rooms in which I have pursued my studies, the hall of prayer, the sound of the bell which has so often awakened me from pleasant dreams to prepare for devotion, and which has frequently fallen on my ear as a death-knell when calling me to the discharge of some irksome duty. Nor will I forget the countenances of my kind professors, the jokes and sport which occasionally obtruded themselves into the recitation-rooms, and the lugubrious expression which sighs from the face of every unprepared student. Above all, I shall remember, "while thought or life or being last," the path which connects the old building with the front gate. How often have I paced that path, feasting my mind with thought, and drinking in the imaginary melody of star-born music; and how often have I given the heavy sigh which burst from a burdened heart to the night breeze that chilled as it kissed the tear from my cheek; and, when my poor frail body has been exhausted, sunk upon the cold step of the chapel and pressed my temples, which have seemed ready to rend with intense pain and the agony which a too sensitive spirit contracted by mingling with the unfeeling.

I bid you all a prospective farewell. My name will soon be forgotten here, but perhaps these sheets will fall into the hands of some kind friend, who, forgetting my thousand faults, will remember my few virtues, and love and cherish my memory.

My frail bark may be dashed against some rock in the ocean of life; but whether, in my dying hour, my head be pillowed on some bosom that loves me, or in distant lands where no friendly hand can wipe away the death-damps that gather on my brow, I wish the last words that tremble upon my lips to be, " I have not lived in vain."

CHARLES M. F. DEEMS.

DICKINSON COLLEGE, midnight,
May, 10, 1839.

I have thus endeavored to trace my history from the first dawn of memory to the present hour. And I must not conclude this sketch without making my acknowledgments to thee, my good goose-quill, for having so patiently accompanied me over these ten sheets without being once mended. Thou shalt soon be lost, perhaps sooner than thine owner, but thou shalt, nevertheless, have the consolation of knowing that thou hast been the wand with which he has called into existence the spirits of long-buried thoughts and feelings.

CHAPTER IV

PROFESSIONAL LIFE COMMENCED, 1839–44

I TOOK my degree of A. B. in July, 1839, and went to Baltimore very undecided what to do. Before leaving the college President Durbin had offered me the choice of two places, positions of very great responsibility; but I had the good sense to decline them. One was the principalship of a large institution for young men and women, at a salary of twelve hundred dollars a year, which was equal to the average salary of college professors at the time. Something was to be done. I intended to make the Christian ministry my life-work. I should at that time have entered the Protestant Episcopal Church but for the doctrine of apostolic succession. For many reasons I preferred it to the Presbyterian or the Methodist Church. I did not believe in Calvinism, and I did not altogether like Methodism. But I could not persuade myself that the doctrine of apostolic succession was true, and without an overmastering belief in its truth I could not become a clergyman in a church which would ignore my father and my grandfather, and such beloved men of other churches as I knew, such as Dr. Duffield, of Carlisle; and so I was very much at sea.

I had not the means of going to a theological seminary, and if I had had there was at that time no seminary in which Arminian doctrines were taught, and I did not care to take training at the hands of those who held other views. My consolation at the time was that I was very young, and that I would better teach awhile, until there came to be some opening of providence. Somehow I felt that the city of New York was to be the great city of the Union, and that would be the place in which a man should begin who looked to a long run of influence and a broadening life.

It so happened that my father's brother, Mr. Henry W. Deems, at that time resided in the city of New York. I corresponded with him, and was invited to go to New York and make his family a visit. I did not have a dollar in the world, and had borrowed twelve dollars and fifty cents from the Rev. Dr. Durbin to pay my last board bill when I left college and to take me to Baltimore. Determining that if I continued in the Methodist ministry not to belong to the Baltimore Conference, of which my father was a member, I felt that there might be better openings for me in New York. When I had been a boy in the city of Baltimore, David Creamer had published what was called the " Baltimore Monument," in which had appeared the effusions of the rising young writers of that city, and into it some of my own productions had been admitted. Very timidly I made known to Mr. Creamer my thought of going to New York ; and while his affection for me prompted him to say that his wishes were for me to remain in Baltimore, his judgment approved my course ; and he loaned me twelve dollars and a half, which barely took me to the rising metropolis.

I shall never forget my arrival there. The possibility is that the latter portion of the journey was made in a steamer commanded by a man with whom a half-century later I was to have most important relations—Commodore Vanderbilt. My good uncle, Mr. Henry W. Deems, was at the wharf. What I knew of New York I had derived from the accounts of travelers and from the " Knickerbocker Magazine," which at that time was far in front of all American periodicals, and from the bright paragraphs of N. P. Willis, who was a favorite poet with collegians. The city was larger than Baltimore, having at that time a population of 312,710. We came up town in the Knickerbocker omnibus, past the office of the "Knickerbocker Magazine," turned into Bleecker Street,—the finest street I had ever seen, the houses seemed so stately,— and came down to Carmine Street, only a short distance beyond which was the terminus of this great transportation line. I think our passage cost us twenty-five cents each. At Carmine Street we debarked, and I went to my uncle's house, which was a short distance around the corner (No. 28). It was a bewilderingly big thing for me to be in New York; twenty years afterward London did not seem larger.

The first thing I did was to find Bond Street. Bond Street seemed to me to be at the top of all human thoroughfares. The local love-stories were laid in Bond Street; the men of wealth lived in Bond Street; in every woman I was to meet in Bond Street I expected to see a peri—such girls as Willis was accustomed to paint in his "Inklings" and "Hurrygraphs." There was a little disappointment, I confess; but I must also confess that I had never seen so many noble mansions on one block in my life as in 1839 I saw on that short street. It must be remembered how small the city was then. Mr. Astor lived at No. 585 Broadway, near Prince Street,—there were no business houses along there then,—and there was no house above that of the Roosevelts, Broadway and Fourteenth Street. Washington Square had been a potter's field a very short time before this, but had been fenced in and made a drilling-place for the local militia and called "Washington Parade-ground." A few houses were built there. Second Avenue was laid out, and was going to be what Fifth Avenue has since become, but there was very little of it. This was just about the time that the avenue idea had taken possession of the minds of the people. Fourteenth Street was the highest street laid out, and very little of that was curbed,—none on the north side,—so that it was a good time to draw Fourteenth Street as the dividing line of the city, just as in former times Wall Street had been considered; and from this time forth the city grew with more regular thoroughfares, the exception being the old Bloomingdale road, as Broadway was called, which continues running its course regardless of rectangles, bearing northwestward toward Albany.

That first Saturday night in New York was clear, with a full moon. I walked up Carmine Street to Fourth Street, and turning round that corner soon came upon Washington Paradeground, with its iron railing. As I came to the East Side, the new university rose in the moonlight, so wonderfully beautiful that it seemed to me that I had never seen such a structure before. I thought it was a church. Across the street was another, and I wondered that two such splendid churches should be together. I recollect my aspiration then: Oh, if I could ever preach in that church! How little did I dream that twenty-seven years afterward I *should* be preaching in that identical building, to a few strangers who would consolidate into a church to be probably as widely known as any other in New York!

The literary celebrity in New York whose name was best known to me was William Cullen Bryant, whose "Thanatopsis" probably every college boy in America knew. I had a natural desire to look upon his face. I found from the directory that he lived two blocks above my uncle's house, just at the bend where Carmine Street became Sixth Avenue, a few doors above Bleecker Street (No. 12 Carmine). On Sunday morning I walked out and stood in front of the house, looking at it with all the reverence natural to a youth of eighteen who himself had a manuscript volume of poems in his trunk, which he hoped shortly to see in print. You see there was a sort of brother-poet feeling, with a sprinkle of modesty which made me feel there was an American poet a good ways ahead of me, and him I naturally wished to look upon. While I was gazing at the house Mr. Bryant came out: a man apparently in middle life, well made, lithe, and active. A little girl was with him. They started up Sixth Avenue, and turned at Fourth Street toward Broadway. At a respectful distance I followed them. Sometimes he would waltz the little girl around him on the pavement, and then go forward with a few dancing steps, and then resume a sober pace, which he would occasionally break with a little waltz. They went to Broadway and then turned north and entered a church, and I followed. It was a Unitarian church, standing immediately in front of the present site of the New York Hotel. The Rev. Dr. Orville Dewey was the pastor, and he preached that day. I stayed through the sermon, and followed Bryant and his daughter on my way back to my own lodgings. I have repeatedly seen Mr. Bryant since that day; but that little girl I have seen only once, and then when I met her she was the wife of Parke Godwin and the mother of a daughter who also was a grown woman.

I set to work at once to do something. My family and the Reeses, of Baltimore, had been friends. At that time there was a physician well known in New York City, David Meredith Reese, who resided on Hudson Street. He was the leading practitioner among the Methodists, and he made me acquainted with the chief people of that denomination—with the Rev. Dr. Nathan Bangs, the chief literary man of Methodism then in America; with the Rev. Thomas Mason and George Lane, who were the book-agents of the Methodist Church, the agency having its headquarters at No. 200 Mulberry Street; with the Rev. George Coles, editor of the "Christian Advocate"; with the Rev. George T. Peck, editing the "Quarterly Review"; with Francis Hall, Esq., who edited the "Commercial Advertiser," and lived one block below Dr. Reese. Immediately below Mr. Hall's was St. John's Park, in front of St. John's Church, and a number of handsome residences were around it. It was one of the aristocratic quarters of the city. In one of its stately mansions lived Mr. George Suckely, a leading Methodist layman. Dr. Reese was an official member of the Vestry Street Methodist Episcopal Church, then called the "First Wesleyan Chapel." This and the Mulberry Street Church, called the "Second Wesleyan Chapel," were the aristocratic worshiping-places of Methodism in New York City. The officials of the Book Concern mostly gathered around Mulberry Street, which also was strengthened by the families of the Harpers, publishers, and the Disosways, merchants. But the West Side Methodist aristocrats worshiped in Vestry Street. Their pastor was the Rev. Charles A. Davis, whom I had known in Baltimore, where he had at one time been stationed. He had been a friend of my father, and immediately took me up and showed me friendship. It was agreed that I should begin a classical school, and all these gentlemen furnished pupils and found others, and I was permitted to use rooms in the basement of the church for my school. I entered upon this work with zeal, and commenced writing so as to make money to pay the debts which I had contracted in closing my college course and in transporting myself to New York. Among other things I wrote a paper for the "Methodist Quarterly Review," on "George Crabbe and his Poems," and I also wrote a little volume which is in print to this day (1886), being a "Life of Dr. Adam Clarke," the great Methodist commentator. Of course this small volume was a simple compilation of the three large volumes in which the doctor's life was originally published in Great Britain. Occasionally, also, I preached in the absence of Mr. Davis, and, when invited, in other churches. I have recollections of three of those occasions.

One Saturday the Rev. Mr. Davis was called away to his dying father, and when I went down to the Bible class on Sunday morning I was told that he had left word that I must preach. I did not know what to do; it was a great surprise. I had at that time preached only two or three times in my life. I took my seat in the chancel, praying and praying that some one might come in. I was not ordained, and so could not administer the communion, and there were the elements on the table in the chancel. I could postpone the administration of the sacrament, on account of the trouble of the pastor, but —the preaching! In the midst of my distress of mind I saw the great lumbering figure of Dr. Bangs, who carried his big head always to one side, as if his neck were too weak to sustain it. I took heart. As he came up I caught his hand and said, "O doctor, what a relief! You will preach for the people this morning?" He whispered to me that he had just got out of his bed; he was ill, but Dr. Reese thought he might come over and administer the sacrament of the Lord's Supper. "But," said he, "you are to preach." I had all a boy's shyness in addition to my reverence for Dr. Bangs, the man of letters of greatest fame in the Methodist Church; and I had also that sense of responsibility which frightens me to this day, so that I never even now go into the pulpit without it, and sometimes it is so severe that I am on the point of running across the river to Jersey and letting things go as they will. After nearly fifty years of preaching (1886) I often make the usher stop just an instant when his hand is upon the door to open it to let me in; so it may be fancied in what a state of mind I went to the pulpit on that day! When they were singing the hymn after the prayer and preceding the sermon, I said to Dr. Bangs, "Oh dear, doctor, what shall I do, what shall I do?" The good old man said to me, "My young brother, trust in God and have no fear of man, which brings a snare. Tell the people what is in your heart." I could hear him praying behind me while I preached. The condition of affairs gave me very considerable excitement, and I finished some kind of a sermon without breaking down, and comforted myself all I could at the holy communion, trusting that God would make up for all deficiencies.

The effect of that sermon upon Dr. Bangs's mind was such that, a vacancy occurring at Sands Street Church, which at that time was the principal seat of Methodism in Brooklyn, Dr. Bangs actually suggested me as the temporary pastor; but this also I had the sense to decline.

I have recollection of another sermon. It was preached for the Rev. Mr. Gilder, pastor of Allen Street Methodist Church. There was a revival. The house was crowded, the aisles being so packed that I think we made entrance through a back window. The magnates of Methodism were here in full force. The crowd and the circumstances naturally excited me, and I was coming to have the dreadful reputation of being a "boy-preacher." I recollect my text on the occasion—"I pray thee have me excused." I preached with might and main, and, following the custom of the denomination, at the close of the sermon I invited penitents to the "altar," as the Methodists call the chancel, although at this day they turn with great revulsion from the use of the word "altar" by their Protestant Episcopal brethren. They came in great number, they knelt three deep around the entire chancel, and it was a very exciting scene.

When I sat down an old gentleman came into the pulpit and asked me if I did not want to go to Wesleyan University, and gave me his name as Dr. Laban Clarke. I supposed it was a proposition to take a tutorship at least, if not a professorship. It was some time before the venerable man succeeded in making me understand that he wished me to go to the university to be educated. Somehow he had not got any of my previous history. When it dawned upon me that he was a traveling agent for that college and was endeavoring to beat up students, I was greatly amused, and shall never forget the expression of his countenance when I told him I was an A.B. of Dickinson College. Next day it dawned upon me that my discourse must have struck the old gentleman as a very crude affair; that he saw in it nothing fulfilled, but enough of promise to justify an effort to give me a college training. This so mortified me that I never had the courage to ask him how on earth he could have made such a proposition to me. The only emollient that I could apply to my wounded vanity was that, in point of fact, I was only nineteen years of age, and weighed only ninety-five pounds. But even so, it occurred to me that the right course for him to have taken would have been for him to turn upon the authorities of the church for allowing such a youth as myself to officiate on prominent occasions.

I have recollections of a third sermon, the record of which requires a preliminary statement. Upon leaving college I paid a visit to Mr. James Inness, a college mate residing in Newark. He had a cousin, a very charming young lady, whose intimate friend was the daughter of a prominent Methodist merchant in New York. This merchant had his country-seat in the suburbs of Newark. The house is now (1886) in the center of the city. This young lady insisted that her cousin Jim should take me to see Annie Disosway, whom I had seen at the carriage when Jim and his cousin and I were driving past the house, and Amanda had stopped to have a little chat with Annie. We walked up the lawn, entered the house, were shown into the parlor, and Miss Annie arose and greeted us; but after a very few words became reabsorbed with a visitor who had entered before us, and who, I learned, was a wealthy young cousin from Philadelphia; she paid little attention to Jim and myself—he was an old neighbor, and I made no impression. I learned afterward that her father drove up from New York as Jim and I were leaving the grounds, and

CHARLES F. DEEMS, AT THE AGE OF NINETEEN, PREACHING IN NEW YORK.

From a silhouette made in New York in February, 1840. Dr. Deems wrote on the back of the original picture, "I esteem this a most correct profile of myself. C. M. F. D."

upon catechizing Annie as to who we were she mentioned my name, and her father thought it exceedingly strange that she had not invited me to stay to tea. Why, she never thought of doing such a thing "with that college boy"! "College boy, college boy, Annie," said her father; "why, that boy is preaching in some of the first churches in New York!" She then awakened to a sense of her condition—that she had not treated me with the respect due even the youngest and lowliest of the servants of the Lord, for she was exceedingly devout, and the ministry in her eyes was a sacred thing.

It so happened that when the family returned to town I was invited by their pastor, the Rev. Dr. Edmund S. Janes, who afterward became bishop, to preach in the Mulberry Street Church. After the sermon there was to be a meeting for some parochial business, and I did not remain. As I passed down the aisle I saw Miss Annie give her brother a sign to go out and speak to me, which he did, telling me when we reached the vestibule how his father regretted not being at home when I was at their place in Newark, and inviting me to visit them at their city residence, which, however, I did not do. Miss Annie had not yet captivated me.

In the spring of the year 1840 the confinement to my school, to my writing, and to supplying pulpits began to have such an effect upon my health as to cause Dr. Reese to advise my removal from the city. I then made up my mind to enter the itinerancy of the Methodist Church, and took a recommendation to the New Jersey Conference. It was presented by my mother's old friend, Manning Force, after whom I was named, and who at that time was presiding elder of a western district in that conference. At the time I was accepted I was on a visit to some college friends in Alexandria. When the appointments were made I was assigned to be the colleague of the Rev. George Banghart, of the Asbury circuit. This happened to be in Warren County, in the extreme western portion of the State, a high, hilly, healthy, and beautiful country. The circuit took its name from a village called Asbury, and that took its name from Bishop Asbury of the Methodist Episcopal Church. Old Colonel McCullough once owned a large portion of that country. He lived like a baron on his estate, and ruled that whole district. His house was beautifully located, and near it he had built a church, which was one of the stopping-places of the old itinerant Methodist bishop, and around the manor had grown the village. Two young fellows from New York had made love to the rich old Methodist nobleman's daughters. One was William Van Antwerp, of a good Dutch family, and the other was Israel D. Disosway, of an equally good Huguenot family. When I reached Asbury Mr. William Van Antwerp, who had two grown daughters, lovely girls, and educated at the best schools in New York, occupied the old McCullough mansion; Colonel McCullough had been dead a number of years. Across the road was the Disosway domain, Mr. Disosway occupying a little cottage preliminary to the building of another large mansion. I went up to my work, saw my colleague, who was a short, fleshy man with bright eyes, a strong voice, and considerable gift at singing. He had the old-fashioned Methodist fervor.

It is to be remembered that I had just passed my twentieth year in December when I went to this region in the following spring. I was entertained at the house of Mr. Van Antwerp, whose family immediately took me up very warmly, and I had a lovely time with the girls, who belonged to the Dutch Reformed Church, their father—at that time a prosperous wholesale hardware merchant on Pearl Street—having contributed largely to the church built by Dr. Mathews on the north side of Washington Square. Now the uncle, Mr. Disosway, who lived on the other side of the road and was building the new mansion, was the father of Miss Annie Disosway. Fortunately for me she was still in the city. I studied in a room I had in

the village, preached at the church there, and took my regular
round on the circuit, which included a village which has since
become the large and prosperous town of Washington. But
at last Miss Disosway was to come up from the city. The
curious thing to me was that while this young lady impressed
me so little, except with her white teeth, her blooming complexion, her ladylikeness, and her little affectations, as they
seemed to me, she appeared to be idolized by all who knew
her: the bishops, the clergy, the leading laymen of her church
who knew the family, her kinspeople, these, her two lovely
cousins, Libby and Mary Van Antwerp, all spoke of her as
being the best girl there was upon the face of the earth, and
the sweetest. Unfortunately for my peace of mind she was
also wonderfully conscientious. I did not know how she was
going to meet me, but she did meet me with a fervor and a
gush of which she herself must have been conscious; for she
blushed to the roots of her hair at the warmth of her saluta-
tion, perhaps checked at the coolness of mine; for in my heart
of hearts I was sorry she had come; I felt she would be *de
trop* in our circle. Her warmth arose from no regard for me
personally; it was simply that she had been brooding over the
sin which she had committed in treating me, a minister of the
gospel, as if I were an ordinary college boy. She had determined, as she afterward said, to make atonement for that by
devoted attention to me when she came to the country. In
alluding to it since I have often playfully told her that I
thought she rather overdid the thing; for when my recognition of the feeling came, when I found that she had the innocence of a new-born babe united with uncommon good sense,
ladylike manners, and a delicate conscientiousness which
shaped her whole life, from dislike to her I went to the other
extreme, and everybody can see what followed.

When I was a boy at school, in Baltimore, I had made up
my mind upon coming of age to go to North Carolina, to

settle in the town of Asheville, in Buncombe County, and marry a mountain girl. The North Carolina project was carried through, all except the settling in Asheville and the marrying a mountain girl—my little Asbury friend prevented the mountain girl. But still I had a strange drawing toward North Carolina. Miss Annie Disosway's pastor, the Rev. Dr. Janes, had become one of the secretaries of the American Bible Society. He was very much interested in my affairs, one of his pet projects being to marry me to Miss Disosway. I wrote to the American Bible Society to know if they had an agency anywhere in the South that I could secure. A letter came back to me very promptly, saying that the society was delighted at my turning my attention to their interests, and they would give me shortly a very excellent position, but at the present there was but one Southern State vacant, and that was one which they would not think of offering to me. In reply to my question as to which Southern State that was, they told me it was North Carolina. It surprised the society to learn that that was the identical State I desired above all others, and that I would take some modest agency for some portion of the State. I was immediately appointed general agent for the whole State. This was stunning; but I had been declining big things so long I thought I would change my tactics, especially as now I was a whole year older than when I was graduated; and, although not yet having attained my majority, I accepted the appointment.

After a year of preaching, making love, and multifarious other businesses pertaining to that peculiar transition period of a man's life, I left to take charge of my Southern work. I never had seen a North Carolinian in my life until I reached Washington City on my way to my field. There I met the Hon. William A. Graham, of the United States Senate, to whom I had a letter from New York. Mr. Graham received me politely. He was an unusually handsome, stately, yet graceful man. If all the North Carolinians I was to meet were to be like William A. Graham, I felt that I had seen no such society. Truth compels me to say that after I became a North Carolinian myself I saw a number of grown men who were not nearly so captivating as the graceful William A. Graham.

I stopped in Richmond, Va., and became acquainted with Dr. Leroy M. Lee, who was editor of the "Richmond Christian Advocate." My headquarters were at the Powhatan Hotel. I saw several leading Virginia lawyers in the courts, and Richmond seemed to me a very charming little Southern city. Just forty-five years after that I had occasion to stop in Richmond on my way South, and went to Ford's Hotel, which had in it something so familiar that I made inquiry and found that that was the hotel which anciently had borne the name of Powhatan.

My entrance upon my work was not brilliant. The first place at which I stopped in North Carolina was Gaston, then a wretched little hamlet, having a little tavern in which everything was as filthy as anything I have ever seen in the way of human shelter in Asia or in Africa. You could touch nothing that would not stick to you—the spoon, the cup; and the cup of coffee was a round lake in which there were floating isles of grease. Everybody that was not drunk was sleepy. There had been a cock-fight the day before my arrival, and I reached Gaston to see a number of young planters who had been carousing during the night till early in the morning and had left nothing fit to touch. I felt that if all North Carolina were like Gaston, and the majority of North Carolinians were like these dirty, tobacco-smeared, tangle-haired, blear-eyed young ruffians, by God's help I would get out of the commonwealth in less than a week. But young as I was, I was too old a traveler to expect to find North Carolina made up altogether of men like William A. Graham or like the young planters of

Halifax and Warren. Down the Raleigh and Gaston Rail-road I proceeded to Henderson. I had heard there was a very estimable Methodist merchant residing there, named Wyche, that this gentleman had been a member of the State legislature, and that he could give me a good start on my mission. Upon depositing my luggage, purposely condensed into a small space, I called upon Mr. Wyche. He gave me the coldest kind of a reception, did not invite me to his house, but informed me that a stage would leave in a few hours for Dan-ville, Va., where I could meet the Rev. Mr. Bryant, who was presiding elder over a district of the North Carolina Confer-ence. It was very plain that this estimable gentleman desired to transfer the charge of me to some one else. Years after that, I may stop here to say, his son, the Rev. Ira T. Wyche, and his son-in-law, the Rev. John Tillett, became my de-voted friends, and I learned from them that Mr. Wyche felt so disgusted that the American Bible Society should bestow its general agency upon such a poor-looking little Yankee as I was that he felt as though he did not want to have anything more to do with the work.

I took the stage, the one mode of conveyance in those days, and went to Danville. It was a long, hard, and doleful ride. I seemed to be going out of the State to which I had been sent. My funds were running low. When I reached Dan-ville the Rev. Mr. Bryant was out of town and would not be back for three days. I put up at a hotel immediately on the riverside to await the coming of this gentleman. I felt that I could not take another step till I saw him; in point of fact, I did not know how to get back into North Carolina. To take the stage in return would exhaust my money and send me into a region whose temperature had been greatly lowered for me by the presence of the cold Mr. Wyche. Whereupon it set in to rain, and it rained three or four days, and I stayed on in the hotel. I must have made a pitiful appearance, for the wife and the sister-in-law of the tavern-keeper plainly took com-passion on me, and I could see on the second day, as I sat eating my melancholy meal, that they were making designs upon me. One of them at last came to me and said I might be lonely up in my room, and, if I chose, any time I could come down and be in the sitting-room of the family, if the children would not annoy me. Now that was quite an open-ing. I felt as Mungo Park did, while staying in the wilds of Africa, when the native women gathered about him and sang him songs of compassion. It *was* a lonely position for a boy twenty years of age, with his first undertaking among strangers, mightily in love and most uncommonly poor. By and by, however, Mr. Bryant came and everything changed.

He was a man much below medium size, with a Jewish countenance, his hook nose a little bent toward the right. He was bright, buoyant, witty, and sometimes impassionedly elo-quent. Mr. Bryant received me most heartily, entered cordially into the matter of laying out work for me, and gave me a good start in my operations. We went down into Caswell County, one of the northern tiers of counties in North Carolina and not far from Danville. Mr. Bryant was to perform the service at the marriage of a young lady in the highest circle of society in that part of the coun ry. It gave me an introduction to the principal people whom I wished to know in Caswell County—to the United States senator, Bedford Brown, to the eloquent lawyer, John Kerr, who was my lifelong friend and who died while on the superior bench of North Carolina, to Dr. Williamson, a physician and planter of great influence and a leading man in the Methodist Church. Mr. Bryant laid out the plan for me, gave me letters, and arranged appointments. At that time the Methodist camp-meetings were going forward, and I was sent out to Iredell County to meet the Rev. Peter Doub, who was a presiding elder and a man of great native power, who had acquired more than usual learning under the difficulties of the Methodist itinerancy. All through the country, as I went preaching and making collections for the society, I heard accounts of Mr. Doub's strength and length of preaching. I was told of sermons extending over three hours, which seemed to be as great as they could be so far as the people could understand them, and how much greater they were beyond that no man in North Carolina had yet been able to determine. I remember that I drove up to the camp-ground in Iredell County, hitched my horse, inquired for the preachers' tent, went in, and found that services were going forward at the "stand," as the pulpit was called, and that Mr. Doub was holding forth. I stood where I could hear the conclusion of his sermon. He was a large man, of great physical vigor and of real mental robustness. I heard only the last few ringing falls of his sledge-hammer on the anvil of his text. The hymn was sung, and after the prayer he came to the tent, where I was introduced to him.

At that camp-meeting I preached every day, and I think it did me a world of good. All young preachers, upon quitting the college or theological seminary, ought to seek a round of camp-meetings and preach whenever they can get a chance —at a real, genuine, old-fashioned camp-meeting; not your camp-meeting on grounds where they have houses three and a half stories high with gable ends to the streets, but where there are tents and wagons, and nothing else to sleep in, and where people are gathered from great distances. No man could read a little twenty minutes' moral essay there; neither men nor angels could endure the ridiculousness of that. He has got to turn himself loose and preach with a swing. I am very thankful to my old friend Doub for keeping me that summer at camp-meetings. Physically and mentally it nearly wore me out, but it loosened my mental joints and made me uncommonly supple. I was taken so young—not yet of age—that I had the full benefit of tuition like this.

At the close of the camp-meetings of Mr. Doub's district I made my way to the town of Salem, in Forsyth County. This is an old settlement by the Moravians. For years they have had a noted female school at this place, which has educated several generations of Southern girls, and many of the leading families of the Southern States, from Virginia to Louisiana, have been represented at this school. The town and seminary were more like my imaginings of a foreign place than anything I had ever seen. I was the guest of the excellent Bishop Van Vleck, not only as agent of the American Bible Society, but also as the friend of the family of his cousin in Newark, N. J., who were intimates of Miss Annie Disosway. Everything was very quaint and very simple and to me very sweet. Every attention was shown me, and I was invited to preach in what might be called their cathedral. I recollect two incidents in that visit. Naturally, love and marriage were favorite topics with me, and so one evening I led the conversation to the method among the Moravians. I said to the good bishop that I did not quite approve this taking a wife by lot. "Why not?" said he. "Oh, it seems to me," I replied, "that it is not only devoid of sentiment, but has the appearance of tempting God." He set his views before me after this fashion. There was no tempting God, but implicit trust in God. All Christian people believe in a special providence; why should not a heavenly Father care as much for the mating of his children as earthly parents do? Moreover, when a Moravian had a wife assigned to him by lot, he took her precisely as if the sky opened and God handed her down to his arms, and she came to him in the same spirit. Now, two people, he thought, marrying in this way would be better prepared to endure the strain made upon them by the prosy and drudging details and often harassing anxieties of married life; they would never think of divorce on account of incompatibility of temper. They might have been brought together just be-

cause of that incompatibility, if such existed; or, having been
brought together of God, perhaps there was no such thing
as this fancied incompatibility.   He instanced his own case,
where his wife had been selected for him at Herrnhut, in Germany.   He had never seen her until he met her on the wharf
in Philadelphia.   " I doubt," he said, looking at the dumpy
little German *frau* with fond eyes, "if I could have made a
better choice if I had taken many years and searched all the
States through."   " Oh yes," I said; "but yours happened to
be a happy union; but really, now, are there not many mistakes made by this method? "   He turned to me and said,
" My young friend, when you come to be older you will find
that there are a great many mistakes made by the other method, where a man has no one to blame but himself for his own
choice."   I felt that there was great force in this, but at the
same time I had a secret conviction that I had not made any
mistake.

From Salem I came to the town of Greensboro, which was
afterward to be my home.   I had a horse and a sulky.
Coming down the hill just west of the town, my horse stum-
bled and broke one shaft in falling, the other shaft as he attempted to rise; but he fell again, and I was drawn across him.
I lay perfectly still until I could gather the reins, and then,
putting my two hands on his side, I leaped as far from him as
I could.   He was up as quickly as myself, and shivering, his
flanks trembling with the splinters which had been driven into
them like arrows.   If I had not made the arrangement with
the reins before I rose I should have been in very great peril.
But having had him now for a number of weeks, we had become friends, and he allowed me to extract the splinters and
fasten him to a fence, which I afterward learned was on
Governor Moorhead's grounds.   Gathering together my little
luggage, I walked into the town and went, as I was directed,
to the house of Dr. Lindsay, the leading physician of the

place, where I found the Methodist pastor, the Rev. Solomon Lea, and his presiding elder, the Rev. Mr. Brock. The first was a scholarly man and had been a school-teacher; the second was a very handsome man, after the style of General Jackson, but not a learned man. His library consisted of but little beyond a Bible, a Methodist Discipline, a Methodist hymn-book, an almanac, and a file of the "Richmond Christian Advocate." Most of his thinking was plainly done without the aid of reading, but he was a very superior man. I had my duster on, and plenty of dust, and my small valise in my hand.

Meeting the two ministers on the porch, we sat and talked for some time. On this, as on almost every occasion upon meeting prominent men in North Carolina, the look was given of wonder that I should be the general agent of the American Bible Society. I knew what it meant; I knew that I weighed only one hundred and one pounds, that I was slightly below five and a half feet in height, and that I looked as if I should be in the junior year in college. My anxiety always was lest this should interfere with the success of my work as agent for the great society, which I was serving not in a perfunctory manner, but with a great delight in being instrumental in distributing copies of the Word of God. Mr. Lea was a nervous man; Mr. Brock was imperturbable. After we had conversed for some time, and I had given an account of the camp-meetings I had attended, I told them at last that my horse was tied to a fence on the roadside and the remnants of my sulky were near him. Mr. Brock sprang up at once and called for a colored serving-man to come with us, and we four proceeded immediately to the scene of my disaster. When about halfway there Mr. Brock suddenly stopped and, looking at me, said, "You'll do; I like you!" "I am glad you think so," I replied, "but why do you like me?" "Because you didn't tell your story until you were ready." "Well," said I, "I can return the compliment; I like you, and for the reason that, although you saw me come into the house in the strange condition in which I was, you asked me no questions until I was ready to tell my story." From that time on till the day of his death, in the far West in after years, Moses Brock and I were fast friends.

The day after my arrival Mr. Brock took me out to another hill at the west of the town and showed me the site of the projected Greensboro Female College, of which he was a trustee and an earnest promoter. I gave him what views I had on the subject of female education, which of course at that time were crude enough, but I had seen some schools at the North. I asked him if he were also trustee of the Randolph-Macon College, the Methodist college for boys in Virginia, belonging to the two conferences. He said no, he had been. When the chief duty of a trustee was to carry a surveyor's chain around the old fields in Mecklenburg County to stake out the campus of a college he felt himself sufficiently endowed by nature and grace for a duty of that sort; but when they called on him to sign his name to a Latin diploma he felt that common honesty compelled him to resign his trusteeship. He was a great man; a small ignoramus would have kept on signing diplomas.

My next point of interest was the city of Raleigh, the capital of the State. This I reached in November, 1841, to attend the session of the North Carolina Conference, to which I intended to transfer my membership from the New Jersey Conference. Here was the seat of the North Carolina Bible Society, whose president was at that time the venerable Duncan Cameron, a wealthy Scotchman, an Episcopalian, and president of the State Bank. My position as general agent of the American Bible Society for the whole State brought me to the acquaintance of the prominent citizens of the several denominations, and made me a subject of great interest to the

North Carolina Conference, which body of ministers received me with very great cordiality. The impression which I had made upon the three leading men of the conference seems to have been most favorable. The impression upon gentlemen of other denominations charged with the interest of the Bible Society seemed also to have been not unpleasant, although on both sides I met at first with that expression of surprise and, as I interpreted it, slight disgust that the American Bible Society should have selected such a stripling for such a work; it seemed to throw contempt upon the venerable commonwealth of North Carolina. I can now see just how those gentlemen must have felt, but the effect upon me at the time was provocative; it put me on my mettle, and I was determined to work day and night in such a fashion as to eclipse all that my large and aged predecessors had ever done in the work of collecting money for the parent society and supplying the State with copies of the Holy Scriptures. It so happened that in the Methodist church, a night or two after the conference opened, I was called upon to lead in prayer, and that prayer seemed to have produced a considerable impression upon the preachers who were present. On Sunday I was invited to preach in the Presbyterian church, the pastor of which was the Rev. Dr. Drury Lacey, afterward president of Davidson College, the Presbyterian institution in the State, and to the day of his death my warm, consistent friend. Here again I seemed to have been divinely aided, and the sermon that day was a turning-point in my life. At that time the Hon. David L. Swain, who had been on the bench of the Superior Court and also governor of the State, was president of the university of the State, at Chapel Hill. He had married Eleanor White, a granddaughter of Richard Caswell, one of the early governors of the State, whose venerable mother was still alive and residing in an old-fashioned mansion on a place occupying a whole square in the city. Her husband had been Secretary of State.

The Whites were Methodists.   Mrs. White's lovely young granddaughter, Miss Felton, had just married the Rev. Ed-ward Wadsworth, of the Virginia Conference, and I had met them in Richmond as I came through.   Governor Swain was on a visit to his wife's mother.   He was an energetic man of great ability and far-reaching policy and of tireless ambition; these qualities were united with a high moral sense, generous disposition, and a keen sense of honor.   He was one of the homeliest men in North Carolina; very tall, angular, with a narrow, towering head and keen gray eyes.   He had an only son, whose baptismal name was Richard, but who had inherited his father's nickname of " Bunk " Swain, Gover-nor Swain being thus familiarly known because he was born in Buncombe County and had represented that county in the State legislature.   Little Bunk happened to hear me preach in the Presbyterian church, to which he had come with his aunt. They both went home with such glowing accounts of "the lit-tle boy what preached," as Bunk described me, that he drove his father into coming to see me and into bringing Bunk with him.   Now it came to pass that at that time Governor Swain was exceedingly anxious to have a Methodist professor in the university.   My age and size were much against me, as I afterward learned, but the governor became interested in me; I was invited several times to dine or take tea at the White residence, and the governor had an opportunity to hear me preach again.   Before we parted a pledge was taken that I should visit the university on my mission in the course of the spring.

After the adjournment of the conference which met in Raleigh, I went to Fayetteville, under the direction of Mr. Cameron, to look after a lawsuit in which the American Bible Society was interested, and which I succeeded in bringing to a satisfactory conclusion.   After that I passed up into the center of the State and recollect very distinctly that I attained my majority in a little town in Chatham County called Haywood. I spent the remainder of the spring diligently working at my agency, visiting and preaching, and becoming acquainted with prominent clergymen and laymen of all denominations, one of my visits being to the seat of the university, where I could not have made an unfavorable impression, as the trustees of that institution the following summer elected me to the professorship of logic and rhetoric. This occurred while I was on a visit to the North, for a change of occupation and for some rest, which I really needed, for I had worked almost incessantly. In the month of March I went to the town of Newbern. The Methodist pastors at that time were the Rev. Dr. John E. Edwards, now (1887) living, having ever since continued in the active pastorate, and an associate, the Rev. John Todd Brame, a young man of very fine intellect, who had been graduated with considerable honors at Randolph-Macon College. I was engaged to preach every day for a week. Full of zeal, I went at it with all my might, preaching twenty-eight times in twenty-six days, holding prayer-meetings, assisting in pastoral visiting, and enjoying the hospitalities of a town so refined that at that time it was called the Athens of Carolina. All this told upon me. It was while I was on a visit to Saratoga that I received the notification of my election to the North Carolina professorship. I submitted it to my friend Dr. Janes, who, while greatly praising me for my success in the agency of the society, advised me to accept the professorship. So also did Miss Disosway's father. I think it was a gratification to him, and I felt that it was a feather in my cap to ask his advice about accepting such an elevation as that. When I first told him I wanted his daughter he burst into tears and said, " I can offer no objection to you at all, but I don't want to see Anna a widow after being the wife of a poor Methodist preacher three years "—a limit which I now think my appearance justified him in making. So I accepted the professorship, upon which I entered in January, 1843, being at that time a little over twenty-two years of age.

[The editors would insert at this point the following article, which appeared in the " Raleigh Christian Advocate " in July, 1885:]

"A POEM WITH A HISTORY

" Forty-three years ago Dr. Deems preached a sermon in Raleigh, after the hearing of which Ex-Governor W. W. Holden wrote a little poem, the history of which our readers will appreciate, and will find in the following letter from Dr. Deems to Governor Holden, which we publish, together with the poem referred to:

" 'NEW YORK, July 13, 1885.

" ' *Hon. W. W. Holden.*

" ' MY DEAR SIR : Yesterday I found in an old tin box an old album, in which were many things pertaining to the transition time of my passing from my " teens," among them this poem. It has occurred to me that perhaps you and your children would be pleased to have the original scrap cut by me from the " Standard " nearly forty-three years ago (!!!), when the reading of it almost took my breath away.

" ' In the album from which it is cut there is a memorandum, stating my suspicion that it was written by you " the day after I had preached upon the soul's paradise state between death and the resurrection."

" ' With best wishes,
" ' Very truly yours,
" ' CHARLES F. DEEMS.'

" ' For the North Carolina Standard.

" ' TO THE REV. C. F. DEEMS

" ' It is a startling and a glorious thing
To gaze on genius in its hour of might,
To hear the rushing of its flaming wings,
To mark its eye as upward through the range
Of the bright worlds of thought it sends its glance
Amid the splendors of the spirit-land.

" ' SPEAKER OF GOD ! thy work is great indeed,
And thou dost gird thyself unto the task
With all the strength of deep humility,
Till thy " boy-spirit," gathering in its course
The power of angels, sweeps untremulous
O'er all time's wrecks, from Adam's paradise
To that far land, shrouded in mystery
Beneath God's throne, and from whose radiant shores
Ascend the anthems of the waiting throng
In thrilling numbers to the gates of heaven.

" ' And what to thee
Is all earth's pageantry, the bannered pomp
Of glittering legions?   What the clarion's tone
Rousing to battle?   What the rending shout
Of the strong multitudes that pave the path
Of mad ambition?   What the laurel wreath
Which blooms forever on the poet's brow?
Thine is a holier mission than the earth,
Robed as it is in beauty, ever gave;
And thine an honor which the worlds shall see
In the great judgment-hour, when all the stars
Which thou hast plucked from out the night of sin
Shall flash their glories, fresh and beautiful
And all undarkened, from thy crown of life.
                                                    " ' H.

" ' RALEIGH, September 5, 1842.' "

When I look back at the period of my life when I accepted
the call to the university, it seems to me unaccountable.   I

have always been afflicted with a large measure of self-distrust, which has been strangely mingled with a sort of obstinate audacity. When challenged to perform any public duty I have invariably shrunk from it in my feelings and yet have under-taken it by sheer force of my will. That at such an age, with so little acquirement, I should go into a faculty of men of ability and experience now seems to me to be the most ridiculous action of my life; but I had determined to undertake it, and so I fell to work in the few intervening months to qualify myself for it as well as I could.

For years the chair of rhetoric and logic had been occupied by the Rev. Dr. William Mercer Green, an Episcopal clergyman, reared in Wilmington, well connected and well known, a gentleman and a scholar—especially a gentleman—a gentleman of very suave and pleasing manners. The duties of the chair were divided and the harder portion assigned to me. I had to take the department of logic, but also assisted in the department of rhetoric, in the correction of compositions, and in the teaching of elocution. Before my advent the only book on logic used in the university was that most absurd and contemptible little treatise by Professor Hedge, of Harvard University, a book bearing the title of logic, with every essential thing belonging to logic left out. I adopted Whately's treatise and commenced with the junior class, in which there was not a single student who could not have taken me by the nape of the neck and put me out of the window, and I managed to make work for the class; so much so that they complained to the president that this young professor was making the department of logic absolutely more difficult than the department of mathematics. The professor of mathematics was Professor James Phillips, an Englishman by birth, who had had experience as a teacher in New York City before coming to the university. He was a man of very considerable ability. The salaries of the professors were not large, and Professor Phillips eked out the support of his family by preaching at a country church. I always liked to hear him preach and had great respect for his brains and acquirements, but have suspected that his son, the Rev. Dr. Charles Phillips, who afterward came to the chair in the university, was the better teacher. Professor Phillips was fortunate in his children, one of whom (Mrs. Cornelia Spencer)* has made many contributions to current literature, especially in the religious papers of her own church, and wrote a book called " The Last Ninety Days of the War," which I published in 1866, the first year of my residence in New York. The elder of his two sons is the professor to whom I have alluded, and the younger, Mr. Samuel Phillips, has been solicitor-general of the United States.

The senior professor was Dr. Elisha Mitchell, who had been brought from Yale College to the university. He had devoted himself to science, had trodden almost every cow-path in the State of North Carolina, and before his death had educated three generations, grandfather, father, and grandson. Dr. Mitchell was a man of commanding appearance and magnificent head. His memory was like a tarred board; every feather that dropped on it seemed to stick. He spared no pains and no expense to settle the most minute questions which had sprung up in his investigations. I have known him to spend forty dollars to secure a map from Europe which would settle the name and precise location of some small village in Mexico or South America. And so he would explore the recesses of any county in the State to strive to find a piece of stone or humble plant, the existence and the characteristics of which it seemed to him necessary to know in order to pursue his studies. It was in this pursuit that he lost his life. He was examining the mountains in west North Carolina to determine the height of the highest when he fell from a height

---

* The University of North Carolina, at its commencement, 1895, conferred the degree of LL.D. on Mrs. Spencer.

into a pool of water, where he expired. His remains were discovered, and great honor was paid to his memory by an assemblage on that mountain-peak, in which the Rt. Rev. Bishop Otey, of Tennessee, President Swain, of the university, and other distinguished gentlemen took part. The professor's name was given to the mountain, which will hand it down to future generations. Professor Mitchell was a genial as well as a learned man, a wit as well as a scientist; and I think we all regarded him at that time as the person who gave the greatest reputation to the institution.

Professor De Bernière Hooper, a descendant of the North Carolinian signer of the Declaration of Independence of that name, was professor of Latin. These were the only members of the faculty of any mark. Governor Swain, the president, imparted his activity to the institution and built it up in many ways. He survived until after the war. I believe that at this writing (June, 1887) all my colleagues are dead.

The duties appointed me upon my first entrance upon the professorship would not have been at all arduous to a man thoroughly prepared for them; but for me, having had no time even to review my college studies on the subjects which I was to teach, it was pretty hard work. I was young and ambitious, and threw myself into it with all my might. In addition to teaching logic, I also had care of the essays written by some of the classes, and took turns in preaching in the college chapel with the senior professor, Dr. Mitchell, and my colleague, Dr. Green, afterward Bishop of Mississippi. It was a prodigious ordeal for a young fellow who had no theological education and no practice in writing sermons. The first of my productions in that line was made for the chapel of the university.

In addition to my college duties, I paid attention to the Methodist church in the village and did all I could to build it up. On Sunday night, in a little chapel on the site of the present Presbyterian church in the village, I took turns with the other professors in preaching. Unrestrained by manuscript, I turned myself loose on the boys and the villagers in earnest appeals. The collegians preferred my crude night discourses to my carefully prepared morning sermons, which, although written out, now seem to me to be about as crude as any young man's sermons well could be.

While I was at Chapel Hill there came a young publisher of the name of Ball, representing the firm of Sorin & Ball, who secured from me twelve of my manuscripts and published them under the title of " Twelve College Sermons."

There is such power and usefulness in ignorance. It does seem to me that the more we know the less we are willing to do, because we become more and more severely critical of our own performances. No twelve sermons that I have produced since I was fifty-five years of age would I allow any house to publish now. My very youth, I suppose, disarmed criticism in a measure; I was phenomenally young for such a position.

In those early days salaries in colleges were not very ample. My salary was seven hundred and fifty dollars; in Chapel Hill, however, at that time it was equal to fifteen hundred dollars in New York, and was not much less than twenty-five hundred dollars probably would be in Chapel Hill at this day. On that sum I determined to marry.

When I became engaged to my wife her father was one of the most prosperous merchants in New York. Between our engagement and this summer the disastrous tide which leveled almost all houses passed over New York, and my fiancée was as gloriously poor as her lover. But I knew that in their most prosperous days the Disosways had trained their children to habits of economy, and that my little sweetheart especially was a woman who by her natural disposition, her acquired habits, and the grace of God which ruled in her heart would be ready to adapt herself to any circumstances and help me in my work; so by correspondence it was arranged that in the summer vacation we should marry. Courtship and marriage did not take me away one single hour from my professorial and ministerial duties; and now (1887) that we have been married forty-four years and have had six children I put it on record that my wife has never for personal or domestic considerations interfered with my work so much as one hour. It seems to me it must be almost unparalleled in the history of a Christian minister that any man could say so much.

Her family were living at the old country-seat in Asbury, in western New Jersey. It was a journey from Chapel Hill to that place in those days. A day was spent in going by carriage from Chapel Hill to Raleigh, then by a miserable little railroad, consisting of rows of hewn logs with strips of iron spiked to them, to Gaston, thence to Petersburg, and so on slowly till we reached Princeton. It took me a good part of a week to do this. At Philadelphia I fell in with a presidential party, the center of which was President Tyler, and we all drew up at Princeton on Saturday night and lay over Sunday. I remember being at a party that night with President Tyler at Commodore Stockton's, although how I got there is to me a mystery to this day. On Monday by stage I reached my destination. There, on the 20th of June, in her father's house, I was married to—well, there is no use of an old man making a fool of himself by undertaking to tell what it was he married.

In time to reach my duties at the university, we started back, visiting my friends in Baltimore and in Raleigh. The condition of the railroads in that day may be made to appear by the following incident. While going from Gaston to Raleigh a rail shot up through the floor of the car between my bride and myself. If it had struck the foot of either of us it would probably have broken a limb. What a road it must have been when the wheels were so small that a piece of iron lying loose on the track could jump a wheel and strike the floor of a car! What a curious piece of iron that rail must have been to perform such a feat! What a slight kind of floor that must have been that could be penetrated by so slender a strip of iron! There was a joke current about this road at that period. A conductor going along perceived a wooden-legged traveler, and as he was lame invited him to board the train and thus get a lift on the journey. The lame man excused himself on the ground that he was in a hurry and could not wait. Nevertheless the accommodations then were better than they had been a few years before, when the whole journey was made by stages. Then it required several weeks and was full of perils; and North Carolina merchants going to New York, or to Philadelphia or Baltimore, as many of them preferred, were accustomed to make their wills.

Collegians make a point of testing every man who enters the faculty of their institution. The boys tested me. I had put on no airs in the recitation-room; I had overlooked many things; had gone straight forward, endeavoring to interest them in their studies, creating discussions in the classes, arraying some portion of a class against another in a logical discussion, taking sides first with one party and then another, sometimes leading my party to victory and then again encountering a defeat, which I always took in good humor, pointing out to the best of my ability to each party why the defeat or the success came.

A part of the discipline of the university was that each member of the faculty took his turn in making a nocturnal domiciliary visit to the rooms of the students, talking with them, helping them in their studies, and also having the responsibility of the care of the campus. There were some wild, rough fellows in my day from the South and Southwest, but they were not such dangerous men as certain boys from some of the older families of Virginia and North Carolina, who could plan and execute mischief with great cold-bloodedness. I knew my time for trial would come. It did. I was visiting the room of one of the students on the first floor in the southwest end of the east building, when certain of the boys, who had taken umbrage at a very plain sermon I had delivered to them in the chapel, managed to fasten the door so that there was no exit to the undergraduate in whose room I was, nor to me. I was the only professor on duty. They commenced stoning the room. It was not only a mischievous, but a perilous thing. I believe every window-pane was smashed. The room was so exposed that there was but one part in which it was possible for two men to stand without being hit if missiles were sent in from every practicable direction, as they certainly were. After the first shot or two, when I found that the combined strength of the undergraduate and myself, who were prisoners, was unable to force the door open, I led him to that point of safety. Our assailants had undoubtedly calculated that we would go under the bed when they had searched the corner with small stones. I calculated as much and gave that bed a wide berth. It was fortunate, as they were drinking and singing and exciting themselves in their attack. Suddenly there came through the window a stone so big and so aimed that it fell in the center of the bed and broke it down to the floor. We were in our corner, however, conversing together until the storm blew over. It was a long time, probably two hours; it seemed to us much longer. At last a tutor coming by discovered the state of affairs and opened the door. The undergraduate found another lodging, for the room was wrecked and piled with stones; and I went back to my little wife, to whom I said nothing about the matter, as I determined never to allude to it in the college.

The boys had tried my pluck once or twice before, and found that I was not scared by having a pistol pointed at me and that I simply did my duty.

Next morning I went regularly to my class with just the same appearance, I suppose, I had any other morning. But Governor Swain, the president of the university, had been told the matter by the tutor and was in a state of great exasperation. I had become his pet, and he was proud of me and could not bear to have any slight or disrespect shown me. He felt as if the older professors could take care of themselves, but as he had induced me to come to the university, he was pledged to give me special presidential support. The trustees were called together. One of the sons of one of the prominent members thereof, of very distinguished family, was in the row, and quite a number of the boys were sentenced to rustication.

I went before the board and pleaded that the sentence should not be executed; that I believed it was a proper one and necessary for the discipline of the college, but, the discipline being vindicated, I had no animosity against these young men, and felt that it was merely a foolish college freak. I succeeded in saving them; and from that day on each man in that outbreak was my friend. Moreover, during the remaining years of my stay at the university I never had a disagreeable encounter with a student. My first year made them believe that I was true, courageous, and unvindictive; that if I was not a great man, I was greatly addicted to doing my duty; and I have no better friends than the Chapel Hill boys of that period.

PART II

MEMOIR

THE YEARS

The years that come to us are dumb,
  Their footsteps rhythmic, low;
We hear not as they swiftly come
  And yet more swiftly go.

Each brings us something we must keep,
  And each doth something take;
Thus we are changing while we sleep,
  And changing while we wake.
                    From " My Septuagint."

CHAPTER I

THE five years of Professor Deems's life in Chapel Hill as a member of the faculty of the University of North Carolina were, indeed, marked by perfect good will between the students and himself, as well as between his colleagues and himself. His home and social life, too, was such that he ever afterward looked back upon that period with pleasure almost unalloyed. It was here that, on May 27, 1844, his first child, a son, was born, to whom was given the name Theodore Disosway Deems. On December 18, 1846, another son, Francis Melville Deems, was born.

Among the members of the faculty none secured a larger place in the heart of Professor Deems than President Swain, as has been seen from the reference to him in the autobiographical notes. This high esteem was never lowered by time; for on May 13, 1869, in the course of an address on the occasion of the fifty-third anniversary of the American Bible Society, in the Lafayette Place Reformed Dutch Church, New York City, Dr. Deems said: " On this program you have an announcement of the death of one of our vice-presidents, the Hon. David L. Swain, of North Carolina. He was my intimate friend, and his death is to me a severe personal bereavement. That great and good man, judge, governor, president of the university, has accompanied me to the cabins of sick servants, and sat reverently while I read to them the Word of God, and knelt humbly on the sanded floor while I prayed. That was in the days of master and servant. The first time I saw him after the war he came into a yard where, on the occasion of the death of a little colored child, I was preaching to an assembly of freedmen, and then he spoke words of comfort to the bereaved mother, and walked with them to the graveyard, where we buried the child amid the solemn services of the church."

The five years at Chapel Hill, from 1842 to 1847, were not only happy, but also busy and significant years. Professor Deems toiled incessantly, laboriously, and fruitfully. As a natural consequence his reputation as a teacher and preacher of unusual ability went abroad. So it is not strange that the authorities of Randolph-Macon College, a Methodist institution, then at Boydton, Va., had their attention attracted to him. By invitation he delivered an address at Randolph-Macon at the commencement exercises of the class of 1847. In a letter to the Rev. Edward M. Deems, from Mr. Richard Irby, the present secretary and treasurer of the college, whose personal recollections of the institution go back to 1839, that gentleman says: " I recollect very well his [Professor Deems's] speech at the old college, and had a copy of it in my collection, but unfortunately that, with many other such things, has been lost in my moving to and fro. The first time your father visited the old college he took part in a debate in the Washington Hall. A young 'limb of the law' took occasion to quote ostentatiously legal authority to sustain his argument; but your father showed he knew more about Coke and Littleton than the young lawyer himself, and floored him, much to the amusement of the audience."

This visit led the authorities to call Professor Deems to the chair of natural science. Had the University of North Carolina been a Methodist institution this call would doubtless

have been declined, but Professor Deems had this one draw-
back to his happiness, the impression that he was not as useful to his church as he might be. Perhaps in that idea he
was mistaken, but he himself used to say, in reference to this
matter, " The impression was deepened by the frequent appeals
of certain brethren in behalf of denominational posts, and
especially by the repeated efforts of the friends of Randolph-
Macon College to draw me to that institution."

Randolph-Macon College was founded by the Methodist
Church in 1830, was opened at Boydton, Va., in 1832, and
moved in 1868 to its present site in Ashland, Va. It is the
oldest Methodist college in the United States, its charter having been granted by the legislature of Virginia at its 1829–30
session. The idea of the college was born as early as 1828,
in the mind of a layman, Gabriel P. Disosway, who received
aid in crystallizing and realizing it from the Rev. Hezekiah G.
Leigh, the Rev. John Early (afterward bishop), and other prominent Methodist ministers and laymen. Mr. Disosway was at
that time living in Petersburg, Va., and was a brother of Israel D. Disosway, whose daughter became Professor Deems's
wife.

Randolph-Macon College was in 1846 the joint property of
the Virginia and North Carolina conferences. Professor Deems
was then a member of the North Carolina Conference. In
1846 the Rev. William A. Smith, D.D., was elected president,
and Professor Deems was invited to take a chair in the faculty.
The question of the wisdom of so doing he submitted to a
number of his ministerial brethren, some of whom urged him
to accept and others to decline the invitation. After much
thought he decided that it was his duty to accept. And so in
December, 1847, he took his wife and his two boys, Theodore
and Frank, and moved to Boydton, Mecklenburg County, Va.,
about one hundred and twenty-five miles southwest of Richmond.

The travelers reached their new home in midwinter, the

ground being covered with snow. Boydton naturally appeared at its worst. It was a very small place, and remote
from the railroad. The cottage into which Professor Deems
moved was in a grove somewhat apart from other dwelling-
houses, and at first the new-comers were very lonely, the solitude of their surroundings being intensified in the spring and
summer evenings by the weird call of the whippoorwill, who
seemed to find in Boydton a congenial atmosphere.

In January, 1848, Professor Deems entered upon his labors
in the department of chemistry, commencing his course of
lectures on January 24th. This he did with an inadequate
equipment for his laboratory, and with no special training or
knowledge of the science which he was to teach. In view of
these facts we have brought out at this time that ambition,
boldness, and faith in divine help which ever marked his character and conduct. One of the rules of his life was to leap
into any work to which he was called by Providence, and then
work or fight his way out. He rarely failed, although at times
he found himself in desperate straits. As professor of chemistry at Randolph-Macon he had in his class, as he often said,
some pupils who knew more about the subject than he did;
although he did not let the young men find that out, for, as
he used to say, laughingly, he kept at least one lesson ahead
of his class, rising often before day to prepare himself, and
when he lacked minute knowledge of the subject in hand he
performed so many and such brilliant experiments that his
young men found no time nor disposition to ask embarrassing
questions.

Among the members of the faculty Professor David Duncan, whose son, the Rev. James Duncan, D.D., became one of
the Southern Methodist bishops, was probably his most intimate
friend. But Professor Deems formed other warm friendships
among his colleagues and among the students. Upon the
whole, however, the one year of life at Boydton had in it more

clouds than sunshine. In a certain place Professor Deems writes: "The year 1848 covers my professorship at Randolph-Macon. It was a bitter year. The failure of a Northern firm stripped me of what little I had saved at the University of North Carolina. I immediately projected the 'Southern Methodist Pulpit,' a periodical intended to assist me. The prospectus was concocted and written in Richmond, and appeared in the 'Richmond Christian Advocate' of December 29, 1847."

The "Southern Methodist Pulpit" was published monthly, and was maintained for four years, the bound numbers making four stately volumes, and containing much interesting and valuable matter.

Naturally Professor Deems's time was closely occupied by the preparation of his lectures, but he managed to find time enough to write quite frequently for the periodicals of the day, especially the "Richmond Christian Advocate."

He found living at Boydton an aged Methodist minister, the Rev. Hezekiah G. Leigh, who owned a number of slaves. From him he hired as cook Lucinda, a negro woman about fifty years of age. She was an earnest Christian, possessing most of the good traits while free from most of the bad qualities of the Southern slave. The family became warmly attached to good old "Aunt Lucinda," and their affection was heartily reciprocated; so much so that when, at the close of 1848, Professor Deems told her that they must part, as he was going to move away, she protested violently. "No, sir," said she, "I will *never* leave you. You've got to buy me. If you don't buy me I will run away and follow you!" So Professor Deems had a slave thrust upon him, as it were. He paid Mr. Leigh about three hundred dollars for the good woman, and until her death at Greensboro a few years later he did all he could to make her lot a comfortable one, and she served him with untiring industry and sleepless fidelity.

While never a rabid pro-slavery man, Professor Deems nevertheless conscientiously accepted negro slavery as a part of God's providential dealings with our race, finding in the Word of God provision made for the righteous attitude of the slave toward his master and the master toward his slave. Wherever he lived in the South he won the hearts of the negroes by his sympathy and self-denying efforts to provide them with the gospel of their Lord and Saviour.

In less than a year after arriving at Randolph-Macon College he began, on various accounts, to feel that he was not exactly where he could best serve the church and the Master. He therefore finally decided to resign his professorship, and, yielding to the pressure brought to bear on him to enter the itinerancy, he became pastor at Newbern, N. C., where he had won many friends years before as the "boy-preacher."

Professor Deems's resignation did not mean the end of his interest in Randolph-Macon College, for he ever afterward cherished toward it a warm feeling of interest. Nor was this a mere sentiment, but a practical thing, for he twice delivered the annual address, once before the war and once after. He aided the presidents in their efforts to secure in New York subscriptions for the college, besides giving liberally himself. He sent the library several of his books, and but a short time before his death aided the professor of physics and biology to furnish his laboratory. He also, by request, sent his portrait, which is now on the wall of the library, surrounded by a number of others, whose originals he was associated with in former days.

But his resignation in 1848 was made in good faith, and was soon followed by his departure from Boydton. Again packing his household goods, he and his family, after another midwinter journey of about two hundred miles, found a home in the parsonage of the Methodist church at Newbern, N. C. Here he continued his work on the "Southern Methodist Pulpit," but gave most of his time and toil to his pulpit and pastoral work. Although only twenty-nine years old, and although most of his experience had been in educational work, yet at Newbern, both as pastor and preacher, he was eminently successful. The church was in every way greatly strengthened by the efforts of the earnest, industrious, and eloquent young pastor.

From a letter of a friend who lived in Newbern and was a parishioner of Mr. Deems when he was pastor there is culled the following interesting extract: "I wish I could write of his beautiful life and work in Newbern. As you probably know, he went there first in 1842 as agent for the American Bible Society. In a protracted meeting at that time he preached a powerful sermon from Judges v. 23: 'Curse ye Meroz, said the angel of the Lord, curse ye bitterly the inhabitants thereof; because they came not to the help of the Lord, to the help of the Lord against the mighty.' This gave great offense, but by it the wrath of man was made to praise God. Hundreds flocked to hear the bold young preacher, and I think the protracted meeting resulted in over one hundred conversions. I once went with him to a Thursday afternoon appointment in the country. For some good reason there were only three persons, besides myself, in the congregation. Instead of dismissing us with a short service, he preached one of the most beautiful sermons I ever listened to from mortal lips. As we left the church I remarked upon it, and he said, 'Yes, that congregation was an inspiration!' He knew they had made great sacrifices to come to church, and he preached his very best for them. Great good resulted from it."

The home circle in the Methodist parsonage at Newbern during 1849 was a very happy one. Mrs. Deems's good mother, Mrs. Letitia Disosway, at this time spent several months with her daughter's family. It was in Newbern that

Mr. Deems's third child was born, and named Mary Letitia. With that playfulness of nature which ever characterized him, and with reference to a certain nasal conformation of his little daughter, he immediately dubbed her " Little Cambric Needle Nose," as he had called his little son Theodore " Theodoric the Goth," or " Ollie de Gok," as the little one himself put it, in his vain effort to echo his father's words. The only cloud which flecked Mr. Deems's sky at Newbern was the fact that his physical powers were unable to keep pace with those of his mind, compelling him for a time to recuperate at Beaufort on the seashore.

While a pastor at Newbern Mr. Deems was elected by the North Carolina Conference as one of the delegates to the General Conference, which met at St. Louis on May 1, 1850. On his way to the St. Louis Conference Mr. Deems first met the Rev. Hubbard H. Kavanaugh, afterward made a bishop, and always a valued friend. In April, 1884, he sent to the Rev. A. H. Redford, D.D., who was writing a life of the bishop, a paper, portions of which are inserted at this point because touching on several points of interest to the readers of this memoir.

" SOME RECOLLECTIONS OF BISHOP KAVANAUGH

" In May of 1850 I first saw Hubbard H. Kavanaugh. I was then a Methodist minister. The delegation from the North Carolina Annual Conference, of which I was a member, was on its way to the General Conference of the Methodist Episcopal Church, South, to be held in St. Louis. The two youngest members elect were, I believe, the Rev. A. H. Redford, of Kentucky, and the writer of these recollections, who was twenty-nine years of age. Our delegation went to Cincinnati by the river. When the steamer drew up to the levee there were several ministers waiting for us. Being young I remained on the hurricane-deck and saw the landing of some of the older members of the Virginia delegation, who had joined us *en route*. While the fastening of our steamer was going on I studied the faces on shore. There stood in the group one whom I had never seen. He made a great impression on me. He was a short, square, muscular man, large for his height, without superabundant flesh, ruddy without being florid, with a *permanent* look, and made to stay. In his eye there was a tremble of innocent fun, and when he laughed heartily he shook all over like a well-filled jelly-bag. I wanted to know him.

"As our delegation lay over in the city it fell upon me to have to preach, and already I had formed the habit of being careful, on special occasions, *not* to try to preach, but on all occasions to do my best. The sermon made Mr. and Mrs. Kavanaugh my friends. She was a charming type of the best kind of Methodist woman, and that is high praise. She was tall and slender, and in every physical, and perhaps mental, quality the opposite of her husband, certainly in the latter his complement. They went down the river with us, and everything I saw and heard of Hubbard Kavanaugh made him dearer to me. Then I felt that that man ought to be a bishop of the church, but knew that his time was not yet.

"From St. Louis I carried back the best remembrances of Mr. Kavanaugh. He was so simple without insipidity, so conscientious without asperity, so earnest without fanaticism, so cheerful without frivolity, so efficient without ambition, that I loved to dwell upon his character and try to form mine after the model. And what a preacher he was, after the first three quarters of an hour! He was an Alleghany thunder-storm turned loose. He could not preach in an expository, quiet, conversational manner. His subject seemed to burn in him like a smoldering fire until it reached a vent, when it suddenly blazed forth and set his whole nature in flame.

"In 1854 we were again elected to the General Conference,

held that year in Columbus, Ga. As few of the North Carolina delegates had seen Mr. Kavanaugh, and none but myself
knew him personally and well, the brethren depended upon
my representations of him, and I urged his name warmly. It
was agreed that we would vote for him. It ought perhaps to
be said that I had never spoken on this subject to Mr. Kavanaugh, and that in the North Carolina Conference there was
no one suffering with the *cacoëthes episcopalis.*

"During the session a Kentucky delegate came to me and
asked me what the North Carolinians desired in regard to the
episcopacy. I told him that we had no aspirations, but would
be pleased to receive suggestions; and he replied that the
Kentucky brethren had not made any choice. 'Well, you
don't have far to look.' 'What do you mean?' he asked.
'Of course you will vote for Hubbard H. Kavanaugh!' was
my answer, and he replied, 'We have not thought of him;
could he be elected?' 'That is not the question,' said I;
'but the whole North Carolina delegation is going to vote for
him because we believe he ought to be elected.' The Kentucky delegate seemed to be surprised, but pleased. The result
was that Mr. Kavanaugh was elected bishop.

"The bishop was known to be given to preaching sermons
that were lofty and long, taking a good while to reach the requisite pitch. After his election, while we were talking it over
in his room, and his natural modesty was really so oppressing
him that he felt as if he could not take the mighty work in
hand, I spoke cheerfully and playfully with him, giving him
two pieces of advice. One was that when he was to preach
at a conference he should commence in the basement, hold
forth about three quarters of an hour, and then *go preaching*
up into the pulpit, and carry everything before him. Mrs.
Kavanaugh said she had given him similar advice. The other
was that he never attend an annual conference without having
Mrs. Kavanaugh with him, assigning as a reason that I had

cast my vote mainly for the female side of the house, for if ever there were to be lady bishops, Mrs. Kavanaugh was my first choice. The first advice I have never heard that he heeded; the second I believe he faithfully observed, to his own great comfort and the profit of the church.

"At the General Conference of 1866 in New Orleans, the last in which I had the honor to represent the North Carolina Conference, who gave me that distinction although I had been removed to New York, Bishop Kavanaugh one day invited me to dine with him. Connected with the house of his host was a garden, in which we walked and talked. At the end of the alley, after we had passed up and down the path several times, he wheeled in front of me, stood and chuckled, and shook with that peculiar motion of merriment so familiar to his friends, and said, 'Deems, the responsibility of my being bishop is on your shoulders.' 'Let it stay there; I am willing to bear it.' 'Do you know what I thought of you when you first mentioned me for bishop?' 'Certainly not; you never told me.' 'Well,' said he, pausing a moment and chuckling again, 'I thought you were a fool.' And he laughed outright. 'Well, bishop, what did you think of a majority of the General Conference when they coincided with me?' Then he shook with merriment and exclaimed, 'Why, I thought they were fools too.' 'And have you never recovered your respect for the General Conference and for me, bishop?' There came suddenly a deeply solemn expression into his face, and he said slowly, 'Never, until our war came. There was a moment of crisis in Kentucky and the surrounding region. The affairs of the Southern Methodist Church were in such position that perhaps there was no man living who could have held the church from destruction but myself. My antecedents and connections in Kentucky gave me the needed influence, and one day in the midst of great pressure there came to me a consciousness of that, but never up to that hour had

I been able to understand the providence which had allowed the church to make me bishop.' A little twinkle came back into his eye, and he added, 'Then it occurred to me that Deems might be a fool, but he was a prophet likewise.' And he put his arm in mine, drew me affectionately to him, and we left the garden.

"When the Round Lake Fraternal Camp-meeting was projected, among the names in the South which I furnished the promoters was that of Bishop Kavanaugh. The church papers, North and South, told how he won all hearts by his modesty, sweetness, and cheerfulness, and how he surprised the great audience who heard him preach by the vast sweep of his thought and the mighty unction of his delivery. There are thousands who will make the impression on their children's children that the man *they* heard at Round Lake was the mightiest preaching bishop in America.

"My last meeting with Bishop Kavanaugh was at Deering Camp-ground, in Kentucky. I suspect that I owed my invitation to that meeting to my dear old friend. It was easy for a man of my style to preach alternately with a man of Bishop Kavanaugh's style, because we were so totally different in physique, and in manner of thought and delivery, that no comparison would probably suggest itself to any hearer; and we were intent on saving souls. A cottage was set apart for us; there we talked together about things pertaining to the kingdom of God, there we prayed together, thence we went together to the pulpit, and there we parted, to meet no more on earth. The next spring, when traveling in the Arabian Desert, going up to awful Sinai, the mount of God, one night I dreamed of that cottage on the Kentucky hill, and thought it was night, and thought I heard the choir singing, as they did one night before that cottage door, the strains of 'Beulah Land,' and the impression was so great that I awoke, and still heard the notes so distinctly that I walked out of the tent upon the cold sand, among my sleeping Arabs and sleeping camels, as if I would find the singers. Then I knew it was an echo from the Kentucky camp, and I seemed to be with Bishop Kavanaugh. I felt that since Moses went that road with Aaron and Hur no purer, loftier soul had gone that way up to the mount of God."

The St. Louis Conference consisted of one hundred and three members, the bishops present being Bishops Andrew, Paine, Capers, and Soule.

Probably the most interesting event of the occasion was the election to the episcopate of Henry B. Bascom, D.D. His ordination took place in the afternoon of Sunday, May 12th, and is referred to as follows in Mr. Deems's account of the conference in the "Southern Methodist Pulpit":

"An hour before the appointed time the large and elegant church where we met was crowded, the aisles were full, the vestibule was blocked up with standing spectators, aged clergy filled the altar and the pulpit steps. The bishop elect opened the services with a chapter from the Scriptures and announced a hymn. Dr. Lovick Pierce followed in prayer, and Dr. Bascom preached. 'God forbid that I should glory, save in the cross,' was his theme. He read his sermon, adhering minutely to the manuscript, and following the lines with the finger of his left hand. His voice was low and husky, so that he could scarcely have been heard by more than half the assemblage, until he arrived at his concluding paragraphs. Occasionally he would look up with an eye all fire, and fling upon the congregation a sentence which had the effect of the touch of the torpedo upon those who heard. His excitement was intense; he trembled under it, and so did we. We were afraid that it was more than he could endure. The last paragraph was ascendingly glorious. After his sermon the bishop elect was conducted by the venerable Drs. Early and Lovick Pierce

to his place in front of the altar. Bishop Andrew read the
collect, Bishop Capers the epistle, Bishop Paine the gospel.
Dr. Early presented the bishop elect. Bishop Andrew moved
the congregation to prayer and afterward addressed and
questioned the bishop elect. The impressive Veni Creator
Spiritus was repeated in alternate strains by the bishops and
other clergy present. The senior bishop was then brought in,
in a feeble state, tottering and gasping for breath. He stood
up—that great wreck of the noble Bishop Soule*—and laid
his large and heavy hand on the head of Dr. Bascom, which
seemed to sink beneath the pressure. The other bishops and
Drs. Early and Pierce then laid their hands upon his. In
the profound stillness of the great congregation, making, as
it were, the last effort of his old age, in a low, tremulous voice
Bishop Soule said, ' Receive the Holy Ghost for the office
and work of a bishop in the church of God.' The Bible was
presented by Bishop Andrew, and the concluding prayer was
offered by Bishop Paine. In a state of exhaustion from the
protracted and intensely interesting service, the congregation
retired from the church."

Meeting Bishop Bascom shortly after the service, Mr. Deems
said to him, "Good-morning, Doctor—Bishop Bascom;" and
his reply, with his husky voice and flushing face, to the acknowledgment of his new honor and authority was, "You tear
my head with a crown of thorns." Impressive as was the
occasion of the ordination of this great and good bishop, its
impressiveness would have been deepened had those concerned
seen that within four months, on September 8, 1850, the good
bishop was to exchange his "crown of thorns" for a "crown
of life."

While the conference was in session St. Louis was suffering
from a visitation of the cholera. Considerable sickness and

---

* Bishop Soule was the framer of the constitution of the Southern
Methodist Church.

panic prevailed among the delegates, but, with commendable faithfulness, they stood at the post of duty, and much important business was transacted before adjournment.

It was while at the St. Louis Conference that Mr. Deems was called to the presidency of Greensboro Female College, at Greensboro, N. C. After due consideration, deciding to accept the position, he returned to Newbern, and, closing his pastorate there, moved his family to his new field of work.

CHAPTER II

MR. DEEMS found the affairs of Greensboro College at a low ebb. The buildings were sadly out of repair and inadequate to meet the demands of any increased patronage; the curriculum was more contracted than that of any similar school in the South; there were virtually no appliances for teaching, such as maps, globes, and philosophical apparatus; the staff of teachers was insufficient in numbers and variety; and the charges for board and tuition were below those of other like schools.

With characteristic executive ability, zeal, devotion, and fidelity, he detected the wants of the college, and by his faculty for inspiring confidence he so aroused the enthusiasm of the trustees that they gave him his way, which meant certain success. During the five years of his life in Greensboro he caused the older buildings to be repaired and new ones to a great extent to be added; the curriculum was enlarged so as to equal any, and in some respects to surpass all, rival female seminaries in the South. He gathered about him—for he possessed rare powers for the appraisement of the fitness of others— a superb corps of faithful and capable teachers. These he inspired with his own ardor, ambition, and breadth of views; and not only by his liberality toward them in the matter of securing for them increased salaries,—for he believed in paying good

108

teachers liberally,—but, above all, by that genial, gracious, just, and generous manner which ever marked his intercourse with everybody and in every relation of life, he so endeared himself to them personally that service seemed but an act of friendship. The college was fully equipped for efficient teaching; the charges for board and tuition were raised so as no longer to underbid other like institutions; and withal, under his able and brilliant presidency, Greensboro Female College took a foremost place among the seminaries of learning for young women; and so deep and broad were the foundations which he laid anew for the reorganized and remodeled school that it has ever kept its high rank.

During vacations, and often during term-time, President Deems was indefatigable in making tours to various parts of the State for the purpose of raising funds for the college and otherwise promoting its interests.

From his Journal, 1852

"March 27th. Visit from the Rev. G. M. Everhart, a tutor in Emory and Henry College, who came to sound me upon taking the presidency of the college, about to be vacated by President Collins, who goes to the head of Dickinson. Do not see that it is my duty to go. Am doing much good here, and should be perfectly satisfied if I had a comfortable house. By 'perfectly satisfied' I mean as much so as I could be in a literary institution. In any situation I must have vexations. I have them here. . . . I am too small, too young, too little learned, to preside over a faculty of older and abler men."

"April 22d, Thursday. Cold and windy. At twenty minutes past nine o'clock in the morning I looked upon the face of my *fourth* child, a boy. There is no name for the young man as yet. His mother insists on calling him Charles, but I protest against this, as I cannot endure the practice of perpetuating names in a family. The use of names is to make distinction. But suppose there should be half a dozen Charleses. Some adjunct to the name would have to be used, as *old* Charles, *young* Charles, *big* Charles, *little* Charles, *swearing* Charles, etc. My plan in names is to make as sure as possible that no other Deems ever had the name I proposed for my child."

Faithful old "Aunt Lucinda," the colored nurse who had served the family so loyally at Randolph-Macon and at Newbern, was a valued member of the household in Greensboro. After a time her health failed. One night, after an unusually hard day, she asked Mrs. Deems to come up to her room and read the Bible to her and pray with her. This was gladly done, for we all loved Aunt Lucinda. Then came the good-night salutations. In the morning when her room was visited, she was found, with a peaceful expression, resting in the sleep of death. It was a terrible shock to the family, and more genuine grief for the dead was never felt than that of our household when Aunt Lucinda died.

Shortly after this there came to the kitchen door and inquired for Mrs. Deems a very neatly dressed colored woman, whose speech and bearing were those of a person of unusual intelligence.

"Well, my good woman, what can we do for you?" asked Mrs. Deems.

"I want you to buy me, Miss Deems." (The negroes never said "Mrs."; it was always "Miss.")

"What is your name?"

"Rachel, ma'am."

"Why do you want us to buy you, Rachel? Have you not a good home?"

"Yes, ma'am, I got a good home, and my master is very kind; but he's got to sell, and he told me I might pick out somebody to buy me if I could. I likes Dr. Deems and you, and would like you to buy me. Can't you, miss? I wish mightily you would!"

Mrs. Deems told her that they did not want to buy a servant at that time, but "Aunt Rachel" persisted, carried her point, and was bought for about eight hundred dollars. As Dr. Deems made it a point not to separate negro families, he hired "Uncle Henry," Aunt Rachel's husband. They were a worthy couple, and a deep attachment existed between them and the family. They were always present at family worship, and received every care and attention. Aunt Rachel could read and was a devout Christian, as was the case with slaves in so many homes in the South.

From his Journal, 1852

"June 30th, Weldon, Wednesday. A mass-meeting, at which I took ground distinctly in favor of the passage of a law prohibiting the traffic in ardent spirits, reviewing the statutes of the State upon the subject. I was about two hours speaking, and the assembly listened with marked attention. Thursday, dined at S. W. Brandis's, took tea with the Rev. Thomas G. Lowe in Halifax, spent the night in Weldon, and next evening reached Stony Creek and the residence of my father-in-law, I. D. Disosway, Esq., where I had the pleasure of meeting Mrs. Deems and the children. On this tour I collected bonds and cash amounting to one thousand dollars for the Fund for Educating Preachers' Daughters."

"July 15th. The college opened its fall session, and fifty-four boarders were in attendance the first day. In about a fortnight we had seventy-seven. This is the largest number ever in attendance during the fall session. We reached seventy-five last Christmas."

"August 1st. The little book 'What Now?' was written

for the class which graduated at our late commencement. It was the product of three weeks' work of scraps and shreds of time, and was sent without copying to the printer. This is very indiscreet, but it was an emergency. May it do much good. Dr. Collins has finally left Emory and Henry College. I have had a visit from the Rev. T. R. Catlett, a trustee, and the Rev. G. M. Everhart, formerly of the faculty. They both urge me to accept the presidency. A letter from my friend Coleman does the same. Do not yet see my duty clear; must be convinced of that, or I do not move. How much easier life would be if we had an angel of revelation to tell us on each occasion what is right! I *think* I desire to do right, but I am very frequently puzzled to know what to do. ' Father, thou art my guide from my youth.' "

" August 16th. Made a missionary collection of sixty dollars, only seven dollars and fifty cents having been collected on the whole circuit last year. This was favorable. On the 20th of August I started at two o'clock in the morning for Halifax, after being up and at conversation or labor all night. The next night, about ten o'clock, reached the court-house and had half a night's sleep. The next day I left Brother Samuel Major's. With him and Brother Sackett and Brother Mallett, whom I met for the first time, I went to the camp-ground at Asbury Meeting-house. There was no preacher from a distance but myself, Brother Bibb (the preacher in charge) and Brother Joseph Goodman being the only other preachers. The consequence was that I had most of the heavy work to perform. It rained almost incessantly after Sunday morning. I collected one hundred and twenty-five dollars in bonds for the college; but it is such hard work."

" August 25th. Rode to Mr. Stovall's, who is senator for the county, and who gave me fifty dollars on my scheme for the college. At night reached Halifax, and started off in the stage, reaching home on the night of the 27th. In all this time I had been in dry sheets only one night, and yet am mercifully preserved."

"August 29th. The sermon which I preached on the 1st of August was remarkably blessed to the conversion of Professor Kern, who has since professed sanctification and is a happy soul. Thank God! I began to feel that I had lost my call. Glory be to the Comforter for this blessed revelation of Himself!"

"Saturday, September 4th. Went to visit Sylva Grove School, Davidson County, N. C., the property of Charles Mock, Esq., twenty-four miles southwest of Greensboro, with some view of purchasing it."

"September 18th. Went to Sylva Grove and concluded the bargain for Mock's place."

"September 25th. Have changed the name of Sylva Grove to Glenanna, in honor of my precious wife."

"October 27th. The Grand Division of the Sons of Temperance held its annual session in Salisbury, N. C., commencing on the 25th of October. I was elected Worthy Associate. Having been put in nomination against L. Blakmer, Esq., I declined votes, desiring to have him unanimously elected, believing him to be entitled to the position. I am glad that I did this. It is always pleasant *afterward* to have denied one's selfishness. I was immediately elected Associate, and the Grand Division appointed Mr. Blakmer and myself to represent them at the National Division to be held in Chicago next June. They give each one hundred dollars to pay expenses. I was also able to help another friend by having the Rev. Peter Doub appointed Grand Lecturer of the State, on a respectable salary. It is so pleasant to have influence to exert in behalf of the good and deserving; it is the highest pleasure of my life, so far as intercourse with my fellow-men is concerned. At this Grand Division I made a move to incite the people of the State to forward legislative action against the liquor traffic.

I made the motion with little hope of seeing it taken up so warmly and prosecuted so vigorously as it was. The Grand Division as a body resolved to petition the legislature, and appointed a committee, of which I was chairman, to draft a memorial to be scattered through the State for signers of all classes. These agents were appointed to lecture and obtain signatures to this memorial until December 15th. The memorial to the legislature does not ask what I desire; it is only such a one as we hope may obtain signers. Believing it a crime in the sight of God to sell liquor as a beverage, I would no more legislate for its regulation than for the regulation of adultery, theft, etc."

"October 29th. Left Salisbury in the stage early in the morning and rode all day to Greensboro. Among my fellow-passengers were the Rev. Peter Doub and Philip J. White, the temperance lecturer. White is the most entertaining traveling companion I ever saw. At night simply stopped at home to have tea, kiss wife, shake hands with the folk of the college, and off again. Sunday evening, the 30th, reached Raleigh and stayed with S. H. Young."

"On Tuesday, November 2d, went to Franklinton depot. Reached Louisburg same evening. Our session lasted eight days and was the most harmonious and pleasant I ever attended. The most important action, so far as I was concerned, was the assumption by the conference of the raising of fifteen thousand dollars necessary to complete the twenty thousand dollars' education fund. It is to be solicited by the preachers."

"December 4th. My birthday. Damp, unpleasant, part of the day rainy. Rode to Pleasant Garden, Guilford, to deliver a temperance address. Am thirty-two years old. How the time flies! Alas, how little I have done! This is the sad song at the close of each year, and the old resolution is entered *to do better*. May God give me grace to make this next year the richest of my life!"

"December 24th. The session of the Annual Conference closed December 15th, and on Monday, 20th, I went to my place at Glenanna. Miss Nixon accompanied me. Met Miss Bronson on the evening of the 20th at John W. Thomas's. She will enter upon the principalship of Glenanna on the first Monday in January. Prepared a circular for Glenanna."

"December 25th. The memorial to the legislature on the subject of the liquor traffic went up on the 20th of December with the signatures of more than ten thousand voters, more than four thousand ladies, and a number of youths, in all over fifteen thousand. This is a most glorious result, far beyond my expectations. For this I thank God, and I thank him that he gave me the spirit of this work and the courage to bring it before the people. The legislature did nothing, but the thing is now before the people, and the discussion will be kept up until we prohibit the traffic."

"December 31st. During the past year I have delivered fifty-two discourses. This was small, but I remember how confined I am, and hope that having preached more than once a week on an average will not be considered too infrequent. The Lord have mercy upon me and forgive all my shortcomings! I desire to be as useful as possible. The total number of my discourses to the close of this year is nine hundred and eighty-eight."

1853

"January 1st. I open the year with labor, commencing a new series of lectures on chemistry. I have also commenced the compilation of a cyclopedia of temperance matter. This is intended to be a work of permanent value.* At the close of the last year I concluded the publication of the 'Southern Methodist Pulpit' after years of labor. In the several peri-

---

* He never finished that undertaking.

odicals and in many letters, I am receiving expressions of great regard for that publication."

" April 24th.   Mrs. Deems and all the children accompanied me to Glenanna.   Wife's first visit.   Went on Friday, 22d, the first anniversary of the birthday of our fourth child, whom we have fully concluded to call Edward Ernest.*   Perhaps it is not much of a coincidence, but my family arrived at Greensboro College the day our third child, Minnie, was one year old."

" May 3d.   Discourse on Odd Fellowship at the dedication of the hall of I. O. O. F. at Salem, N. C."

" May 19th.   Our annual commencement."

" June 10th, Chicago, Ill.   I was in attendance upon the National Division.   Here became acquainted with Judge O'Neal of South Carolina, Neal Dow of Maine, General Carney of Ohio, Oliver of New York, and other co-laborers in the great temperance work."

" July 10th.   A family meeting was held at my father-in-law's, Mr. Disosway's.   The Rev. John Bagley thus signalized the event in a newspaper article:

" ' On last Friday morning a pleasant ride of about forty miles from Richmond, on the Petersburg and Raleigh railroads, brought me to the depot at Stony Creek, where I found a friend waiting with a carriage, in which I was conveyed to Pleasant Grove, the residence of Israel D. Disosway, Esq., the father-in-law of Dr. Deems, where I spent several days in the most agreeable manner.   Here I found one of those deeply interesting family gatherings which are so often seen in old Virginia.   Brother George W. Deems, of the Virginia Conference, Dr. Deems, his gifted son, with their wives and children, had left their fields of labor for a season to meet once more on earth, probably for the last time that *all* would enjoy such a meeting.   Eleven children and thirteen adults formed

* He was finally named Edward Mark.

the social band who had been thus brought together by the mysterious providences of God, to sit around the family board, to talk and sing and pray, to go to the house of God together, and then to take the parting hand and in different spheres to engage in the great battle of life.

"'As Dr. Deems had made an appointment to preach at Hall's on Sunday, Brother Covington had embraced the opportunity to hold a meeting of several days. It was my privilege to hear Dr. Deems and his father preach on the same day to quite a large country congregation. Owing to the smallness of the house, which would not accommodate all the female portion of the congregation, the services were conducted under an arbor. The doctor's text was John v. 40. For about an hour and a half the eloquent preacher enchained the attention of the congregation while he held up before his hearers the reasons why the glorious gospel of the Son of God is rejected by the mass of mankind. It is not my intention to attempt an analysis of the discourse. It was well adapted to produce conviction on the minds of sinners. It came like the breath of spring on the cold, frost-bound heart, and I trust that it produced in some the buddings of good desires, the blossoms of holy resolutions, and that it will yet bring forth the ripe fruit of faith, hope, and love.'

"The degree of doctor of divinity was conferred upon me by the authorities of Randolph-Macon College, June, 1853."

"October 27th. At the meeting of the Grand Division of the Sons of Temperance in Wilmington I was chosen to be the Grand Worthy Patriarch by a very large vote."

"November 12th. At the conference held in Raleigh I was elected to the General Conference at the head of the delegation. The confidence of brethren is pleasant."

"December 5th. My thirty-third birthday fell on the Sabbath, and was spent at home, the first so spent in many years."

"December 25th. My father and his family visited me in

November. The first number of the ' Ballot-box ' * issued in December. My soul, I hope, has greater desires after holiness! During the past year my discourses amounted to forty-eight, of which twenty-five were new. The total number of my discourses to the close of the year is one thousand and thirty-six. Oh, how deeply I feel my feebleness!"

1854

" The Rev. Professor Jones enters upon his duties. May we be mutually profitable."

" On Monday, April 24th, started, in company with the Rev. Dr. Carter, to attend the General Conference of the Methodist Episcopal Church, South, to be held in Columbus, Ga."

" April 28th. Reached Augusta, Ga., and early next morning we were in Macon, thence to dine in Columbus. My residence was with Joel Early Hunt, Esq., at Wynnton, a delightful residence. My room-mates were the Rev. H. N. McTyeire, editor of the ' New Orleans Christian Advocate,' and W. H. McDaniel, P.E., Talladega district, Alabama. The principal work done was the determination to establish a Southern Book Concern, and the location thereof in Nashville, the improvements in missionary and publishing plans, and the election of three bishops, Pierce, Early, and Kavanaugh. The first was elected on the first ballot, the second upon the fifth, and the third upon the seventh ballot. For the election of Dr. Early and Mr. Kavanaugh I may hold myself responsible, as I suppose that without the effort I made they would not have been chosen. Believing them to be best entitled to the place, I am happy in reflecting upon the part I took in this matter."

" On Monday morning, May 22d, was born my fifth child and fourth son, George Israel. May God consecrate him to Himself and set him apart to a high and holy work!"

* A small periodical devoted to the cause of temperance legislation.

"July 30th. Elected president of Centenary College, Louisiana."

The North Carolina Conference met in Pittsboro in 1854. During its session it passed the following resolutions:

"WHEREAS, We have learned that the Rev. C. F. Deems, D.D., has been elected to the presidency of Centenary College, Louisiana, and is now considering the acceptance of the same; therefore,

"*Resolved*, That, while we appreciate the honor thus conferred upon one of our body by one of the highest institutions of learning in the country, and while we regard him in the highest sense in every way qualified in intellect, integrity, and learning, yet we beg our brother to consider the state of the work in North Carolina, both as regards the pastorate and institutions of learning, and if he can find it consistent with his duty to the church, that he decline the presidency of Centenary College."

Following a copy of these resolutions in his journal for December, Dr. Deems writes:

"I did decline the call, and my reasons are embodied in my letter to the Rev. Dr. Drake, dated November 18, 1854. Upon declining the presidency of the largest institution of learning in our church, I could not reconcile it with my sense of propriety to retain the headship of a more limited sphere, and so I resigned the presidency of Greensboro College, and was appointed to Goldsboro circuit, the Rev. Ira T. Wyche being presiding elder."

Thus it appears that ever within he heard the old call that he had heard when a student in Dickinson College, where he had solemnly consecrated his whole life to "preach Christ, and him crucified." Therefore, when he had securely assured the future prosperity of the college by showing on what lines it should be conducted, he determined to take up again the

regular ministry.   It need hardly be said that while rendering
these great special and substantial services to his denomination, the Methodist Episcopal Church, South, and to the cause
of education in general, Dr. Deems was also rapidly increasing his own personal fame and greatly widening the circle of
his loving admirers ; for in this, as in everything he had so far
seriously undertaken, he displayed the possession of qualities
not often found in the same person.   The brilliant pulpit orator had shown himself to be an almost ideal college president.
He had a rare faculty for maintaining discipline, and so rare
was this that the writer feels himself unable satisfactorily to
describe it.   He was not a severe man in either appearance
or disposition, but quite the opposite in both of these respects.
He appeared to have ruled by a kind of moral authority and
persuasiveness, unless he did so by the profound respect for
his sincerity which he inspired in all who were brought into
close relationship with him.   There was a moral dignity about
him in such exercises that seemed like the judicial ermine and
other insignia of right to rule.   Whatever that gift of ruling
may be, whether a single quality or a union of qualities, Dr.
Deems possessed it in a notable manner and to a high degree.
But by the time he had reached the close of his Greensboro
experience he had shown himself to be also a thorough business man.   He was a whole committee on ways and means
in himself when it came to the devising of schemes and
methods for the raising of funds.   Much of this he had
learned in the hard school of poverty through which we have
seen him passing while as yet even a mere boy.   The youth
who could help pay his way through college by writing
" poems " for the press had become, with all his higher achievements, a systematic, painstaking business man in his habits
and methods, while his innate sagacity had developed by experience until he was able to, and did, put this poor college
on a paying basis.

CHAPTER III

APPOINTED by the North Carolina Annual Conference of 1854 to the Everittsville circuit when he resigned the presidency of Greensboro Female College, Dr. Deems went to his work early in 1855, making his home at Goldsboro, the county-seat of Wayne County, and the largest place on the circuit. He entered the little parsonage Saturday, January 13, 1855. Goldsboro was, and has continued to be, quite a railroad center, being one of the principal stations on the Wilmington and Weldon Railroad, which was the main route from the North to the South. The Methodist Episcopal Church, South, had a female seminary in Goldsboro, whose president, the Rev. Samuel M. Frost, was a good friend of Dr. Deems, as was also the Rev. Dr. Ira T. Wyche, who was then the presiding elder of the Newbern district, which included the Goldsboro circuit.

In a letter from New York City, written November 2, 1880, Dr. Deems thus writes about the good presiding elder of the Newbern district:

"How shall I write of Ira T. Wyche? He was my friend from the earliest years of my ministry until he went up higher. He was a good man, so true, so faithful, so forbearing, so persistent in duty! He served his friends in darkness as in sunshine, and his friendship looked for no reward. He served in every department of conference work and served so faithfully! He could be trusted with anything and everything. I know that my friends regard me as no judge of preaching, and I suspect they are right. My talent for *hearing the Word* is so great that it neutralizes any little critical ability there is in me. But I delighted in the preaching of Ira T. Wyche. It struck me. One discourse of his, preached long ago, so fixed its outline on my memory that on several occasions I have used it, so modifying it as to make it available for my style of delivery. It has been blessed to the conversion of many souls. There is a little incident connected with this discourse. A few years ago I was engaged one week-night to preach in the Episcopal Church of the Holy Trinity in this city. By some mismanagement a marriage party had possession of the church, and the rector caused the great congregation to be turned into Dr. Hepworth's. There I preached this sermon. At the conclusion of one passage the Rev. Dr. Tyng was so warmed up that he shouted out a hearty 'Amen.' As we rode home my wife said that she never expected to hear an Episcopal clergyman saying a loud 'Amen' to a sermon preached in a Congregational church. 'Ah, my dear, it was Ira T. Wyche's sermon, and any man can say "Amen" to almost anything of his.' That sermon has since been printed and circulated widely. The Lord will reward each man according to his work. For the pleasure of his intercourse, for the fidelity of his friendship, and for his influence upon my personal character, I owe our dear departed friend so much that when the telegram reached me announcing his death, this new bereavement, following so soon on the departure of Mrs. Nicholson, melted my heart within me. I have reached that time of life when the majority of my comrades and friends are on the other side of the river. Now Ira T. Wyche has joined not only the majority, but the innumerable company of those who have washed their robes and made them white in the blood of the Lamb."

The only record of events in the life of Dr. Deems in Goldsboro is contained in a small pocket-diary, and even this has only brief jottings, evidently hastily entered while engaged in the restless and absorbing work of an itinerant Methodist minister. Most of his time was spent away from his family at the various points on his circuit. From his record of sermons preached we learn that his preaching appointments were Goldsboro, Everittsville, Live Oak, Providence, Falling Creek, Indian Springs, Friendship, Smith's Chapel, Ebenezer, Salem, and Pikeville. Some of these churches were out in the pine woods, and attended by people who had to walk or ride for miles in order to hear the gospel.

In the opinion of some, a change from the presidency of a college to a Methodist circuit might be regarded a degradation. Dr. Deems looked upon it as a promotion, and flung himself into his work with a zest and ambition never excelled at any other period of his life. He preached to his congregations in the villages and woods of the Everittsville circuit in the spirit of the Master as he poured into the rapt soul of the woman at Jacob's well the wonderful spiritual truths recorded in the fourth chapter of John's Gospel. Nor were Dr. Deems's labors lessened by his exchange of a college presidency for a circuit; the rather did they become more abundant and pressing. No greater mistake could be made than to suppose that the life of an itinerant Methodist preacher in North Carolina in those days was an easy one.

On some circuits the preacher finds large compensations for his trials in picturesque scenery and invigorating air; but the Everittsville circuit was not favored in these ways. The roads were either very sandy or ran through swamps whose mud was bottomless, and they stretched through a generally flat and uninteresting country, whose monotony was somewhat relieved by vast fields of green and waving corn or glistening white cotton. Moreover, in summer the heat was intense and the air freighted with malarial gases from the swamps. Dr. Deems found his compensation in his joy at being able to preach again, and in the keen and affectionate appreciation of his labors by the people on his circuit, among whom were many bright and refined women and able, earnest, prosperous, hospitable, and godly men.

Dr. Deems himself gives us a most interesting insight into his life on the Everittsville circuit (1855–56) in a letter to the "Raleigh Christian Advocate" of April 15, 1885, written on the occasion of the death of one of his most faithful friends and co-workers :

"A few weeks ago a North Carolina paper brought us the announcement of the death of David B. Everitt in Goldsboro. My whole family felt a sudden sorrow. The younger members had so often heard their parents speak in loving terms of the man who bore that name that they felt a claim to be his friends.

"When I quit the presidency of Greensboro Female College in 1854 I was sent to Everittsville circuit. I think that was its name, although it embraced Goldsboro. There I met David B. Everitt. His plantation was some miles from the village which bore his name, where he lived near a little church which was one of the preaching appointments on the circuit. We were not long in becoming fast friends. We were as unlike in body and mind as two men could well be, and perhaps *therefore* we loved each other. He was very large, bluff, loud of speech, sometimes boisterous, but gentle of heart as a woman. He was a thorough Methodist; perhaps he was considered by some a bigoted Methodist; but he was simply a brave, conscientious, earnest soul—a soul that had been *converted.* He had no doubt of that; neither had any of his friends. He was not a mere church-member; he had been *converted.* He no more doubted it than he doubted his birth.

Converted under Methodism, he knew no other way. But he was not bigoted; he had friends in other churches and he loved and honored them—but he was a *Methodist*. I know men of that type among Baptists, Presbyterians, and Episcopalians, and it is always a charming type to me. These men do not deny the good that is in other churches, but they are not familiar with it, while they do know the good that is in their own. In them what superficial observers take for ignorance is mere innocence. Of all guile, malice, meanness, and uncharitableness David B. Everitt was as free as any man I ever knew.

" And then, I think he had a great desire to know the truth. This was shown in whatever interested him. Many things did not interest him; they lay beyond his circle of thought; but if anything did attract his attention he was earnestly solicitous to go to the bottom of it. He could listen wonderfully and question closely.

" He was very ardent in his friendships, and steadfast. Within three miles of him were two other men, his intimates, William Carraway and David McKinne. Such another trio I never knew and probably never shall know. They were so large and so loud. I venture a sketch to show the characteristics of these men. I remember the first time I saw them together. They had gone down to Indian Springs, where the new preacher was to hold forth. We four started together for Everittsville and brought up at William Carraway's. In the after-dinner conversation the talk turned on some question of the yield of crops on their several plantations. It waxed warm. Sometimes all three talked together. Carraway roared, McKinne bellowed, and Everitt yelled. They were all red in the face, and their faces were very large. It was an unhappy moment for me. I had never been in Mr. Carraway's house before, Mr. McKinne I had just met, and Mr. Everitt was a recent acquaintance. What should I do? If those ' bulls of

Bashan' locked horns what was I? I could not prevent a general fight. And just from church! And all official members of the church of which I was pastor! At last I ventured very meekly to suggest, in most modest terms, that the 'brethren' might all be right, or if all wrong, was it really a question for neighbors, members of the same church, to be excited about? At this suggestion they all looked at me, and then at one another, and then burst into roars of laughter that literally jarred the house. They were accustomed to 'chaff' one another in this free, rough manner, and it never had occurred to them that a stranger might take it for quarreling. When they saw from my face that I *did* regard it seriously, the ludicrousness of the situation was too much for them. Mr. Everitt laughed until tears ran down his face.

"After that, how often I have seen tears on those great faces, when those three men have engaged with me in prayer for the spiritual improvement of the neighborhood or the conversion of some special neighbor! And they have all crossed the flood before me!

"Gentlest at heart of them all, perhaps, was David B. Everitt. How much I have desired in the last two years to see him! And I was planning to enjoy that pleasure when the news of his death came. I have seen no notice of his last hours and heard nothing. It is not needful that I should. Such a man's life, of gentleness and force, of cheerful sobriety, of fixed principle, of humble, happy faith, is the testimonial most precious to his friends. May some other in his church be raised to take his place, and may his children be Christians after the manner of their father! Very dear to me forever will be the cherished name of David B. Everitt.

"CHARLES F. DEEMS.

"CHURCH OF THE STRANGERS,
     "March 31, 1885."

While editor of " Frank Leslie's Sunday Magazine " in New York City, many years afterward, Dr. Deems, writing of another of his parishioners of a very different, but equally interesting, type, said:

"Some years ago, among the churches to which the editor of this magazine ministered in North Carolina was one called 'Smith's Chapel.' It would seat about two hundred white and one hundred colored people. But in that climate a large part of the year a considerable portion of the congregation sat outside. The nearest house to the little chapel was the dwelling of a gentleman who was one of the most famous school-teachers in his native State. He was the college-mate of James K. Polk, and the first time we ever saw him was when he had just completed a walk of fifty miles to meet his old college friend at the university.

"Mr. John G. Elliot got his middle initial from his resemblance to a ghost. He was usually known as 'Mr. Ghost Elliot.' Small, thin, washed out by multitudinous ablutions, built after the architectural design of an interrogation-mark, with a disproportionately large head, the white hair on which was cropped to a length measured exactly by the thickness of the comb, he was a man whose appearance attracted attention everywhere. In some departments he was very learned, and his solid acquirements dominated his eccentricities and won for him the respect of a large class of citizens. He was what the colored people would call 'a powerful hearer of de Word.' Upon warm days he would walk into the meeting-house, throw his coat, if he had one, over the back of his seat, pull off his shoes to cool his understanding, and propping his head against his left hand and supporting his left elbow with his right hand, he set himself to penetrate the speaker with auger eyes. The thing his soul most hated was nonsense. He had no kind of reverence. He would take up a slave or the Archbishop of

Canterbury with equal patience, and by Socratic methods exhibit to him the ridiculousness of his errors.

" If within the reach of practicability, Mr. Ghost Elliot was always at any service this editor held within his range. There are readers of this magazine in North Carolina who, when they peruse this article, will recollect how sometimes, when an assertion had been roundly made by the preacher, Mr. Elliot would rise in his place and say, ' Doctor, what is supposed among theologians to be the proof of that?' Or, ' Doctor, I have heard that circumstance stated quite differently.' Or, ' Doctor, that statement of yours has been publicly denied in the papers.'

" There was no laughing. Mr. Elliot was the oracle of that neighborhood. There were boys about there whom his skeptical ideas had infected; there were people in that audience not to be surpassed in what is called ' a Boston audience'; and Joseph Cook never ran a severer gantlet in the Athens of America than the young professor from the university ran in that chapel in the pine woods. No one laughed; every one listened; and if Mr. Elliot had frequently got the better of the preacher the preacher's occupation would have been gone.

" To this day we feel the healthy influence of that instantaneous criticism. To this day, in preaching every now and then, it occurs to us that somewhere in the church there may be a ' Ghost Elliot,' who does not ' speak out in meeting,' but carries the objection away in his soul. Would it not be better that men should speak out?"

Saturday morning, February 17, 1855, Dr. Deems preached at Salem. While driving home he met with an accident, from which he suffered greatly and by which he was confined to the house for about two weeks. He thus speaks of this experience in the entry in his diary for the above date: " Flung from my buggy coming home. Badly hurt, but, thank God, preserved." By this accident his ankle was sprained, and so seriously as to trouble him all his life thereafter. During his confinement at this time he wrote his lecture entitled "Trade Life," which became quickly very popular in North Carolina and the neighboring States. It was while returning from Petersburg, Va., where he had been for the purpose of delivering this lecture, that he was shocked by the intelligence of the death of his little baby boy, George, who at eleven o'clock at night on Wednesday, March 14th, had fallen asleep in Jesus. As he has not only embalmed the precious little one's memory, but also brought out an interesting truth in his characteristic style, in an article, published in 1880, entitled "The Czar and the Babe," we here give our readers the article in full.

"THE CZAR AND THE BABE

"On the 17th of March, 1855, I was coming from Petersburg, Va., to my home in North Carolina. In the car was a gentleman with New York papers bearing the intelligence of the recent death of Nicholas, autocrat of all the Russias. He was gone. A man of great stature, of iron will, of vast energies, a born king, ruling fifty millions by his simple word, he had bowed to destiny and death and dropped the scepter which swayed an empire. He had died at a crisis in which he was the most conspicuous and important personage among men, at such a juncture in affairs as will draw an arresting line across the page of human history. He had roused the world to arms. He had brought thousands into fortified towns and stretched tents and camp-fires along miles of hills and valleys. The stride of his ambition had made troops of orphan children and thrilled the nation with woe. He was known to all the world, and his history, his words, his deeds, his policy, were the study of all who read or thought. But he had gone. Europe stood still and held its breath as the curtain dropped upon the colossal actor on a stage trembling with the thunder of artillery and red with the gore of the gallant. And then the cabinets of all governments, and the traders upon the marts of the busy nations, began industriously to calculate the probable effects of this great departure upon all the operations of mankind; and Russia was preparing to bury the 'father' with mingled barbaric pomp and civilized splendor.

"I was not indifferent to the importance of such an event as the death of the emperor, but it stirred my heart very little. *I was far off.*

"Twenty miles farther south I heard of another death. In this case it was a babe only ten months old. He was heir to no great estate or title. He was known to very few, and very few had any interest in him; he had never uttered a word. He was in no one's way. His life made no great promise. He had always been delicate. He was a mere intelligent, 'pretty little fellow,' as his father was fond of calling him. He was dead. How sad, how very sad a thought was this to me! *He was 'our little George.'*

"All the potentates of Europe might have died and my heart have felt no pain. But this was a near grief. This was the first departure from the little flock. There was no pomp at his funeral. He lay calm and lovely in his little coffin—beautifully dead. His brothers and his little sister stood in the awe which the first invasion of the invisible feet makes in a family. A few friends went from the humble house of the bereaved living to the humble resting-place of the shrouded dead. No retinue, no plumes, no emblazonry of ostentatious sorrow, marked the child's removal to his last home.

"But he was our babe. How little thought his mother of the grand griefs of a European empire! Her little kingdom was darkened. While we had read accounts of the slaughters which marked the Crimean campaign, and shuddered at the desolations they must have brought thousands of homes, none of the thrilling reports had penetrated and agonized us like the sight of our own dead. Nothing I ever read or saw or felt transfixed me with such cold pain as the kiss of the little hands folded over the heart of our serene and breathless boy. They were beautiful hands. How often I had admired them as he clapped them when his earnest gaze had brightened into a smile and broadened into infantile glee! How often had they pressed their soft little palms upon my aching head, and buried their little dimples under my chin! Death had not discolored the lovely flesh, but had made it clearer and finer, as if it had been purged of all taints of corruption. And so I could hardly believe him dead. But when I stooped to kiss those hands for the last time they met my lips with such an unexpected chill that I felt stricken. It was as though I had been stabbed in the heart with a dagger of ice.

"Oh, how different the far and the near! A quarter of a century lies between that death and this writing, but that dead babe to-day has more power over me than any living man. He walks the streets with me. He goes to all the funerals of infants. Before his death I did not know how to talk at the funeral of a babe. Now I know at least how to sympathize with the parents. When a man comes into my house and tells me with quivering lips that there is a baby lying dead in his home, I go with him, led by the hand of a little child whose mortal body was buried a quarter of a century ago.

"CHARLES F. DEEMS."

During the month of May a fruitful revival of religion rewarded Dr. Deems's work at his Indian Springs appointment. Thirty-four were added to the church. Of those added more than half were heads of families, and quite a number were past middle life. Dr. Deems baptized twenty of these converts, eleven of whom he immersed in the river. It was a most gracious season, in which some signal victories were achieved by the Holy Spirit's conversion of persons regarded as hopelessly ungodly. Similar works of grace occurred in other portions of the circuit, which were most cheering to the faithful pastor.

About this time, greatly to his gratification, he was invited to preach the commencement sermon at Greensboro Female College. This, on May 15th, he did most acceptably, and while in Greensboro at commencement he was honored by being made president of the board of trustees of the college.

From Greensboro he made a visit to Glenanna. This was a seminary for young ladies which Dr. Deems founded while he was president of Greensboro College and owned and supervised for a number of years. The object of the school was to prepare young ladies for college, especially for Greensboro College. It was situated in Davidson County, one mile from Thomasville, which was on the Central Railroad. The location was picturesque and healthful, and the school was a center of refined culture and influence. While this school was a care and responsibility to Dr. Deems during his itinerancy, yet it was a source of intense gratification that while preaching he was also teaching for the Master.

Notwithstanding the inevitable interruptions in his life on the Everittsville circuit, he did considerable writing for the press, and in September published a new edition of his " Twelve College Sermons." An idea of the public estimate of this book may be gained from the following criticism by the " Home Circle," of Nashville, Tenn. :

" Dr. Deems is one of the most racy writers of our acquaintance, and the public will expect to find in this volume a fine specimen of correct and elegant rhetoric. In this they will not be disappointed; but they will find that its *belles-lettres* merits are, as they should be, the merest accessories to the great end of preaching. When it became known to us that these discourses were produced by a very young professor of *belles-lettres*, which the author was at the time of their composition, we expected to find in them an undue amount of 'fine writing.' We were agreeably disappointed. If there be anything of the sort in them, it is not more than the reader will relish; and we feel bound to say that, as far as we have observed, every artificial merit that they possess promotes the religious purpose of the sermons. Every rill that sparkles through them helps to swell the tide of the author's exhortation; every vine has its cluster; every flower brings fruit."

It was at this time that Dr. Deems wrote to the Rev. Dr. Sprague, of Albany, the letter referring to Summerfield quoted in the autobiographical notes. By both pen and tongue he also did all in his power to assist the cause of temperance, so dear to his heart from his youth, being an ardent advocate of legal prohibition, and being greatly in demand as a lecturer on this theme. His temperance oration delivered in the hall of the South Carolina Institute at Charleston, on June 6th, elicited from the press the most glowing encomiums.

From his diary we learn that on Saturday, June 23d, Dr. Deems delivered a masonic address at Long Creek, Duplin County, having been invited to do so by his masonic friends in that region. He had been raised to the sublime degree of Master Mason by the Greensboro Lodge, No. 76, on October 4, 1852. He had been made a Fellow-craft Mason by the same lodge on September 7, 1852. The record of his being made an Entered Apprentice Mason has been misplaced. For the above facts we are indebted to Mr. W. D. Trotter, of Greensboro, N. C., who was Worthy Master of the lodge in 1884. Dr. Deems kept up his interest in masonry all his life, taking the degrees beyond the " Blue Lodge " as far up as the commandery. At the time of his death he was a member of Kane Lodge, Crescent Chapter, and Palestine Commandery, all of New York City, and in all of which he was for years chaplain. Among his many friends Dr. Deems had none more faithful and enthusiastic than his masonic brethren. In

1846 he had become an Odd Fellow, but he did not keep up active membership.

Fever and ague, eye troubles, and other physical ailments annoyed him exceedingly during the latter half of 1855, but do not appear to have cooled his zeal or lessened his labors. On July 10th he wrote the prospectus of the " North Carolina Christian Advocate"; on Sunday, July 29th, he dedicated Smith's Chapel, Wayne County; in September he commenced work on "The Annals of Southern Methodism," of which more will be said later; and attended the Annual Conference in Wilmington, N. C., Wednesday, November 14th, where, among other things, he delivered an address on " Education," and was reappointed to the Everittsville circuit.

Leaving Goldsboro on Saturday, December 1st, Dr. Deems went to Petersburg, Va., to attend the annual meeting of the Virginia Conference, at which Bishop Andrew presided. The business which took him to this meeting was of a most painful nature; although only thirty-five years old, he was to be one of the principal figures in an important and complicated ec- clesiastical trial. As the chief personages involved are dead and in heaven, and as they forgave one another before their ·death any and all real or imagined injuries they had sustained, and as a complete account of the affair would fill a volume, we see nothing to be gained by giving names or going into details. But to ignore altogether what is history, and what at the time excited the Methodist Church, South, more than any other controversy (that concerning slavery excepted), would be a fatal omission in any biographical account of Charles F. Deems, who, though the innocent cause of it all, became thereby involved in a miserable tangle of miscon- ception, misrepresentation, and malicious persecution, which, while it temporarily clouded his *reputation* in certain quarters, yet stimulated the development of his mental and moral char- acter and enabled him to present to those who followed him

closely through the long, hot trial—and they were thousands—
a splendid example of moral courage, unswerving integrity,
Christian forbearance, and fearless candor. On Tuesday,
December 18th, Dr. Deems delivered his closing argument in
the case. This address was in many particulars the master-
piece of his life. It was four hours long, but was heard with
breathless attention by the vast congregation assembled.
When the vote of conference was taken the defendant in the
trial was acquitted by a bare majority of his brethren.

Nevertheless Dr. Deems found that he had suddenly leaped
to a lofty place in the esteem of the people of the South as
being an able, eloquent, and godly man. In Petersburg itself,
although he had been the prosecutor in the trial of an eminent
doctor of divinity in the Virginia Conference, he received a
remarkable ovation, costly family Bibles and elegantly bound
hymn-books and glowing resolutions and elaborate silver
plate being the visible tokens of the popular verdict.

When he returned to North Carolina he was received like a
conqueror; and such he was, but greater than the victor in any
bloody battle, for he had by his courage, self-control, and
splendid genius won a victory for public truth and justice.
From every part of the State, from Weldon to Wilmington,
from Goldsboro to Greensboro, public meetings were held and
resolutions were passed, and the name of Charles F. Deems
became a household word throughout all her borders, and so
remains to this day. The older children in Dr. Deems's family
well remember the opening of a box which came a few weeks
after the Virginia Conference adjourned, and was addressed to
the Rev. Charles F. Deems. The brilliant contents when set
forth were dazzling to our young eyes. The box contained a
very beautiful and costly service of silver plate. With painful
eagerness we deciphered the following inscription: " Presented
by the citizens of Petersburg, Va., to Charles F. Deems, Doctor of Divinity, ' in the dew of his youth,' as an evidence of

their appreciation of his virtuous life and exalted worth, and especially as a memento of their admiration of his moral courage, his powers of speech, his Christian spirit, as displayed by him on the trial of —— —— before the Annual Conference of the Methodist Episcopal Church, South, in Petersburg, Va., in 1855."

We remember also the advent of a large and splendidly bound copy of the Holy Bible, on the fly-leaf of which was this inscription: "Rev. Charles F. Deems, D.D.: Accept the Holy Bible as a token of esteem and affection. May a good and merciful God long spare your life, and may you continue to be, as you have been, a faithful and able expounder and defender of its sacred truths; and may it ever be a lamp unto your feet and a light unto your pathway, guiding you to heaven, is the sincere prayer of the givers. Petersburg, Va., December 18, 1855."

That prayer was answered in every particular and to the uttermost. Upon the volume was laid a sumptuously bound copy of the hymns of the Southern Methodist Church, with the following note: "This little volume is gratefully presented to Dr. Deems as a tribute to his splendid talents, Christian purity, and gentlemanly bearing through this trying controversy. The following ladies are proud to bear testimony in his favor and to subscribe themselves his admirers." The ladies of Petersburg, after their names, signed themselves, "Members of the Episcopal Church."

In the corner of the parlor of the little Goldsboro parsonage stood a goodly number of ebony canes with gold heads, bearing each the name of Charles F. Deems, D.D., the name of the donor, the date of the gift, and an indication that it was an expression of appreciation of the genius and character of the recipient, especially as brought out at the Virginia Conference of 1855.

And so it came about that a year which at one time

threatened to close with dark clouds closed flooded with sunshine.

Sometime during 1855 Dr. Deems conceived the idea of "The Annals of Southern Methodism," and during the latter part of 1855 and in 1856 and 1857 he published an annual volume of about three hundred pages with that title. The author's purpose was to furnish once each year a volume which should present in a collected form all that was desirable for full information in regard to the workings and growth of the Southern Methodist Church. The titles of the chapters of the volume for 1856 are as follows: "The Episcopacy"; "The Annual Conferences"; "Dedication of Churches"; "Missions"; "Colleges and Schools"; "Sunday-schools"; "Tract Society"; "Southern Methodist Literature"; "Our People of Color"; "Historical Sketches"; "Biographical Sketches"; "Personal Notices of the Living"; and "Miscellaneous." The editor gleaned his information from a multitude of books, periodicals, and persons, at the cost of much time and tedious toil. Four volumes came out, which by their variety, logical arrangement, and accuracy of detail showed what a many-sided mind the editor possessed. In reviewing the volume for 1855, the "Home Circle," of Nashville, Tenn., said: "There can be no sort of doubt about the success of this book. It will have an enormous circulation. One can scarcely think of a question in the last year's history of Southern Methodism which is not answered here. The idea of making an annual contribution of this sort to our literature is a happy conception. Another egg stands on end! How can we, after this, do without it? Why was it not thought of sooner? The editor's rare talents and tireless industry have been worthily employed, and he is entitled to our thanks—not so much for the copy sent us (we could have bought it cheap at five times the cost, one dollar), but for the *invention* of the thing and for the promise of an annual series."

By request, Dr. Deems attended the commencement exercises at Hampden-Sidney College, Virginia, in 1856. On June 25th he delivered before the Philanthropic Society a lecture on "The True Basis of Manhood." While he had delivered other lectures, this one first attracted public attention to Dr. Deems as a lecturer. The "American Phrenological Journal," in its sketch of Dr. Deems's life, states that "of this effort a distinguished logician of the South said, ' It shows the highest capabilities as a thinker and a writer.' "

Dr. Deems's interest in education was so great, his experience so wide and varied, and his talents as an orator so conspicuous, that he was in great demand every summer at the various college and school commencements. These visits to educational institutions did not interfere with his regular work on the circuit, which was prosecuted with vigor and success, while he continued to win souls and build up saints on their most holy foundation.

On September 30, 1856, his heart and home were gladdened by the birth of his sixth child, a daughter, who was named Anna Louise. All who knew Dr. Deems when living remember his fondness for babes. He always took them in his arms when administering the holy sacrament of baptism and kissed them. The little ones ever seemed by instinct to recognize in him a friend, and it was most unusual for a child to refuse to get into his outstretched arms.

CHAPTER IV

THE North Carolina Annual Conference for 1856 was held in Greensboro from November 12th to November 20th. Bishop Early presided. Dr. Deems was appointed to the Front Street Methodist Church in Wilmington. The Rev. D. B. Nicholson was presiding elder of Wilmington district, and was held in the highest esteem by Dr. Deems, as were all of the Nicholson family.

Wilmington was then, as it is now, the metropolis of the State and an important center of influence, because of its situation on the Cape Fear River, with a commodious harbor and extensive internal navigation and railway connections. The Front Street Church was one of the strongest stations in the conference, which paid Dr. Deems a high compliment when it sent him there. He entered upon his work in January, 1856. To the gratification of all concerned, he was reappointed to the Front Street Church by the conference which met at Goldsboro in December, 1857.

The Front Street Church was a spacious building, situated on a corner and in a desirable part of the city. It had galleries which were always reserved for the colored people of the congregation, for whom the doctor also held special Sunday afternoon services, and among whom he quickly became popular. The membership, already large, greatly increased during the two years of his pastorate. Into the work of organization, pastoral visitation, and preaching he here flung himself with characteristic energy and ability. Invitations to preach at revival services, to address schools and colleges and other institutions, poured in upon him, and his letters during these two years show how frequently he had to decline such calls. But to a few of them he responded favorably, because of special claims upon him—as in the cases of the Goldsboro and Greensboro female colleges.

Not long after the home was established in Wilmington a little incident occurred which is of interest and might have had a tragic conclusion. His family, fearing a breakdown from overwork, persuaded him to tear himself away from his studies and other toils and go fishing with his three sons. Accordingly, one day the little party of four, armed with fishing-rods and supplied with luncheon, tramped up to Hilton Bridge on the Cape Fear River. While they were strung along the bank and watching their corks with eager expectancy, their father ambitiously attempted to walk across some logs lying in the water and thus reach a very "fishy"-looking place in the river. But alas! one of the logs turned with him, and in he plunged, going in over his head. While the youngest of his sons wept and wrung his hands, the two older boys with great difficulty managed to get their father on shore. But he was drenched, and had to walk some miles in wet clothing; moreover, this experience brought on sickness, from which Dr. Deems took months to recover. It is to this incident that he alludes in the following article, which appeared in the "Christian Intelligencer," November 30, 1892, and which we insert as showing his opinions and habits with regard to hunting and fishing. To the best of our knowledge and belief, Dr. Deems never fired a pistol or shot-gun in his life; he had neither time nor taste for entrapping or slaying the inhabitants of the woods and waters.

"WHAT I KNOW ABOUT FISHING

"From what I have accomplished in the piscatory line, if any one should infer 'what I know about fishing,' he would conclude that I was as well up on that subject as my old friend Horace Greeley was on another, when he wrote 'What I Know about Farming,' and allowed people to see his Chappaqua farm.

"My two boys, who now have sons that can fish, I think could tell of a time, years ago, when they went with their father a-fishing in the Cape Fear River; and how he trod upon a loose log and went a-ducking, and had to walk home in wet clothes, and on the way caught a cold, which was the only catch of that expedition.

"Long since then, after eight years of constant labor in the Church of the Strangers, I went one winter to St. Augustine, and, just for a total change of employment, one day took a canoe and went fishing on the river. I had never read a page on the subject and I had had no personal instructions, but as rapidly as I could drop my line into the water up came a fish, until I had all I could well carry back to the hotel. That was phenomenal. The fish seemed to want to jump into my canoe. I could not understand it. I am not superstitious,— I belong to the Thirteen Club,—but from that day until the summer of 1892 I have taken no part in the original business of the apostles.

"But last summer, after a month of twenty-two lectures and speeches in thirty days, I did what never occurred before in my ministry of fifty-three years—when I was not sick and not out of the country: I spared the churches three whole Sundays. In all that space of time I did not speak in public; I hardly had strength and sense enough to pray in private. But I was on Dr. Bethune's old fishing-grounds, and worship-

ing in the church which stands to his blessed memory, and—
I went fishing. I went once with a beloved friend and twice
with my beloved self. The results were as follows:

"1. I caught a fish. Mark 'a fish'—one fish, only one,
and that was not very large. Brethren of the rod, is it not a
triumph of grace that I am able to tell the exact truth on such
a subject?

"2. I caught another fish. While the first came to me in
a normal manner, the latter was hooked by the tail. My
only theory for this is that that fool fish was just flouncing
around in the neighborhood of my hook and got caught in
that ignominious manner. Another possible theory is that he
looked at my hook and bait, and desired to express his contempt for the whole concern, and in flirting away struck the
wrong place with his tail.

"3. But I caught a thought or two about fishing, and that
being all the rest of my game, I frankly express it to you.

"What is the object of fishing? There is but one which
can satisfy a highly rational and deeply conscientious nature,
and that is to obtain food for one's self or for some one else.
To fish for any other purpose must be both foolish and wrong.
I ask myself this question: Am I so small in resources that I
cannot amuse myself without inflicting pain upon a fellow-
creature? And then I reflect upon the prevalence of the slurs
that are made upon the veracity of fishermen. I believe they
generally take the form of ridiculing the reports made of the
number of fishes, or of the *size*, or of both. There may have
been occasions when my brethren of the rod have yielded to a
temptation in that direction, but if so, I think I caught on the
bank of that Manhattan Island which is in the great St. Lawrence River something which may be morally helpful to all
my brethren in moments of violent temptation.

"Settle it with yourself once for all that the number of fish
caught has nothing to do with the importance, the grandeur,

the beauty, or the utility of fishing. Let it be understood that when one goes fishing there is an object one has in view higher than all kinds and any number of fish, and that that object is the better secured the longer time he is out and the fewer the fish he may catch. Going a-fishing does not at all necessarily involve the bringing home of fish. That may be an incidental, but it ought to be made a subordinate, consideration. In every case, where a man is not actually trying to get his food, holding a rod over the water on the bank of a river or lake, outdoors, hour by hour, without hurling up the swimmers in the water, is very far from being a bad business. Its success depends upon the fewness of the fish caught and the length of time one has to wait.

"Just settle that as a fundamental principle of your philosophy and you have gained much. A quick catch would spoil the whole thing, and many fish would knock the bottom out of the whole business. This was my summer discovery, namely, that going a-fishing does not involve catching any fish whatever. The relation of fish to going a-fishing is of the most abstract possible character. Any fellow can have a lovely old time catching the biggest fish in a couple of hours, but he may come back morally no better than when he started. Not so the fisherman who for six hours never budges and comes back with no more in his basket than he took out. Morally, he must be better as a man, and this can be shown to be the case philosophically. If there were time I believe I could prove this merely on the doctrine of conservation of energy, but I forbear.

"I caught one story which illustrates my theory. A boy was on the bank, and a man came by.

" 'Why, what are you doing?'

" 'Fishing,' replied the boy.

" 'Been at it long?'

" 'Four hours,' the boy did say.

" ' Caught anything? '

" ' Yep.'

" ' What? '

" ' Patience.'

" The gentleman, who was a railroad man, immediately employed that boy at twelve dollars a week and his board to take charge of the information bureau at a neighboring station on the trunk-line."

Among Dr. Deems's letters was found one written from Wilmington, N. C., and dated August 31, 1857. It is addressed to his friend the Hon. John A. Gilmer, of Greensboro. After congratulating Mr. Gilmer on his recent election to Congress, Dr. Deems goes on to confer with him as to the sale of Aunt Rachel, the colored cook. This extract is deeply interesting and significant as showing the relations which existed between the Southern master and slave. No satisfactory purchaser appearing, Aunt Rachel and Uncle Henry continued to live in the Deems family until her death.

" You know that I own a woman whose husband belongs to General Gray, of Randolph. I hire Henry to keep him with his wife, and then hire him out here to pay me back. But it is a risk, and next year I may be stationed where I cannot get a situation for him. So I would like to sell Rachel to a good master in your county. I do not wish to separate them. And then, my dear friend, I am probably too poor to own her. I have not sought lucrative stations in the church, you know. I have worked hard, spent my time and talents to build up the church in North Carolina, given freely, helped to educate other people's children, and if I were sold out and my debts paid perhaps I might give each of my own five children twenty-five dollars apiece. At nearly thirty-seven years of age this is rather a gloomy prospect, isn't it? It would be if it were not for the reflection that I have endeavored to do good, live unselfishly, and have faith in the final rewards.

" But to return to Aunt Rachel. She is a nice woman, has improved much since she came to me, and would readily bring twelve hundred dollars from the speculators here; but I would not sell her to them, nor, indeed, would I either sacrifice my interests or let her go to a master who would not serve her properly. It has occurred to me that if you knew any gentleman who wants a good, honest, faithful woman for his lot, who lives within range of General Gray, say in Davidson, Guilford, or Randolph, I would sell her for something in the neighborhood of nine or ten hundred dollars. And if I could sell her in that vicinity to a good master, it would be doing her a service and enable me to 'square off' matters. She and her husband are very loath to hear me speak of parting with her, and I do not wish this matter at all spoken of unless you can put us on the track of making a satisfactory arrangement."

The tone of Dr. Deems's letters during the year 1857 is in the main most cheerful; but in places they show that he was tempted to be depressed by physical infirmity, pecuniary anxieties, and the detractions of certain evil and envious men. In a letter written to an intimate friend in the fall of 1857 he says: " What an immense deal is couched in the promise of that heaven where ' the wicked cease to trouble, and the weary are forever at rest '! My troubles have seemed to produce a complex effect upon my character. They have hardened the muscles of my spirit and they have bruised also. I can bear more, lift more; but there is a very sore *inside* spot, and I have continually to watch it, lest it fester and break out. And then I have a sensitiveness lest it be discovered. I have inaugurated street-preaching in this city, and last Wednesday night, October 14th, I rang our new bell, mine being the first hand to employ it in calling the people up to worship. This

is an event.   My steeple is going up.   Last week I spent in
Goldsboro and was sick all the while.   Mrs. Dr. Annin, of
Newark, N. J., Anna's playmate in childhood, has been our
guest some weeks."

To Miss Mary Reamy

"September 1, 1857.

"Our baby girl is one of the cutest, sharpest, liveliest little
things you ever saw, and so small and plump!   We call her
partridge, snow-bird, rice-bird, everything we can think of
which is expressive of brief plumptitude."

To His Son Theodore

"WILMINGTON, N. C., November 4, 1857.

"My dear Son: We were much gratified yesterday by
the reception of your letter, and much pleased to know that
you were growing fat.   Upon the failure of your letter we
wrote to Mr. Wilkinson, and he told us of your punctuality
and praised you in terms which gladdened us.   I wish, my
dear son, you could look into your father's heart and see how
it grows happy when he learns that you have done anything
to please others and make them happy.   None but a parent
can know a parent's anguish at the misdeeds of a child.   We
pray daily that our dear Theodore may always bless us.   I
shall be willing to be an old man if my children will only so
act that they can maintain a good position in society.   If this
gives us concern, how much more anxious should we be that'
our children stand well with God, who knows all hearts and
who will fix our places in eternity!

"All the children send love.   Louly is *so* sweet!   Our kind
regards to Mrs. Hook and Uncle Everitt's family.

"Affectionately your father,

"CHARLES F. DEEMS."

The North Carolina Annual Conference of the Methodist Episcopal Church, South, was opened at Goldsboro on the second day of December, 1857, Bishop Pierce presiding. Dr. Deems was present and took an active part in the proceedings, especially as chairman of the Committee on Education. He was elected one of the delegates to attend the General Conference, which was to be held at Nashville, Tenn., the following spring. It was at this conference in Goldsboro that Robert S. Moran, D.D., then a local elder from Genesee Conference, New York, was readmitted into the traveling connection. Dr. Moran was a man of brains and culture, and Dr. Deems and he became devoted friends for life.

The closing weeks of 1857 were largely devoted by Dr. Deems to preparing the third volume of "The Annals of Southern Methodism." With this exception, he had done but little literary work for two years; so we find him writing to the editor of the "North Carolina Christian Advocate," early in 1858: "For two years, except a few scraps, I have given nothing to the press. My personal matters, as you know, have kept my faculties in their full employ, and in Wilmington, you know, a man has hardly an hour to himself."

Being devoted to children, it was a constant source of sorrow to Dr. Deems that his duties separated him so frequently from his family. In April, 1858, he sent his two elder sons, Theodore and Frank, to an excellent boarding-school at South Lowell, N. C. Writing to Mr. Joseph Speed, the principal of the school, he says, among other things: "When Wilberforce once entered the nursery of his own house and took up his own little child, it cried, and the nurse informed him that it 'always did so *with strangers.*' That is one of the great afflictions of being a public man and the servant of the whole community. Perhaps I do not know my own children as well as others do." He then proceeds to speak of the dispositions and needs of his two sons in a way which shows how thoroughly he did know them. All his children can testify that never was a father less deserving of the title "stranger." On the contrary, he was their companion and most trusted friend. All their little joys and sorrows they took straight to their father, ever assured of finding in him a true sympathizer. No father ever found greater comfort in, or showed truer devotion to, the babe in the home than did Dr. Deems. In a letter to a friend written shortly after the one just referred to, he writes affectionately about all his children, concluding this part of his letter by saying: "The pet of the house is 'Louly' [Anna Louise], our Goldsboro bud. She begins to expand beautifully, after very little promise. She is exquisitely sweet. The dear child now makes attempts at a few words and keeps up an enormous amount of jabbering and chattering. This morning she woke like a birdling and opened on us with the sweetest twitterings and attempts at songlets." This same letter is full of characteristic expressions of affection for his wife. And a few weeks later, in the midst of a business letter to his father, he suddenly breaks off to say: "I *love you dearly* for all your goodness, tenderness, and devotion to me. You are just one of the dearest and best fathers that ever a boy had—and I write that out of my heart, with tears in my eyes. God bless you! And if I live when you are gone I shall survive to bless your memory." He did outlive his father and most faithfully fulfilled his promise to bless his memory.

To His Infant Daughter Louise

WILSON, N. C., July 29, 1859.

"Poppa's darlin' Nits, pop's goin' to yite a itty letter to. 'Most all his work's done, and he's goin' in the tars to Wi'm'ton. Pop do want to see Pidfit TO mut. No itty Looloo to teep in itty bed 'side poppa's; no mama in the yoom; no Sis Minnie. P'ees, Looloo, do tum home to poppa. Poppa will hud and tiss, and tarry on wid, and div it tandy. My gayshus!

won't pop be g'ad? And won't Fide dump? Itty Fide been all way up in Johnson Tounty on a visit. When pop dot home Fide 'most eat him up. Looloo ought to see how he 'make his tail went.' Looloo 'member 'Missie,' Miss Honfluer's itty dog? Well, yesterday pop went to see it; and it was so g'ad. It 'most talk, and would stay by pop. Poor Missie t'ou't pop could tell her 'bout her mittit. Looloo, 'et's all tum home—mama and Min and F'ank and Eddie and Bud Teedy and pop. And 'et's hud and tiss powerful.

"Hud F'ank for pop, and tiss Eddie, and skeeze Sis Min, and eat mama up. Dood-by, darlin' itty bitty teet dal! Tell danpa and danma and Untle Markey and Aunt Mary and the chillun they must tum home wid Looloo!

"Your owney-downey

"POP."

Dr. Deems's tenderly affectionate and demonstrative spirit was manifested toward many outside as well as those of his own family circle, and was one of the secrets of his popularity and success; for all felt that it was genuine.

In March, 1858, in the Front Street Church, and in fact in all the churches of Wilmington, a work of grace was manifested. This was most cheering to Dr. Deems in his ministry, and to the editor of the "North Carolina Christian Advocate," Dr. Heflin, he thus writes:

"The Lord has been pouring out his Spirit upon this church during the last fortnight abundantly. The humility, earnestness, and zeal of the membership have been greatly increased. We have had two meetings daily. The prayer-meetings at noon have been largely attended and have proved precious seasons. Persons of all classes have been penitent at our altar, and more than thirty have made a profession of religion. Last night there were twenty-nine penitents. The intervals of public service are spent in private conversa-

tion with 'mourners.' Of course I have little time for anything else.

" 'The Lord of hosts is with us; the God of Jacob is our
refuge.' "

About the middle of May Dr. Deems went to Nashville,
Tenn., as one of the delegates from the North Carolina Conference to the General Conference of the Methodist Episcopal
Church, South, which meets once in every four years. Although kept very busy all the time he made many friends, and
returned to Wilmington refreshed and stimulated in spirit,
though weary in body. Writing from Nashville, May 15th,
to a member of his church, he says, among other things: " I
made my North Carolina tour safely, reached this city 'right
side up,' and, as they say in Georgia, 'pitched in' *ad*medi-
ately. . . . Last night I preached in the Methodist cathedral
called McKendree Church. It was a very large congregation, a very hot time, a very slender discourse, and a very attentive crowd. You cannot tell how I long to be at home.
My labors are excessive. I am confined to the conference-
room during the morning, and the afternoon is spent in committees. I am secretary to the most laborious committee, that
of revisals, and have to write out the reports thereof. This is
laborious, as our committee has the revisal of the whole subject of our church Discipline." When conference was adjourned, about June 1st, Dr. Deems wrote home that he was
almost blind with exhaustion, and that his hand was giving
him continuous pain from constant use of the pen.

The summer and fall were spent in faithful, fruitful work
in the interests of his Wilmington parish, wherein he was
greatly blessed. His birthday, December 4th, found him
in improved health and excellent spirits, as may be seen by
the following letter to an old New York friend.

To Mrs. Caroline R. Dend

" December 4, 1858.

"MY DEAR SISTER DEND: This is my thirty-eighth birthday, and I reserve for it my correspondence with my most
intimate friends. Do you remember that just *nineteen years
ago* (!) you were so kind to the boy who had gone to New
York to try his fortunes and begin his ministry? What trials,
what conflicts, what fightings, what fears, since that time!
How hard has been his life, how good his God! And amid
it all he has never forgotten one single act of your kindness
and goodness. To-day my people fête me. Never has there
risen upon me a birthday that had more clustering blessings.
In arranging, as I always do before conference, all my worldly
affairs as if I were going to die, I have never been in so comfortable a condition. And now from all these comforts my
heart goes back to a time when I really did not know how to
replace my threadbare coat with another, and when a lady, as
I walked with her down Canal Street, so delicately begged me
not to be offended if the ladies presented me a suit of clothes,
as they intended to do the same to Dr. Bangs. *You* know
who that lady was, but you do not know how acceptable was
the gift. The Lord God bless you abundantly. . . .

"My future is somewhat uncertain. They have again
elected me president of Soule University, Texas; but my North
Carolina friends seem determined that I shall not leave them,
and are projecting the purchase of a residence for my family
in this city. In the meantime two wealthy gentlemen offer
me two seminaries in the same town (Wilson, N. C.), the title
of the property to be in me in fee, the rectory of which is all
I shall have to take; that is to say, I could have my conference appointments as now; and my occasional work and constant oversight would yield me a handsome profit. And to
bribe me to accept their munificence, one of the gentlemen

offers me five hundred dollars for a brief European tour. If I accept the latter I shall probably see you in February.

"Please write to me, and 'keep a-lovin' me,' as the darkies say. Mrs. Deems joins me in sentiments of high regard."

The Annual Conference of the Methodist Episcopal Church, South, in North Carolina, met at Newbern, in the African Church, Bishop Kavanaugh presiding. Dr. Deems was present, and of course had a delightful reunion with his many friends in his former parish. In the "Daily Progress" for December 15th, the following item appeared:

"C. F. DEEMS, D.D.

"We understand it was stated on the floor of the conference yesterday that this distinguished divine has been invited recently to the presidency of a university in the State of Texas. This promises to be the richest and best endowed and one of the most influential institutions in all the South.

"We also learn that Dr. Deems has been called to the pastorate of a popular church in the city of New York.

"It is certainly gratifying to his friends—and their name is legion—to know that he who is so much loved at home is held in such high estimation abroad. We hope North Carolina will offer such inducements to Dr. Deems as that he will be content to forego these splendid offers and remain among us. Though an adopted son, there is no one more loyal to the 'Old North State,' and who has a warmer place in her great beating heart. The ties that bind us are strong, and we trust they will never be severed."

Conference, in making its appointments, at this session did not send Dr. Deems back to Front Street Church, but promoted him by making him presiding elder of the Wilmington district, within whose bounds were at that time fourteen churches.

CHAPTER V

THE next thing after the conference of 1858 to receive Dr. Deems's attention was an appeal from certain citizens of Wilson, N. C., for him to establish and maintain in that place a seminary for young men and women. This is the offer referred to in the last chapter in his letter to Mrs. Caroline Dend. He decided to accept the invitation, and in a letter to a friend, dated December 24, 1858, says: "Conference has adjourned; we are breaking up; all things about us are in confusion. We are to live in—Wilson!! Your old home. But it has grown greatly. They have erected a large seminary and presented me two thirds of it; that is, I pay one third of cost, and have the whole in fee simple and the whole control. I expect next month to open a large school for boys and girls, and to expand it, as my time and powers allow, into the greatest and best thing in the State of North Carolina."

From His Journal

"Monday, January 3d. The circular announcing my school in Wilson published at noon. My first Quarterly Conference was held at Fifth Street Church in the preacher's office. Rev. T. W. Guthrie, pastor."

"Tuesday, January 4th. At work on 'Annals of Southern Methodism.' Very perplexing. The book has to be finished at such a busy time of the year. My engagements now are very pressing. The 'Annals,' my district, the opening a new seminary—all at once! I go to my office by starlight in the morning. 'As thy days, so shall thy strength be.'"

"Monday, January 10th. Closed up affairs. Started with Mrs. Deems and 'Loulie' for Wilson. Mrs. Coffin (who is to be matron of the seminary) and daughter accompanied us. At Faison we gathered up all the other children. Stayed all night at Wiley Daniel's in Wilson."

"Wednesday, January 12th. The first meal at the new seminary at supper. Present, Mrs. Deems, Mrs. Coffin, Miss Sarah Brown and Miss Kate Shackelford, of Wilmington, Miss Mary W. Speed, Maria Coffin, Professor Radcliffe, Minnie, Theodore, Frank, and Eddie Deems. In the name of the Lord have we set up our banners."

The newly erected seminary cost seventy-five hundred dollars. It was amply provided with rooms for boarding pupils, class-rooms, and one entire wing devoted to a residence for Dr. Deems and his family. Ample grounds and outhouses, such as a kitchen, barn, etc., made a complete institution. In connection with the seminary Dr. Deems secured an indefinite lease on another lot having on it a large two-story house, a school for boys, with dormitories and recitation-rooms.

The town of Wilson is about one hundred and twenty miles north of Wilmington and is the county-seat of Wilson County. It was a bright place in 1859, but has grown and improved wonderfully since that time. After energetic and careful effort Dr. Deems secured a faculty for his schools, furnished them, and began the first term on January 13, 1859. On that day the new seminary was dedicated. It was named "St. Austin's Institute." The Rev. J. W. Tucker read Psalm xci. and offered prayer; Dr. Deems delivered the address of the occasion; and the benediction was pronounced by the Rev. N. A. H. Goddin.

Fifteen boys and sixteen girls were entered as scholars for the ensuing session.

When the first scholastic exercises commenced, on Monday, January 17th, there were in attendance twenty-four boys and twenty-four girls; but by the end of the year there had been enrolled in the seminary for young ladies eighty-two, and in the military academy ninety-three, a total of one hundred and seventy-five. Miss Mary Wade Speed was principal of the ladies' seminary, and Captain James D. Radcliffe of the military academy. They were both experienced teachers and eminently fitted for the positions which they held. Professor Radcliffe was a graduate of the South Carolina Military Academy. In addition to the English, mathematical, and classical branches, the pupils had the advantage of the infantry drill of military academies. To secure interest and success in this an ample supply of cadet muskets was provided, and a neat, plain, and inexpensive uniform. The uniform proved a great help in securing discipline and preventing extravagance; and the drill, while not interfering with the studies, favored the physical and intellectual training of the boys and young men. The pupils of both departments came chiefly from North Carolina, but also a few came from neighboring States.

In addition to engaging teachers and professors of unusual ability for the various departments, Dr. Deems secured for the institution a very fine and ample selection of chemical and philosophical apparatus, and one afternoon in each week was devoted to lectures illustrating to the pupils in both departments the laws of matter and of motion, mechanics, hydraulics, hydrostatics, pneumatics, electricity, optics, magnetism, electromagnetism, chemistry, and astronomy. In addition to these regular scientific lectures, gentlemen from abroad were occasionally employed, and the rector, Dr. Deems, addressed the classes upon such subjects of personal interest as he thought

most important. While St. Austin's was an undenominational
school, it yet made provision for the spiritual culture of its
pupils, both branches being opened and closed daily with the
reading of the Scriptures and prayers; and on Sundays especial instruction in the Bible was given.

Dr. Deems was, of course, profoundly interested in his Wilson schools, and put into them not only four of the best years
of his life, but also his whole heart and mind. Nor were these
bestowed in vain; for in return he made a host of friends,
educated a large company of young people, and received a
mental and spiritual discipline without which he could never
have made the mark in the world which he afterward did. He
never forgot the generosity and aid of the patrons of St. Austin's in Wilson and elsewhere, and held in tenderest memory
both his associates in the faculty and his pupils in the ladies'
seminary and the military academy.

In addition to the care and toil involved in the founding
and carrying on of his Wilson schools, Dr. Deems during his
whole life in Wilson kept up vigorously and successfully his
work as presiding elder of the Wilmington district. The bulk
of his time was given to this work, and the schools received
the remainder. To give the reader an idea of his life at this
time we insert here the following

Extracts from His Journal for 1859

"Saturday, January 22d.   Left Wilmington on early train.
Weather inclement.   Mr. Tom Ashe invited me to his brother's.
Found the family of the Hon. William S. Ashe very agreeable.
Mr. Tom Ashe particularly interesting in California stories.
Walked over, or rather waded, to Rocky Point Church.   No
one there."

"Monday, January 24th.   Rose at three o'clock and rode
with Mr. James to the Marlboro station.   Thence to Wil-

mington by railroad. Shopped all day. Left in afternoon train and reached home at night. Wednesday, 26th. At home; very unwell. Wednesday, February 2d. Working on the 'Annals of Southern Methodism.'"

"Saturday, March 12th. Dr. F. W. Potter carried me to Zoar, in Brunswick County, over a most wretched road to a wretched 'meeting-house.' Lot said truly, 'It is a little one.' Met the Rev. A. D. Betts. Held Quarterly Conference. Then went to the Rev. C. C. Mercer's, where we spent the night. Doleful country."

"Monday, April 11th. At night [in Wilmington] heard Edward Everett deliver his famous oration on 'Washington,' and was sadly disappointed. Every gesture was *put in* precisely where it should have been; every sentence was balanced, every tone studied. As a *literary* performance it was polished to perfection. Some of the gems were exquisite. But at the conclusion I had not once felt my blood stirred, nor did I feel a greater veneration for Washington. Whereupon I concluded that, with all its merits, it failed both as a philosophical inquiry and as an oration."

"Friday, June 3d. Friday afternoon went [from Wilmington] in the steamer 'Fanny Lutterloh.' Just before daylight was put out at Purdie's Landing. Lost my way—night—storm—finally succeeded."

"Sunday, December 4th. My thirty-ninth birthday! 'Few and evil;' yet how old I am! I have *felt* so much. Stayed last night with Mr. John C. Bowden. Administered the sacrament of the Lord's Supper in the morning to the whites, in the afternoon to the colored people."

"Wednesday, December 14th. Conference opens at Beaufort, N. C. Bishop Early presides."

"Monday, December 19th. Very sick with my ear. At night I *fainted!* A new sensation. Am I weakening?"

"Tuesday, December 20th. The physician put me on my

feet, and I made an address before conference in behalf of the 'Advocate,' and secured thirteen hundred dollars to meet its liabilities. The news reached town [Beaufort] to-day that I had been elected to the professorship of history and elocution in the University of North Carolina."

During the 1859 session of the North Carolina Conference two things occurred which gave the greatest gratification to Dr. Deems: one was the admitting into that conference and the appointment to the Topsail circuit of his father, the Rev. George W. Deems, from Petersburg, Va.; and the other was Dr. Deems's election by the University of North Carolina to the chair of history and elocution. The Wilmington "Herald" of December 21st, commenting on the call to the university, said: "The trustees show their appreciation of sterling talent and ability in their selection of Dr. Deems. We do not think, however, that the doctor will accept. He has year after year refused tempting offers of a similar nature, and we do not believe that he wishes to leave the regular work of the ministry. Besides, he has now in the full tide of successful operation a large and flourishing school at Wilson, which he can superintend without interfering with his duties as a minister of Christ." Although urged to do so by conference, Dr. Deems, after mature deliberation, decided not to go to the university.

From His Journal

"Saturday, December 31st. Raining and cold. Spent the last night of this year [in Wilmington] in the quiet house of my friend Mr. Van Sickle. God has been good to me this year. I have not missed an appointment on my district through sickness, and only one elsewhere. My schools have prospered. We have had about one hundred and twenty pupils. My receipts have fallen short of my expenditures by about two hundred and fifty dollars, but I have purchased more than sixteen hundred dollars' worth of furniture. I thank God and take courage. Oh, that I may be a better man next year! So pass our years into eternity; the unalterable record is made."

Almost every thoughtful man sooner or later is possessed with a desire to travel, especially in foreign lands; so it is not strange that for many years Dr. Deems had eagerly wished to visit Europe. At last, in 1860, the way seemed clear for him to do so. During 1859 he had put his Wilson schools in good working order and had become familiar with and systematized the work on the Wilmington district, over which he was presiding elder. Moreover, friends of means and generosity had placed at his disposal five hundred dollars toward the expenses of a European trip. Besides all this, he had been for years under a mental and physical strain which imperatively called for some such experience as this. He accordingly decided to travel, and prepared industriously for a six months' journey abroad.

From His Journal

"Wednesday, March 21st. My dear children met me in my study and we had a pleasant family chat. Thursday, March 22d. Left the seminary with Mrs. Deems, Minnie, and Loulie for the cars. Many of the pupils assembled. It was hard parting, but my wife was with me and that cheered. At Weldon married a couple at the hotel. Reached Mr. Disosway's [at Stony Creek, near Petersburg, Va.] in the evening. Friday, March 23d. At three o'clock to-day parted from my dear, dear wife for six or seven long months. It was tenfold more bitter than I thought it could be. Traveled all night."

On his way to New York Dr. Deems stopped off to visit friends at Washington, Baltimore, and Philadelphia. He reached New York City Wednesday, March 28th, and put up at first at the Astor House, but afterward made his headquarters at the residence of his wife's uncle, Mr. Cornelius Disosway, who lived at No. 36 West Forty-fifth Street, and who showed Dr. Deems every attention during his stay in the city. Saturday evening, March 31st, he went to Albany, where he was the guest of the Rev. Dr. Sprague, author of "Annals of the American Pulpit," for which Dr. Deems had written sketches of Brame, Summerfield, and Emory. On Sunday he preached in Dr. Sprague's pulpit both morning and evening. Monday was spent delightfully in visiting in Albany, a most pleasant interview with Palmer, the sculptor, being one of the features of the day.

Leaving Albany Tuesday morning, he stopped a few hours at West Point, where he was introduced to Professor O. O. Howard. Arriving in New York in the afternoon, he heard in the evening William Cullen Bryant's oration on Washington Irving at the Academy of Music. Edward Everett also spoke, and Dr. Deems saw on the platform, among other celebrities, Bancroft and General Winfield Scott. It was Irving's birthday. The next few days were spent in sight-seeing, hearing addresses and sermons by famous men, and in securing his passage for Europe.

It was at this time that Dr. Deems first came in touch with "Commodore" Cornelius Vanderbilt. On this subject he wrote years afterward:

"In the year 1860 I had occasion to visit Europe. For that purpose I left my pastoral charge in North Carolina and came to New York. One day, while standing on the corner of Broadway and Bowling Green, my wife's uncle, Mr. Gabriel Disosway, found me there in a brown study. I told him that I was just considering the question whether I should venture to take passage in the steamship 'Illinois.' He said he had a friend in the neighborhood who could tell me all about it. 'Who is it?' said I. 'Cornelius Vanderbilt.' I had heard Mr. Gabriel Disosway's brother, my father-in-law, many a year ago speak of his early acquaintance with Mr. Vanderbilt, both these gentlemen having been Staten Islanders. I requested him to take me to Mr. Vanderbilt's office.

"When we entered he was standing at a desk alone. He was a magnificent-looking man. 'How are you, judge?' said he, addressing Mr. Disosway. My wife's uncle then presented me and told my business in general terms. He looked me straight in the eye; I shall never forget the man's face and expression. I stood returning the gaze and said: 'Mr. Vanderbilt, I am going to Europe; I haven't too much money; I want to expend as little on the passage as practicable, that I may have more to spend abroad. The "Illinois" advertises passage at twenty dollars in gold less than the other lines; twenty dollars is an amount worth my considering, but I think too much of myself to put my life in peril for twenty dollars. Do you think the "Illinois" will make the trip?' He looked me straight in the eye and said, 'Doctor, she will reach the other side.' I instantly responded, 'Then, if I am alive, I shall be with her. Good-morning, Mr. Vanderbilt,' and I walked out.

"I never forgot that brief interview, but supposed that of course it had long ago passed from his memory. Sixteen years thereafter, a few days before he died, while propped up in his invalid's chair in his front room in No. 10 Washington Place, I alluded to the circumstance. A gentleman of the party said, 'Oh, the commodore has forgotten all about that.' 'No,' said he, 'I haven't.' And then the dying man detailed the whole interview, and not only remembered me as well as I had remembered him, but gave a history of the 'Illinois,' describing her build from stem to stern with tenfold the fullness with which I could have done it, although I spent fifteen days on her. He followed it up with a minute account of her subsequent history."

From His Journal

"Saturday, April 7th. At twelve o'clock was on board the 'Illinois.' State-room 7 ; Captain Seabury ; bound for Havre. Beautiful day. Quiet in heart. Not sick. Interested in the sea. After to-day shall keep a copy of the captain's log."

The sea voyage was marred in a measure by wind and rain, and was made in fifteen days. Dr. Deems preached on the steamer's deck April 15th and April 22d. He thoroughly enjoyed his experience on the Atlantic notwithstanding its roughness. Southampton was reached Monday, April 23d, and Tuesday, April 24th, the steamer was at her pier in Havre.

Before going abroad Dr. Deems determined not to correspond with any newspaper and not to write a book, for he wished his travels to be unclouded by any form of responsibility. His diary is filled with sketchy memoranda made with lead-pencil and in very fine handwriting. He wrote frequently and fully to his family and friends, and sent especially interesting letters to his Wilson schools, which were brought together from time to time to hear these letters read. On account of time and war and the death of many of his correspondents, all of Dr. Deems's letters are lost, save one which he wrote to his wife on reaching the British Channel. The doctor traveled rapidly and covered a great deal of ground ; but he observed acutely and intensely and thought deeply on what he saw, thus making his six months in Europe an epoch in his mental and spiritual life. In going to Europe he had three especial objective points: Rome, Oxford at the commencement season, and Oberammergau at the time of the passion-play.

To the more important places in his itinerary he gave weeks, and to those of less interest, days or even hours. His longest stops were at Paris, Naples, Rome, London, Oxford, and Berlin. During most of the time he had delightful American and British traveling companions and was in excellent health; but at other times he suffered from loneliness and depression of spirits, and once he was quite ill for a few days while in Holland. What interested him most in his travels was not scenery, but historic places, painting and statuary, and people of high and low degree with their peculiar thoughts and customs. The cathedrals especially impressed him, leading him to exclaim, while under the spell of one of the most impressive of them, " Thank God for the dark ages!"

In Paris he saw everything of note, and, among other sights, was permitted to see the emperor and empress, the little prince, and Prince Jerome, his son, and his wife. He admired the elegant simplicity of the traveling costume of the Empress Eugénie, who at the time was leaving France for a visit to the British queen. He spoke to the little Napoleon, and said he then looked like his illustrious uncle.

Naples, with its historic and picturesque surroundings, was deeply interesting to Dr. Deems.

From His Journal

" Thursday, May 8th. Woke this morning near Naples. Beautiful for situation. Vesuvius active—beggars too. Detained two hours; then landed. Examined by police, baggage examined by custom-house officer. At last allowed to go to our hotel and get breakfast at eleven. Passports kept."

Besides delightful sight-seeing in Naples, Dr. Deems made excursions to Pompeii, Herculaneum, Vesuvius, Virgil's tomb, Baiae, Castellamare, and Sorrento. Just before leaving Naples on Saturday, May 10th, Dr. Deems wrote in his journal, " Garibaldi has taken Palermo and is expected to march on

Naples. Most of the strangers leaving." He reached Rome
at 8 P.M., May 20th, and in his journal indicates his emotions
on arriving in the Eternal City by giving the word " Rome "
three heavy underscorings. He spent ten intensely interesting
days in Rome, meeting many noted people, including the pope,
and seeing most of the great sights. He says in his journal
that on Wednesday, May 23d, he took a night walk "*à la*
Marble Faun*," and on Thursday mounted St. Peter's into the
ball. The Vatican with its treasures of art and antiquity received especial attention and thrilled him. He did not fail to
explore the catacombs, climb Hilda's Tower, and otherwise
study and enjoy Rome.

After Rome the principal northern cities of Italy were visited,
Florence, Venice, and Milan giving him especial delight. At
Verona he was taken for a spy. The " Diamond," a little
amateur journal, edited and printed for a short time in New
York City by the young nephews of Mrs. Cornelius Vanderbilt,
in its issue for June, 1887, printed the following account of this
episode :

" We heard Dr. Deems tell the following story : ' In 1860
I came near dropping out of the world. In a party of
travelers at Venice were a New York merchant, a Brooklyn
physician, an English acquaintance, and myself. My English
acquaintance and I went to Verona. We parted at night
with the understanding that he should join the American
friends from Venice the next morning, while I went to Mantua. Rising early, I put on my duster, and, taking a guide-
book, ascended the castle steps to enjoy the splendid view of
Lombardy. I sat upon one of the steps taking notes and
sketches. Once or twice I heard the door at the top open
and shut, but before I could turn my head the opener had disappeared from sight. At last I got a view of the head as the
door closed. In a few moments a strong-armed Austrian soldier came lumbering down the steps and laid his hand on my

shoulder. It was easy to see that he meant that I should follow him. Serenely and innocently I walked behind.

"'After a few steps we met an officer. Some conversation followed, which I was not able to understand, my conductor showing him the book in my hand and turning to the page which had the plan of the fortifications. He was directed to take me below. All at once I awoke to a sense of my condition. A gentleman had lately, to the great distress of his family, been kept in an Austrian prison on suspicion of being a spy. It struck me that that was to be my fate. When we came to a certain platform about nine feet above the street there was a fork in the road; my conductor, evidently expecting me to follow, had turned to the left.

"'I made a calculation of my ability to leap. After he had taken three steps I wheeled to the right, sprang down the steps into the street, doubling until I reached a church, where I went in, got behind the altar, stripped off my blouse, wrapped it into as small a compass as possible, turned my cap inside out, and by doubling reached the hotel, where I quickly settled my bill, secured a conveyance, and got into an eastern-bound car, where I found our whole party. I explained my escape to them. A European sitting near and hearing the story said, "Well, no doubt you did some rapid running?"

"'"Running!" I replied. "I am an American; do you suppose an American ever runs? But to be candid with you, sir, if you had seen me from the bridge you would have seen some tall walking."

"'If I had been imprisoned I should have disappeared. The last trace made of me would have been at the hotel whence my English friend expected me to go to Mantua. There the clue would have broken. It was a close call, and I was very glad to get off so well.'"

While in Europe Dr. Deems was three times in London, and on each visit made good use of his time in sight-seeing.

Probably what interested him most was seeing and hearing the great men in Parliament. He heard Gladstone, Lord Palmerston, Lord Brougham, and others. Among the preachers whom he went to hear were Spurgeon, Mr. Punshon, and Dean Stanley.

On Saturday, June 23d, he wrote in his journal: "The greatest day of England in this generation. The great 're-view of volunteers.' Walked and stood and leaned for seven hours. Saw thirty thousand volunteers and certainly seventy thousand people. Was opposite Buckingham Palace. Saw the queen distinctly, and Prince Albert and the Prince of Wales, and the 'whole lot.' What people! what crowds! what splendor! what beauty!"

From London Dr. Deems went to Oxford, and the five days which he spent at this ancient and classic university were after-ward often spoken of with glowing pleasure. He probably enjoyed no part of his travels more than his stay at Oxford, which he reached on the 27th of June. Here he packed every minute with the sweet toil of inspecting Oxford buildings, men, and methods. As it was the commencement season, many men of learning and rank were present, and among other addresses which Dr. Deems heard was a discourse by Mr. Huxley, which he afterward thought "had in it the main points of the article of his which appeared in the 'Westmin-ster Review' of that year, afterward published in his volume, in which he gives his reason for rejecting the hypothesis of the direct creation of species."

In speaking of the various college buildings and grounds, he always awarded the palm—and who would not?—to Magdalen College, with its quiet, studious cloisters adorned with ivy, its ample parks with their stately shade-trees, green-sward, feeding deer, and, the glory of all, "Addison's Walk."

Neighboring points of interest were visited: Woodstock,

where he saw Blenheim's beautiful grounds, drank of "Rosa-mond's Well," and looked upon Chaucer's house; Shotover, Mary Powell's home; Forest Hill, with Milton's courting-walk; Cumner, where Amy Robsart died, and near which Alfred was born and Hampden fell. In the midst of his memoranda of these excursions he writes in his journal: "Delightful walks and sights. Beautiful, dear old England!"

When in the midst of his rambles through the English lake district he visited Rydal Mount, the home of the poet Words-worth, on Wednesday, July 18th. There he saw and talked with James Dixon, who had been for thirty-five years a ser-vant in the Wordsworth family, and from whom Dr. Deems bought a most interesting chair, which the poet had used in his study, and which is still preserved in the Deems family as a precious relic.

The latter half of August, all of September, and half of Oc-tober were spent on the Continent, visiting the principal points of interest in Holland, Belgium, Germany, and Switzerland, touching again at Paris on his homeward way. Naturally the cathedrals and art galleries received the largest share of his attention.

No paintings appear to have impressed him more than Ru-bens's two masterpieces in the cathedral of Antwerp. We find lying in his journal a loose sheet of note-paper, on both sides of which is a closely written discriminating criticism of these two noble works of art.

The Rhine, Heidelberg, Berlin, Dresden, and Oberammer-gau, as well as other points on the Continent, were seen and enjoyed as only a man like Dr. Deems could see and enjoy them. Then he turned his face homeward, and after touch-ing again at London, and spending a few days in visiting Cork, Dublin, and the Killarney Lakes, he boarded the steamer "Edinburgh" and sailed for America on Thursday, Octo-ber 25th.

From His Journal

"October 26th. This morning it was very rough, and for the first time in my life I was somewhat seasick. My roommate is Mr. Mirzan, a native of Smyrna and now living in Boston. October 28th. To-night was flung down and bruised my arm badly. It was in the engine-house. A most furious blow all night. Rolling, terrible waves; water poured in; women and children cried; a time! Preached on shipboard from Psalm lxv. 5. November 2d. In the night reached banks of Newfoundland. The morning foggy, the day rainy. November 5th. A day of debate on American politics. November 6th. A wonderful waterspout rising to the south of us and coming across our stern a few hundred yards behind; a most extraordinary exhibition when a black background of clouds made it very visible; the rapid waving ascent into the air and its agglomeration into feathery clouds; its colors, white, lead-color, and copper. November 7th. At ten o'clock to-day dropped anchor in the river. On landing, learned that Abraham Lincoln had been elected President of the United States. Heard of the conversion of my children. Took train for Wilson at 6 P.M. November 8th. In Baltimore at eight. Went to Washington, where we remained until 6 P.M. Strolled through Patent Office and Capitol. Sad feelings. Perhaps this may never be occupied by the Congress of the United States again. November 9th. Reached Wilson at 2 P.M. (after several stops on the way from New York City). *Joyful meeting with my wife and children.*"

Thus closed one of the most interesting and significant epochs in Dr. Deems's life, a period which, had its close not been shadowed by war-clouds, would have been looked back upon by him as one of almost undimmed sunshine.

CHAPTER VI

THE WAR, 1861–65

> " Where we lay,
> Our chimneys were blown down; and as they say,
> Lamentings heard i' the air; strange screams of death;
> And prophesying, with accents terrible,
> Of dire combustion, and confused events,
> New hatched to the woeful time."

A S Dr. Deems landed upon the wharf in New York City that bleak November day in 1860, the first thing he heard was that Mr. Lincoln had been elected President of the United States. Remembering all that had transpired in the deep and angry slavery debates between the extremists on both sides, and especially the John Brown raid, which was virtually the first battle of the war, he foresaw clearly that Mr. Lincoln's election meant civil war, and lost no time in rejoining his family. Arriving at his home in Wilson, he found himself confronting a situation which was indeed so menacing, so intricate and perplexing, that few men knew what best to do. The conflict of opinion had reached the explosive stage; madness seemed to rule the hour. The warning voices of sober men who would promote peace were raised in vain or silenced amid the mighty clamor; individual and even State efforts to check the impending and tremblingly poised avalanche were seen to be utterly in vain; the strong undercurrent of conservative good sense and calm reflection was overborne by the elements of strife and revolution.

Posterity and future history will render a different and more impartial verdict in favor of the mass of the people of the South, especially of North Carolina. Already we have seen much of the unjust harshness and rancorous asperities of the post-bellum sentences eliminated or softened down by the justice of time. It is now seen that it is possible for a few opposing extremists in power to plunge a whole people, despite themselves, into war.

With the peace- and Union-loving patriots of that day Dr. Deems was in cordial sympathy. When the war broke out there was no man in the State of North Carolina who was personally known to so many people as he; and since the war, with the sole exception of the late Senator Z. B. Vance (war governor of North Carolina), no man ever was known personally to more North Carolinians than Dr. Deems, thanks to his popularity, his eloquence, and the itinerant feature of the Methodist ministry. He was opposed to his State withdrawing from the Union, believing such a course to be not unconstitutional, but inexpedient; but when North Carolina decided to secede he went heart and soul with his people. As to slavery, while he was not its rabid advocate, yet he knew that as it existed in his State slaveholding was not a crime, that slaves and slaveholders were Christians, and died as Christians, and were buried side by side, and that much that was said about the abuses of slavery was absolutely false, so far, at least, as North Carolina was concerned.

In common with the majority of Southerners, when the war closed and slavery was abolished Dr. Deems was glad that it was gone. He was of those who believed that slavery would have been abolished eventually by the process of gradual voluntary manumission. Living on the ground, he did not see those horrible things which were said of the abuses of the relationship of master and slave; but residing in the South, he did see certain things that in his opinion sufficiently ameliorated the state of affairs to warrant the nation in getting rid of slavery by less bloody measures than a gigantic civil war. So it must not be supposed that Dr. Deems regarded the course of the Southern people as wrong. He did regard secession as *inexpedient* and deemed its advocates mistaken. He, in common with many good men, believed in the "sacred right of revolution for the redress of insupportable grievances."

In these memoirs we would fain pass over those four years of fratricidal strife, from the spring of 1861 to the spring of 1865; but this cannot be done, for they are matters of irrevocable history and played an important part in molding Dr. Deems's character and shaping his destiny. It will be seen from the extracts from his journal and letters that, never having been a preacher of partizan politics, he did not begin to be one when war came. Being a minister of the gospel, he did not bear arms; but he did toil indefatigably to comfort the bereft at home and inspire the heroes at the front. He gave his oldest son, Theodore, to the army, to fall with a mortal wound fighting heroically on the second day of Gettysburg's bloody field.

While visiting and toiling in the Wilmington and Newbern districts, over the latter of which he was made presiding elder in December, 1862, he also canvassed the whole State in the interests of a fund for founding and supporting a "College for the Orphans of Southern Soldiers." Soon after the commencement of the war the young men and boys of his military academy either went to the army or were taken home by anxious parents; so that it was only a matter of a few months before that department was closed. But the seminary for young ladies was with great difficulty kept up until the close of 1863, when it seemed best to Dr. Deems to sell his Wilson property, close his school, and move to Raleigh. But we will let him speak for himself of these and other interesting matters.

From His Journal, 1861

"Tuesday, January 1st. The new year makes its advent in gloom. The secession of South Carolina and the events consequent thereupon have thrown the whole country into trouble. Every day the telegrams become more distressing. No one now sees what is to be the result. The greatest pressure exists in trade."

"Saturday, April 13th, Providence, Duplin County, N. C. Heard that yesterday General Beauregard had opened the assault upon Fort Sumter. This is the beginning of our Civil War. The excitement rises."

"Sunday, April 14th. Fort Sumter last night fell into the hands of the Confederate troops. No one killed on either side, except three men by accident after the surrender. The excitement of war news growing intense."

"Tuesday, April 16th, Wilson, N. C. The news to-day is that General Scott has resigned and that Virginia has seceded."

"Wednesday, April 17th. Lincoln's proclamation has stirred the country. North Carolina is in revolution. Forts Caswell [near Wilmington, N. C.] and Macon have been taken by the Confederates. An order came to-day for the Wilson Company to proceed to Fort Macon. The ladies are at work on mattresses and shirts. All the country astir."

"Thursday, April 18th. Had hard work to keep my boys from breaking up and going to the war. The Wilson Company left in the two-o'clock train. John W. Dunham, my assistant, is with them. Patriotic speech to the troops. Virginia seceded to-day at 4 : 20 A. M. It was proclaimed at noon."

"Sunday, April 21st, Clinton, N. C. Heard to-day that the Baltimoreans had withstood Northern troops and there had been loss of life."

"Monday, April 22d, Wilson, N. C. At night the Georgia troops passed through and I addressed them at midnight."

"Friday, April 26th. Went to Wilmington. Stayed with the Rev. M. Robbins. Many of the men of the town are at Fort Caswell. My son Theodore came down with me."

"Saturday, April 27th. Met the Rev. I. B. Bailey (at Prospect, New Hanover County) and held Quarterly Conference. Theodore (seventeen years of age) went to Fort Caswell to go into the fort as secretary to Captain Hedrick. Returned to Wilmington. Tea with the Rev. T. W. Guthrie. Went down to the evening train and saw the Hon. Alexander Hamilton Stephens, Vice-President of the Confederate States of America. Small man, big head, clear voice, rapid enunciation. Good talk. He was much jaded, was just from Richmond, taking Virginia into the Confederation."

To His Son

"WILMINGTON, April 29, 1861.

"MY DEAR SON: Your note of yesterday gave me much pleasure. That to your mother will go up to-day. On Saturday evening Vice-President Stephens passed through town and made a short speech. In private he said that the march upon Washington was mere newspaper talk, that of course it would not be made until war should be declared by the Southern Confederacy, and that that would not be done, of course, before the assembling of Congress. We have, however, plenty of work to do in perfecting our home defense and drilling our men. We must not go too fast. The North is putting itself in complete array and the feeling is deepening.

"For yourself, I can give you no better advice than that of the town clerk of Ephesus: 'Do nothing rashly.' Your surest place is the post of duty. Rise by doing just what is needed in your position. Your work will often require *haste*, never *hurry.* Be thoughtful. A slight mistake in a subaltern may produce very disastrous consequences. You will be noticed early enough and advanced. Let all about you acquire confidence in your judgment, coolness, reliability, and promptness. Guard against the infection of moral evil in the camp. ' My son, if sinners entice thee, consent thou not.' If your course of carefulness cause a sneer at first, it will produce respect afterward, and perhaps at the moment may strengthen some weaker soul in the struggle with the tempter. Attend to your private devotions and study God's blessed Word.

" Collect all the facts you can this week, and I will endeavor to be down next Monday, and we may be able to decide upon something. You need make no haste in that, however. If you are useful in your present position, that is enough. Preserve all the letters you receive; when you become an old man they may be highly interesting and important as showing the temper of these trying times. May the Lord keep you.

" Your affectionate father,
" CHARLES F. DEEMS.

" T. D. Deems,
 " Fort Caswell, N. C."

From His Journal, 1861

" Thursday, May 2d, Wilson, N. C. My male school nearly broken up. The boys who have not gone to the war have been recalled by their parents."

" Monday, May 6th. Went down [from Wilmington] to Fort Johnston and thence to Fort Caswell. Mrs. Deems and Minnie returned. Frank and Eddie stayed with me all night in the fort. Preached at the fort, Philippians i. 21. Very many of the soldiers were present. An impressive time. The singing of ' Old Hundred ' was remarkable."

"Tuesday, May 7th. Slept last night in the hospital, Fort Caswell. This morning, with Lieutenant McIlhenry, went in a boat to Fort Johnston. We swamped and were obliged to be put into a lighter. Preached at Fort Johnston, but was interrupted by the steamer bringing troops. From Fort Caswell we carried the Wilmington Light Infantry to Federal Point."

"Wednesday, May 8th. There was an alarm in Wilmington this morning that troops were landing on Oak Island to attack Fort Caswell. Turned out to be false, but made much excitement."

"Monday, May 20th. Went to Raleigh. Was present at the convention, which adopted the ordinance of secession whereby the State of North Carolina resumed her sovereignty. At the close of the voting Governor Ellis and I went to the west window of the capitol and gave the signal for artillery discharge. Great enthusiasm."

"Tuesday, May 21st. Had an interview, at his request, with the governor. Gave him many of my views on matters and things. Do not like the way they manage matters. At the request of Weldon N. Edwards, president, I opened the convention with prayer, the first prayer after North Carolina had become one of the Confederate States. At night the ordinance was signed."

"Tuesday, May 28th. Theodore went to Norfolk."

"Monday, June 3d, Wilmington. At tea Frank arrived with Theodore's commission as second lieutenant, Company K, Seventh Regiment, North Carolina Volunteers."

"Tuesday, June 4th. Returned to Wilson, where I found Theodore, who had accepted the appointment of second lieutenant, etc. Battle of Bethel Church."

"Thursday, July 4th. Fourth of July! Eighty-one years and the country disrupt! Was to have delivered a speech in Cheraw, S. C., to-day, but here I am on a bed of sickness in Wilmington. 'Man proposes, God disposes.' "

"Thursday, July 18th. All interest seems absorbed in the war."

"Friday, July 19th. Left for Wilmington. Heard of a great battle fought yesterday at Bull Run in Virginia, in which the Confederates were victorious. A few such conflicts ought to terminate the war."

"Monday, July 22d. Great news to-day of the splendid victory achieved yesterday by our forces at Manassas Junction."

"Tuesday, July 23d. Very anxious to hear the particulars of the great battle, a number of our Wilson men being in it. Sad, sad war!"

"Tuesday, July 30th. Left Wilmington in 5 A.M. train and reached Wilson at noon. Rode much of the time in mail-car, where I met Lieutenant Blocker. At Wilson, Arthur B. Davis, of Georgia, shot and instantly killed Captain Charles H. Axson, of Charleston, S. C. I cared for the corpse, and after the inquest directed and aided in washing, dressing, etc. Melancholy task."

"Saturday, August 17th. Preached at Fifth Street Methodist Episcopal Church, Wilmington. Sometimes one seems inspired in preaching; so this morning. Never can repeat this sermon."

"August 29th, 30th, 31st. News reached us that the batteries at Hatteras had been taken by the Federals. Dull hearts. The Hatteras news very troublesome. The people flying from Newbern. I went to Goldsboro. Saw very many of my friends. A great crowd going to Western villages. Went to the graveyard to see little George's grave."

"Monday, September 2d. At work in the schools. Dull times. Wilson greatly deserted, and all depressed by the Hatteras news."

"Tuesday, September 10th, Wilmington. Bought the girl 'Nicey' from the estate of James Sampson [a free negro who owned many slaves]; paid five hundred and twenty-five dollars."

" Wednesday, December 4th. My forty-first birthday. The Lord God have mercy upon me and pardon me all my past sins and delinquencies! And the Lord smile upon me, and bless me, and lead me to devote all my coming life thoroughly to his service! The bishop [Andrew] having failed to arrive, the conference [at Louisburg, N. C.] elected me president. Did much business."

1862

" Monday, February 10th. Went by rail to Wilmington and there heard of the terrible disaster to our forces at Roanoke Island. A gloomy season. Went to Goldsboro, where General Gatlin seized the train, turned out the passengers, and put in soldiers. I was permitted, however, to come on, and had a pleasant ride with Colonel Levinthorpe."

" Tuesday, February 18th. Great gloom over the community by reason of the fall of Fort Donelson. Our men are said to have fought well and to have been overpowered by numbers. It is the hour of darkness with the Confederacy."

" Friday, February 21st, Wilmington, camp of Twenty-eighth Regiment, North Carolina Volunteers. This being a day of fasting announced by the mayor, at the invitation of the chaplain I preached for the regiment. Great attention. Hope good was done. Went in steamer ' Hunt ' up the Cape Fear River. Read German poetry on the way."

" Saturday, February 22d. This morning at five left the steamer at Mr. Guion's landing, because the flood in the river kept me from landing at Major Richardson's. Mr. and Mrs. Guion very kind. Mr. Guion sent me to Wesley Purdie's. Took boy and horse and crossed the river, and took down fences, finally reaching Bethlehem in time to preach and hold Quarterly Conference. Then dined at Dr. Richardson's and stayed all night at Major Richardson's. Pleasant visits."

" Friday, March 14th. The battle of Newbern fought to-day. Our forces were defeated by overwhelming numbers of the enemy. They retreated and fell back to Kingston. Not knowing of the disaster, I went with a squad to Goldsboro, but before night the trains began to pour in, bringing wounded, the baggage, refugees from Newbern, and soldiers. The rout was terrible. The excitement in Goldsboro was intense. I waited on General Gatlin and urged that he should arrest the fugitives, reform them, and send them back. Stayed all night at Frank Kornegay's. Dr. Foard, who was in the battle, slept with me. The Rev. Dr. Closs arrived in town, looking for his son."

"Saturday, March 15th. This morning we finally started the train for Kingston. I went with them as far as Mosely Hall on the railroad. My friend Z. H. Greene was with me. It rained. At Mosely Hall I met my friend Miss Harriotte Cole, of Newbern, and went with her to Mr. Joyner's, where I was politely treated. Mrs. Lavinia Roberts, Miss Cole's sister, is with her; also three children of Mrs. Roberts, two of Mrs. Taylor; also Captain Hugh L. Cole. Mr. Wooten, seventeen years of age, from Fayetteville, with a bad wound in his arm, is here. In the evening I aided Dr. Adam Davis to dress the wound. Have had a most fatiguing day. Have persuaded my friends to go with me. Oh, horrible war!"

"Sunday, March 16th! How unlike a Sunday this has been! This morning, after a scuffle, I succeeded in putting all the Cole family and servants on board the cars, except 'Hattie,' with all the baggage, numbering over thirty pieces. But after the train was in motion I saw that Hattie was left. I leaped off and let all go. Finding Hattie, I took her in Dr. Adam Davis's buggy to Goldsboro. My shawl had been stolen, but all else was complete. At night I succeeded in putting all the baggage, except five or six pieces, on the cars, and before midnight we were all in Wilson. What a day of exertion! O Lord, how long?"

"Monday, March 17th. Great excitement in the country. Troops passing and repassing. Tuesday, March 18th. At home keeping the school going. Wednesday, March 19th. Went to Goldsboro with stores for the hospital. Found many poor fellows wounded. Returned at night."

"Sunday, April 20th. Should have been at Queen's Creek, Onslow County. The enemy have possession of that county. A dark day. Hour and power of darkness. In my weakness [he was ill] all past troubles came back like a tide, and the future darkened. At night Anna and Hattie came to my rescue, talked to me like Christian women, soothed me, and sent me to bed quiet as a child. 'Lord, save, or I perish!'"

"Thursday, April 24th. To-day went into the school and taught a little, Mrs. Deems being unwell. I have suffered from an attack of a bilious nature and then with an inflammation of the right eye. It has been a tedious time. Dr. B. B. Williams has waited on me most skilfully, and Mrs. Deems and my friend Hattie Cole have devoted themselves beautifully to me. April 25th. After twenty-two days' confinement to the house I walked out for the first time. April 26th. A long, dark, gloomy, rainy day. I should have been at Shallotte Camp, in Brunswick, attending to the Smithville Quarterly Conference, but for my sickness. The Lord's will be done."

"Saturday, May 3d. All day long under the influence of quinine. The afternoon was so beautiful I rode with Mr. Greene to the country. In the evening several friends called. Dr. Dickson thinks I can preach once to-morrow if I am willing to have a fever after doing so. It has been so long since I spoke a word for Jesus that I think I am willing."

"Thursday, June 26th. Went to Petersburg, Va. Called on the Brownleys. The first discharge of artillery which I have heard came booming over Petersburg to-night, and distinct flashes could be seen in the northeast. Shook the windows all night. Was very sick all night. June 27th. Felt very sick this morning, but took the train after breakfast, went to Richmond, and put up at the Exchange Hotel. The Secretary of War gave me a pass, but I could not find passage to the camp. The great battle of Richmond began yesterday. A terrible fight. We are succeeding. All the city in an immense stir. Saw John Dunham to-day."

"June 28th. To-day I went with the ambulance to the battle-field over Meadow Bridge on the Chickahominy, up by Mechanicsville, down by Ellison's Mill, where there was such carnage, and out to Beulah Church. Oh, the sights! Dead men and horses. Wounded men and horses. Great crowds of wounded hobbling along or carried in ambulances. Platoons of prisoners being marched in. The dust immense. Went to hospital at Hood's brigade. More than a hundred lying with every kind of wound. Went over to Beulah Church. Saw Drs. Stith and Pearsall, of North Carolina. A hundred wounded and dead men here. Came home at night, and reached the ladies' seminary at eleven o'clock with twenty-two wounded men. Went to Kent, Paine & Co.'s hospital, and saw Clark, of South Carolina, in the agonies of death."

"Sunday, June 29th. Heard the Rev. Dr. Minnegerode this morning. No services in the churches the balance of the day. Visited John Dunham and spent the rest of the time in the hospitals. What scenes of suffering, and how bravely our men bear it!"

"Monday, June 30th. To-day Dr. Basham let me have his horse, and I went out the Williamsburg road two miles, then down the Charles City road. Met Basil Manly's company of artillery coming round to reinforce General Longstreet. Fell in with General Ransom's brigade. Dined with General Ransom, Colonel Ransom, Colonel Cutts, Colonel Vance, Ashe, Broadnax, *et al.*, on a cracker and a half. Went on to camp of Twelfth Virginia Regiment; then forward, where I overtook the regiment of Dr. Frank Disosway, my wife's brother.

Saw him.   Had several broken interviews near Mrs. Fisher's.
Went on to White Oak Swamp.   The enemy had cut down
obstructions and made a stand.   An artillery fight of two
hours ensued, and I was caught in it.   The shells went over
and around me.   It was fearful.   God was my stay.   Returned
to Richmond at ten, dreadfully tired."

"Tuesday, September 16th.   Have been revolving in my
mind a plan to obtain an endowment for a military college to
educate the orphan boys of such of our fellow-citizens as shall
fall in this war.   At night mentioned it to my wife and to
Messrs. Daniel and Moses Rountree, who approve.   Wednesday, September 17th.   Am thinking more and more about
my plan for endowing orphan college.   O Lord God, guide
me ; take away all wrong and selfish motives and help me to
be pure and do purely.   Thursday, September 18th.   Day
of thanksgiving appointed by the President.   After preaching
a sermon (Isa. lv. 12, 13) I proposed my plan for endowing
a military college for soldiers' orphans to several gentlemen,
who approved.   Mr. Zeno H. Greene dined with us.   We
opened a subscription, which at bedtime amounted to fifty-one
hundred dollars.   *Laus Deo!*   Thursday, September 25th.   To-
night we held our first regular meeting of subscribers to the
orphan college.   Our fund has gone up to eighty-two hundred dollars."

"Friday, October 3d.   Engaged in teaching in the school
and in bringing up my correspondence.   Heard from my son
Theodore through a letter from Dr. Frank Disosway, the first
intimation in three weeks.   Saturday, October 4th.   Went to-
day to —— and found —— on the car.   He had heard of
Theodore's safety in camp.   Great relief.   Had pleasant time.
Mrs. —— is always charming ; her heart seems like a trap
to catch sunbeams.   Tuesday, October 7th.   Came home.
Found a long letter from my son Theodore, which was a
great relief."

"Sunday, November 9th. The pastor being absent, I preached. In the afternoon visited the hospital. About three hundred soldiers there. In the evening alarming news came of the enemy arriving at Greenville in gunboats. Mr. Russell came for his daughter. Monday, November 10th. Things more quiet to-day. Some aggravation of the news from Greenville in the evening. It is said that fifteen gunboats are in the river. What am I to do with this houseful of women and children? The Lord direct me!"

"Wednesday, December 3d, Raleigh, N. C. The twenty-second session of the North Carolina Conference was opened in the African Methodist Episcopal Church, the Rev. Bishop Early presiding. As usual, I am thrown upon a number of the hardest-working committees, besides being presiding elder. Monday, December 8th. Conference adjourned to-night, and I was appointed to Newbern district."

"Monday, December 15th. We hear that General Lee has repulsed the enemy at Fredericksburg, but we can learn no particulars. The enemy are apparently advancing upon Goldsboro. Tuesday, December 16th. The fighting has been going on about the Neuse River below Goldsboro. The enemy seem to have crossed at White Hall. We learn that they destroy houses and other property in their march. Wednesday, December 17th. Many of the wounded are being sent from Goldsboro. Saturday, December 20th. On a freight-train came to Goldsboro with my son Frank. The enemy have beat a retreat and are below Kingston. Thousands of troops are around Goldsboro. The bridge over the Neuse has been destroyed."

"Monday, December 22d. Was carried in a wagon [from Goldsboro] by a man named Smith to the Neuse River, across the county bridge, finding troops of soldiers. Walked with the Rev. D. C. Johnston and others to Everittsville, where I dined with Mrs. Everitt. Went to William Carraway's, where

I spent the night. The enemy had burned the railroad bridge and torn up some rails. Tuesday, December 23d. Carraway gave me an account of his captivity; was prisoner seven hours. The enemy have stripped some houses of everything, leaving many of the poor in great suffering. To Faison's by carriage. To Wilmington by train, arriving at 2 A.M. Wednesday morning."

" Wednesday, December 31st. Closed the day at a prayer-meeting in the church. It is solemn to take leave of another year, with its sins and follies, its efforts and successes and failures, its joys and sorrows, its losses and gains; and it is very solemn to stand at the door of another year, to watch it open upon the invisible future. Blessed be God for all his mercies! God be merciful to me a sinner!"

1863

" Wednesday, January 28th, Wilmington. Bought one hundred bushels of ground-peas [peanuts] to send to Petersburg, Va., for sale to make oil. I am in St. Paul's case when he was reduced to tent-making to support the outward man while he preached the gospel, with this difference, that I do not know how to make tents and must do what is within my capabilities. The war has reduced us to this. Settling up my salt affairs. [He was interested in some salt-works on the coast. — EDS.]"

" Friday, May 8th. These several days we have been exceedingly solicitous to hear from our boy Theodore, who has been in the terrible battle near Chancellorsville, in which General Lee has defeated the enemy and General Jackson has been seriously wounded; but had to leave home without hearing a word. Went to Goldsboro. Monday, May 11th. Compelled to leave for Columbus. No news from my dear boy. My strength seemed failing, when a young gentleman

informed me that a letter had been received from Theodore;
that he was well. Just afterward Miss Hattie Cole handed
me a letter from him. Bless the Lord, O my soul! Went
on my way rejoicing."

"Tuesday, June 2d. Believing that Lee's forces are about
to move, at the advice of my wife and the Rev. Mr. Cunning-
gim, I started for Virginia to see Theodore. Rode all night
on the cars. Thursday, June 4th. About nightfall reached
on foot camp of Iverson's brigade. My son much surprised
at seeing me. After supper went over to wagon camp, where
I lay down upon the ground with very light covering, but
slept sweetly. Wednesday, June 10th. Parted [at Culpeper
Court-house] with my son, perhaps for the last time in this
life. [This proved prophetic, for Lieutenant Theodore D.
Deems fell at Gettysburg.] Reached Richmond and put up
at the Powhatan House."

"Thursday, July 9th. Reached home [from his district]
very much fatigued, and while at my desk bringing up my
correspondence received a telegram from Captain West that
my dear boy Theodore had been severely wounded at Gettysburg. At last this suffering comes! Was up nearly all night.
*First night of my life in which I did not sleep a moment from
sunset to daybreak.*"

His journal then goes on to tell of an intensely interesting
but painful visit which Dr. Deems immediately made to the
front in search of his wounded son. But his efforts were vain.
All he could learn positively was that his son had been left,
wounded, near Gettysburg, and had probably fallen into the
hands of the enemy. So he sadly returned to his home and
his duties. The most conflicting rumors came to the family:
that the wounds were slight, that they were fatal, that Lieutenant Deems had been seen in a Northern prison, and so on
until the family were harassed beyond measure. At length,

about two months after the battle of Gettysburg, on Monday, September 14th, while attending Quarterly Conference at Goldsboro, through a letter from a Rev. Mr. Skinner, Dr. Deems received certain information of the death of his beloved Theodore. He returned to Wilson immediately to carry the sad intelligence to his wife and children.

From His Journal

"Wednesday, 16th, Thursday, 17th, Friday, 18th, Saturday, 19th. Sad, mourning days, spent in condoling with my family, in writing letters to friends, in arranging the papers of my dear departed boy."

"Wednesday, September 23d. My servant Rachel fast sinking."

In the course of time it was learned that in the absence of Captain Taylor, of Company G, Fifth North Carolina State Troops, Lieutenant Deems was on the first day acting captain, and while enthusiastically leading and cheering on his men during one of Gettysburg's desperate and bloody charges, fell wounded in two places, the wound which proved fatal being in the hip. He was taken prisoner and kept, with other wounded men, on Hanky's farm. He here lingered until about July 17th, when his brave spirit was released and took its flight to that blessed realm where the horrors of war are forever unknown.

Lieutenant Deems was a devout Christian and expected to devote his life to the ministry in the Protestant Episcopal Church. He was universally beloved, and his death was a dreadful blow to his home and friends. Happily he was not entirely without the ministry of kind hands and sympathetic hearts as he approached and walked through the valley of death. A Northern gentleman and his wife, of the Christian

Commission, finding out from Lieutenant Deems that he was
the son of a Methodist clergyman, did all they could for him,
and were so thoughtful and good (God richly bless them!) as
to cut off a lock of his hair and see that it, together with the
lieutenant's sash and diary, finally reached the hands of his
parents. Moreover, they marked the soldier's grave, and wrote
to Dr. and Mrs. Deems in such a way that at the close of the
war it was found by his family, and the remains transferred to
the cemetery at Wilmington, N. C.   By a strange providence,
long after the war, Dr. Deems met this same gentleman while
traveling on a train in the North, and met his wife while
traveling in the South.   Acts of Christian kindness toward
enemies on both sides of the line, such as the one just recorded,
relieve our Civil War of some of its darkness and make us
hopeful for humanity.

After the death of his soldier son Dr. Deems flung himself
into the work of teaching, preaching, and the soldiers' orphan
fund with, if possible, even more consecration than ever.
During the fall he was saddened by the fatal illness and death
of his faithful servant Rachel, to whom he makes a touching
allusion in his journal.   At the close of 1863 Dr. Deems saw
that it was useless longer to attempt to carry on his school;
so he rented a house in the suburbs of Raleigh, sold out at
Wilson, and in the face of fearful odds moved to the State
capital.

From His Journal

" Monday, December 28th, Wilson.   Still amid the horrors
of packing, and no prospect of removal.   All things are dreadfully upset, but this evening I have been casting my care on
the Lord and remembering what is written : ' Call upon me in
the day of trouble; I will deliver thee, and thou shalt glorify
me.'   ' Remember the word unto thy servant, upon which
thou hast caused me to hope.' "

"Tuesday, 29th, Wednesday, 30th, Thursday, 31st. These three days have been as the past, only more abundant. The trouble, care, physical labor, perplexity, and loss of a removal are so distressing that I think I will never move again. I go to Raleigh. If the capital of my State fall, I go down with it. If not, I hope to remain until peace comes; then if I must move I will sell out wholly. It has been the darkest year of this war, and still there is no light. Our arms have few successes, the enemy many. Our legislators seem stricken with madness. All is dark. O Lord, teach me to stay my heart upon thee! My property is greatly diminished, my home is totally broken up, my first-born hath been slain, my servant is dead, my children's prospect of education is restricted, and many of my friends are wounded or prisoners, or in the enemy's lines, or in great bereavement. 'Our light affliction, which is but for a moment, worketh for us a far more exceeding and eternal weight of glory.'"

The year 1864 opened in gloom for the South, especially for Dr. Deems. The first days were spent in moving his family into the Raleigh house, which was named "Villula." The claims of the Newbern district kept him away from home most of the time, and the irregularities of trains often led to his sleeping on benches and goods-boxes in railway stations. These exposures aggravated his physical ailments in his eye, his ear, and his lame ankle. Nevertheless he wrought prodigiously and successfully, bringing up the soldiers' orphan fund to one hundred thousand dollars. In November the state of affairs was such that he was again compelled to break up his home.

From His Journal

"Tuesday, November 22d, to Friday, November 25th, Raleigh. Days of extraordinary labor and trouble. Broke

up my establishment at Villula and put my furniture about at
different places in Raleigh. Cold weather and very heavy
work. I could not have gone through my toils if the blessed
Lord had not sustained me with the promise, 'As thy days, so
shall thy strength be.' Saturday, December 31st. Blessed be
God, who hath kept my feet from falling, my eyes from tears,
and my soul from death! Amen."

At length Dr. Deems entered upon the eventful year 1865.
War matters for the first three months engrossed the attention
of everybody. When the end came in April it found Dr.
Deems's family living in the home of the Hon. D. M. Barringer, in Raleigh.

From His Journal

"Saturday, March 18th, Raleigh. Johnston meeting Sherman below Raleigh. Monday, March 20th. Generals Beauregard and Jordan spent the evening with us until eleven
o'clock. Mrs. Barringer's entertainment very handsome, and
Beauregard's conversation agreeable. He appeared thoughtful and a little sad, I thought. He nevertheless expressed
himself as hopeful of the Confederate cause."

"Wednesday, April 5th. News came that Richmond had
been evacuated. A terrible catastrophe. April 8th. Minnie
came out of the lines with Colonel McKoy. Joy at the
safety of my child. April 10th. Governor Vance to-night
informed me that the enemy were advancing upon Raleigh.
Tuesday, April 11th. Great excitement in the city. People
leaving. I am making preparations to go.

"On Wednesday morning, April 12th, I left Raleigh in a
box-car with several other persons, on my way westward to
keep in advance of the army, as General Johnston is falling
back and Sherman will press forward. On my way to Greensboro I heard that General Lee had surrendered to Grant.

The news is a terrible blow to our hopes of the final success of the Confederate cause. While in Greensboro Johnston made his headquarters near the town, and an armistice was held between Generals Johnston and Sherman, and terms were submitted which we supposed might secure something to us from the wreck.

"In the meantime the news reached us that President Lincoln had been assassinated. It was doubted by many, but it seemed to me to be true and *dreadful*. It will be greatly to the injury of the South. We seem to have a succession of horrors. I was ill all the while in Greensboro.'

"Easter Sunday, April 16th. No services were held in any of the churches of this city to-day. My son Frank arrived, with Hospital No. 7, from Raleigh. Sunday, April 30th. Preached in Salisbury. The armistice ceased, whereupon Johnston surrendered. *The war ended and our cause was lost!* Oh, the precious blood and treasure expended! But as 'the blood of the martyrs is the seed of the church,' so all this sowing may arise in a glorious harvest hereafter.

"'O God, clouds and darkness are round about thee, but righteousness and judgment are the habitation of thy throne.'

"But it is horrible to have no country!"

After recovering in a measure from the blow caused by the tragic close of the war Dr. Deems boarded in Raleigh and to the end of the year wrought with what heart he could as presiding elder of the Newbern district.

The North Carolina Conference, which met in Raleigh in December, elected him a delegate to the General Conference, granted him permission to go to New York City and establish a religious newspaper, whose purpose should be the promotion of the spirit of unity between North and South, and passed handsome resolutions concerning him.

From His Journal

"Tuesday, December 19th.   Left Raleigh, left dear North Carolina, started to my new Northern work.   O God, if thou go not with me, lead me not up hence!   Friday, December 22d.   Reached New York at night.   Saturday, December 23d. We are staying at the National Hotel on Cortlandt Street. Sunday, December 24th.   Attended services at Trinity.   Monday, December 25th.   Christmas!   Services in Trinity.   All the remainder of the year engaged in securing lodgings, office, and contracts for printing.   Put my family at French's Hotel, corner of Frankfort Street and City Hall Square.   Office [of the ' Watchman '] at No. 119 Nassau Street, Room 21.   Printing done by Gray & Green, corner Jacob and Frankfort streets."

CHAPTER VII

STUDENTS of the Civil War between the States have often expressed wonder over the fact that after such a long, desperate, and stupendous strife there should have ensued such a speedy, real, and complete reconciliation. Is there any other explanation of this grand historical fact than that, first, it was not really a popular war,—a people's war,—but one sprung upon them; and, secondly, that the Southern people, as a rule, did *sincerely accept the decision of the war?* There was no general desire upon their part to destroy the Union. Those who were participants in that great conflict, whether so voluntarily or, as was the case with the vast majority, such by the force of circumstances, and all fair-minded students of the war, recognize the fact that, but for certain unnecessarily harsh and vindictive post-bellum legislation, reconciliation of the two sections, and consequently rehabilitation of the South, would have obtained much sooner than it did.

To cite but one of hundreds of similarly significant episodes, recall how men gazed with wonder, and all patriotic men with hearts full of joy and satisfaction, at the spectacle of the most prominent Southern generals acting as pall-bearers to those whom the fortunes of war had aforetime made their vanquishers; the now feeble, gray-haired ex-Confederate leader, Joseph E. Johnston, following the bier of Sherman, and white-

191

headed old Simon Buckner following Grant's body to the grave! All such things showed the existence of a patriotism which, outlasting the war, made speedy reconciliation not only a possibility, but a fact, and the presence of influences which said, even before the echoes of the last gun had died away, "Now bring together, readjust, and insure those conditions most favorable to the speediest reunion!"

Filled with such true patriotism, Dr. Deems looked over the desolate field, and considered himself, and came to the conclusion that he could do the most good, with his special talents and influence, by publishing in the North a religious and literary paper devoted to the timely and supremely important mission of bringing about a good state of feeling between the sections.

Before leaving North Carolina he laid the plan of his paper before the people and secured six hundred dollars in subscriptions. This was the extent of the financial basis of the "Watchman" enterprise. More than half this sum was expended in publishing the first number, which appeared January 10, 1866. It was a bright, clean, elegant-looking paper, and drew out high encomiums from the best periodicals in both the North and the South.

The undertaking was bold almost to rashness. All the members of the family who were old enough assisted in some way to get out the first issue. Fifty-two numbers were published. All the editing and most of the correspondence, bookkeeping, and mailing were done by Dr. Deems and his eldest son, Francis M. Deems. There was a gratifying growth of the subscription list, but the high quality of the paper, the lack of capital, the torn state of the country, and the poverty of the South made the publication of the "Watchman" an increasing burden. Harassed in body and mind, Dr. Deems, usually most sanguine, toward the end of the year went through seasons of deepest depression. In October the following four entries in his diary speak volumes: "October 22d. Exceedingly gloomy. October 23d. Very nervous. October 24th. Threatened with congestion of the heart. October 25th. Oh, that I had the wings of a dove; then I would fly away!" The "Watchman" ceased at the close of one year, but not without having accomplished much good. In view of the many limitations under which it was published, it must be conceded that the late James Harper, one of the original members of the firm of Harper Brothers, was correct when he pronounced it "the greatest feat of publication ever achieved in New York."

The failure of the "Watchman" was to Dr. Deems an almost deadly blow, and he appeared to be confronted by defeat in his whole life. But God had some better thing in store for him, as we shall soon see; nor was he left entirely without faith and hope, for we find the following entry in his diary written across the week beginning December 12, 1866: "A week of darkening prospects so far as the 'Watchman' is concerned. But my faith in the heavenly Father, that he will overrule all things for my good, is triumphant."

This brings us to the supreme point in Dr. Deems's life, the founding of the *Church of the Strangers*. The story can never be told again as well as it has been in that deeply interesting little book, "A Romance of Providence; or, A History of the Church of the Strangers." We refer to this work the reader who may care to enter more deeply than we can into the details of the organization and work of this unique church. As Dr. Deems personally supervised and approved of this account of the Church of the Strangers, written in 1887 by Mr. Joseph S. Taylor, of New York, a valued friend of Dr. Deems and an officer in the church, we have secured Mr. Taylor's permission to insert in these memoirs all that follows in this chapter.

"It was amid Dr. Deems's terrific struggles with the 'Watchman' that the first steps were made which led toward the

Church of the Strangers. It will be remembered that Dr. Deems was a clergyman of the Methodist Episcopal Church, South, still in such good standing there as to have been elected by his conference to the General Conference of his church, which was held in New Orleans in April, 1866, at which a number of votes were cast for him as bishop. This conference took him one month from his work on the 'Watchman.' He had no ecclesiastical associations in New York; the differences between the Northern and the Southern Methodist churches never were so great, the feelings never so bitter. Dr. Deems had been in the Confederacy through the whole fight, and, as he once said, walked the streets of New York and engaged in his daily work with the weight of Andersonville prison around his neck. Neither his own family nor Southern people coming to purchase goods could attend church in New York; for almost everywhere the pulpit resounded with denunciations of 'rebels' and the 'rebellion,' and the voice of the gospel seemed hushed in the land. Dr. Deems has said that every Sunday through the winter and spring he had received a lashing in church. One Sunday afternoon, as he was then boarding in Fifteenth Street, he went to St. George's Church, of which the senior Dr. Tyng was rector. He was very tired, having worked hard during the week. The sexton refused to show him a seat; he must wait till the pewholders were in. He stood twenty minutes, until he became so weary that he was compelled to return to his room without having the comfort of the service. He said that that made him determined, if ever he had rule in a church, no man should have to stand one minute who came in one minute before the service opened. Now (1887) St. George's is a free church, free to all strangers.

" Invitations to deliver addresses began to reach the doctor. The American Bible Society, which had sent him as its general agent to North Carolina, asked him to make a speech at its anniversary; this called attention to him afresh. There were

noble Christians who rose above sectional strife and acknowledged Christianity wherever they saw its fruits.

"On Sunday, July 15, 1866, Dr. Deems was invited to
preach a sermon before the Young Men's Christian Association of the Hedding Methodist Episcopal Church, in Jersey
City. Among those who were present was the wife of Mr.
Frerichs, the artist. That lady had known the doctor when
he was president of the college in Greensboro, N. C., but had
not seen him for years. After hearing this sermon she followed him to the house where he was dining, and accompanied
him to the ferry-boat, and employed the time with importuni-
ties that he should begin preaching regularly in New York.
His replies that there was no church of his denomination in
the city, that there would be no propriety in attempting to establish a Southern Methodist church, that he was making a
violent effort to support his family and pay his debts, seemed
to make no impression upon her. She spoke as if she regarded
herself a prophetess sent to direct a servant of the Lord. As
they parted she concluded her appeal by saying: 'I am very
sure that God intends you to preach in New York. I do beg
of you to promise me that you will preach just four weeks
somewhere in New York, even if it is in a garret or a cellar or
a tub!' The promise was extorted that an effort would be
made to gratify her desire.

"In accordance with this promise, next day Dr. Deems went
to the university on Washington Square (of which institution
he is now, 1887, one of the councilors) to see what he could
do. He had seen the announcement of some preaching there.
Upon his arrival he found a quiet, meek-mannered little janitor. The doctor asked him if a place for preaching could be
hired in the university. 'For whom?' inquired the janitor,
inspecting the doctor from head to foot. 'For me,' was the
reply. 'No,' said the janitor; 'we have no place to suit *you*.'
This janitor died shortly after, and Dr. Deems never became

well enough acquainted with him to ask what he meant by
stating that there was no place that would suit *him*. It appeared that while the eloquent Rev. Dr. Hawks was occupying the large chapel of the university an eccentric preacher
was holding forth every Sunday afternoon in the smaller
chapel, and that the latter apartment could be obtained for
morning service at twenty-five dollars a month. That seemed
to be within his reach; at any rate, he determined to give out
of his poverty that much to the Lord. On Saturday, July
21st, he put this notice in the New York 'Herald': 'The Rev.
Dr. Deems, of North Carolina, will preach in the chapel of
the university to-morrow at eleven o'clock.' On Sunday, July
22, 1866, he repaired to the chapel, where he had to be his
own sexton and precentor, and employed in the service such
hymns as everybody knew, for there were no books. The
congregation consisted of sixteen persons. The persons not
of the preacher's family were, it is believed, the following: Mr.
W. H. Chase, Mr. Clement Disosway, Mrs. and Miss Frerichs,
Mr. Nehemiah Pratt, General Richardson, of Tennessee, J. M.
Roberts, Dr. N. W. Seat, Mr. S. T. Taylor, Mrs. Mary E.
Tucker, Mr. W. J. Woodward, Mr. A. C. Worth. (Six are
dead [1886].) The text was, 'Philip went down to the city
of Samaria, and preached Christ unto them.' At the conclusion of the service it was announced that the doctor would
preach on the next Sunday, and on the following Saturday the
announcement was repeated in the 'Herald.' On Sunday, the
29th, there were over thirty persons present. On Sunday,
August 5th, there were over seventy persons present. As the
preacher's promise did not bind him beyond the month and
as he saw no way of continuing this work, he announced at
the close of the service that for three weeks he had enjoyed
Paul's pleasure of preaching in his own hired house, but that
Paul must have found tent-making in the East more profitable
than the preacher found journalism in the West, and that con-

sequently the next Sunday would close this series of sermons, as he could not afford to preach for nothing and supply a place for service. A large number of those who had been attracted to the service were Southerners. One of them, General Richardson, of Tennessee, asked the doctor whether, if a place were provided, he would continue to preach; and the reply was that the preacher's Sundays were wholly unoccupied and he would willingly preach for those who desired to hear him. Whereupon it was proposed that a collection be taken up and that Dr. Deems be requested to continue preaching. The collection a little more than paid the month's rent. On the following Sunday, the 12th of August, the chapel was packed; there had dropped in many whose churches were closed. It was then proposed that there be some regular organization to afford a free place of worship for strangers from all parts of the world who might be in the city.

"At the close of the service it was resolved to form an executive committee of gentlemen of different denominations to provide for keeping the place open for worship. They had the following card printed, to be distributed through the congregation and around the neighborhood:

"'THE STRANGERS' SUNDAY HOME

"'In the chapel of the university, Washington Square, New York, under the pastoral care of the Rev. Dr. Deems, of North Carolina, there is a congregation composed of members of the different denominations of Christians. Divine service is conducted every Sunday, and no distinction of sectarianism is allowed. The worship of God is the simple object of the assemblage. It is specially designed for strangers who visit the city and for particular pastoral oversight of the young men who have recently engaged in business in New York. A Sunday-school assembles at nine o'clock, and the public service begins punctually at half-past ten o'clock. *The seats are free.* All

are cordially invited.   Visitors to the city, if sick or needing
a pastor, can have the services of the Rev. Dr. Deems, whose
residence for the present is ——.

" ' This enterprise is maintained wholly by voluntary contri-
butions.   You are respectfully requested to assist us.   We so-
licit donations or weekly subscriptions.   If you are residing in
the city, please say how much you will pay weekly, and on
Sunday deposit your contribution in the basket, in an envelope
with your name upon it, so that you may be duly credited.
The executive committee are: Major C. L. Nelson, 23 East
Thirty-seventh Street; Dr. Gardner (of Evans, Gardner &
Co.), 380 Broadway; Colonel B. B. Lewis (of Lewis, Daniel
& Co.), 21 Nassau Street; S. T. Taylor, 349 Canal Street;
Dr. Seat, 23 West Thirty-first Street; J. M. Roberts (of Ring,
Ross & Roberts), 86 Front Street; K. M. Murchison, 188
Front Street; Dr. F. M. Garrett (of Garrett, Young & Co.),
33 Warren Street; R. C. Daniel (of Lewis, Daniel & Co.), 21
Nassau Street; and J. L. Gaines (of Harris, Gaines & Co.),
15 Whitehall Street.'

" It will be observed that the pastor's residence was left in
blank; the income was so small and he was so compelled to
study small economies that he had to look out for the cheap-
est boarding-place in which he and his family could live in any
degree of respectability.   It is proper to add that a Sunday-
school was formed in the very beginning, and put into the
charge of Mr. R. C. Daniel, of Kentucky, of the firm of Lewis,
Daniel & Co., then brokers in Wall Street.

" The large chapel of the university was a much more commodious apartment than the little chapel in which we worshiped.   It was very beautiful.   It has since been cut up into
rooms for office purposes.*   At that time it was occupied by

---

* In 1895 the university building was taken down and a new structure
erected on its site.

a Protestant Episcopal congregation, in charge of the Rev. Dr. Francis L. Hawks. Dr. Hawks was a North Carolinian, and had distinguished himself at the bar in his own State before he entered the Episcopal ministry. He had been rector of the old St. Thomas's Church when it stood at the corner of Broadway and Houston Street. He was magnificently gifted, a man of great natural eloquence, of varied learning, and of surprising powers of elocution. During the Civil War he had some trouble in New York and had gone to New Orleans. On his return to New York his friends rallied about him and were preparing to build him a new church, the nucleus of which was then the congregation of the large chapel of the university. Dr. Hawks died on the 26th of September, 1866. In his last illness he frequently sent for Dr. Deems. They had both recently been elected to chairs in the University of North Carolina, and had both declined. In one of the latest interviews between the two gentlemen, Dr. Hawks said to a friend that his chief ambition had been disappointed; that for years it had been his desire to be president of the University of North Carolina and have Dr. Deems as his lieutenant, in the assurance that they two could make the university one of the greatest institutions in the country. He once said: ' Dr. Deems, three times I have been offered the miter, and three times have I put it aside. Never let your church make you bishop; God has some better thing for you. Your calling is to preach Christ—Christ crucified. Pursue that steadily and have no doubt that God will give you great success in this great city.'

"The year 1867 was a struggle for existence. Upon the death of Dr. Hawks, negotiations were made for the occupancy of the large chapel; but the ' Strangers' Sunday Home ' could not be removed till the first Sunday in May, 1867. Its accommodations were then increased fourfold, but it was still a mere assembly without church organization.

" In the autumn of 1867 many persons expecting to remain

in the city, some a longer, some a shorter time, some perhaps permanently, came to Dr. Deems offering their church letters; but there was no 'church.' These repeated offers led to much thought and prayer; consultation also was had with the authorities of the church of which Dr. Deems was then a minister, and with other godly and learned persons. The result was a determination to organize, in the city of New York, a free, independent church of Jesus Christ. On the last two Sundays in December, 1867, it was publicly announced that on the first Sunday in January, 1868, such a church would be organized. The following was the paper read by Dr. Deems:

" ' It is probably known to all present that I am a minister of the gospel in good and regular standing in the Methodist Episcopal Church, South, and a member in particular of the North Carolina Annual Conference.

" ' In July, 1866, at the urgent request of Christian people of several denominations, I began preaching in the university of this city. At their urgency these services were continued until a congregation was formed of many who hold this as their regular place of worship, and of many others who are in occasional or very frequent attendance. The wants of many strangers visiting New York, and of many residents whose ecclesiastical connections have not been permanently formed, seem to demand the existence of such an institution. So strong .is the conviction of intelligent and devout people that such an undertaking should be persevered in that they united in a request to the bishops of the church of which I am a clergyman, that I might be returned as pastor of this flock which God's providence has seemed to commit to my charge. In accordance with this expressed wish, the bishops at their annual meeting directed me to remain, and, in accordance with that action, the bishop presiding at the session of my conference, lately held, has appointed me to this work.

" ' That all things may be done decently and in order, as

the Apostle Paul directs, it appears to be necessary that some organization be made which shall give us a place among the churches of Jesus Christ. All of you who are communicants naturally desire to be acknowledged as regular members of the church militant, and that, when providential circumstances indicate the necessity of removal, you may be able to bear with you the evidence of having been orderly disciples of Christ and under Christian pastoral direction.

"'In Article XIX. of the Church of England, and in Article XIII. of the Articles of Religion of the church of which I am a minister, it is set forth that: "The visible church of Christ is a congregation of faithful men, in which the pure Word of God is preached and the sacraments duly administered according to Christ's ordinance in all those things that of necessity are requisite to the same."

"'In the preface to the Book of Common Prayer of the Protestant Episcopal Church in the United States of America it is said that: "It is a most invaluable part of that blessed *liberty wherewith* CHRIST *hath made us free,* that in his worship different forms and usages may without offense be allowed, provided the substance of the Faith be kept entire; and that, in every Church, what cannot be clearly determined to belong to Doctrine must be referred to Discipline; and therefore, by common consent and authority, may be altered, abridged, enlarged, amended, or otherwise disposed of, as may seem most convenient for the edification of the people, 'according to the various exigencies of times and occasions.'"

"'In its Form of Government, Chapter II., Section IV., published with its Confession of Faith, the Presbyterian Church in the United States of America sets forth that: "A particular church consists of a number of professing Christians, with their offspring, voluntarily associated together for divine worship and godly living, agreeably to the Holy Scriptures, and submitting to a certain form of government."

" 'Christianity exists *subjectively* in the rule of Christ in simple individuals, *objectively* as an " organized visible society, as a kingdom of Christ on earth, as a church." " The word ' church,' like the Scotch *kirk*, the German *Kirche*, the Swedish *kyrka*, and like terms in the Slavonic languages, must be derived through the Gothic from the Greek κυριακός, i.e., belonging to the Lord. It may signify the material house of God, or the local congregation, or, in the complex sense, the organic unity of all believers."

" 'Believing these to be correct statements of the truth as touching this matter in the liberty wherewith Christ has made us free in the fear of God, and that for your edification the gospel may be preached and the sacraments duly administered and orderly discipline maintained, it is proposed that all who are like-minded do form themselves into a congregation of Christian people, of which I am to be the pastor so long as the providence of God and the authorities of my own branch of Christ's church shall continue me in this special office and ministry.

" 'That I may surely know who are minded to be thus under my pastoral charge, I shall, if God will, on the next Lord's day, being the first Sunday in January, A.D. 1868, receive into this society all the following persons, to wit:

" '(1) Such as present letters showing their good standing in any branch of God's visible church; (2) such as declare that they have so been and desire so now to be, but by reason of circumstances which they could not control are not able to present letters of membership; and (3) such as desire to join upon their sincere and hearty profession of faith in that statement of Christian doctrines commonly known as the Apostles' Creed, and of an earnest " desire to flee from the wrath to come, and to be saved from their sins."

" 'It is understood (1) that all such applicants have been baptized or desire to receive Christian baptism in such mode

THE CHURCH OF THE STRANGERS, EXTERIOR.

as they may of conscience elect, by sprinkling, pouring, or immersion; (2) that all things thereafter necessary for the proper ordering of the things which Christ hath appointed to his church shall, so far as this congregation of faithful people may be concerned, be by them determined "according to the various exigencies of times and occasions"; (3) that nothing hereby or herein done shall be considered as affecting the relations to any branch of Christ's church now held by any, except so far as they themselves shall choose; nor as in any way or degree touching the ecclesiastical relations of the pastor, or as modifying the present position or relations of such pewholders in this chapel* or other attendants upon the ministry in this congregation as may not feel perfectly free to enter this Christian society.

"'Wherefore, as many as desire to avail themselves of the benefit of this organization will present themselves on the next Lord's day at the holy communion, that their names may be taken and registered as members of the Christian society to be known for the present by the name which in the past has distinguished it, the Church of the Strangers.'

"On the fifth day of January, 1868, thirty-two persons enrolled themselves according to the terms in the above paper, and formed themselves into the Church of the Strangers; whereupon the sacrament of the Lord's Supper was administered.

"The Mercer Street Church was organized by the Third Presbytery of New York, October 25, 1835, with twenty-eight members, coming from six different churches, but the great majority of them from the Laight Street Church, a branch of the Spring Street Church.

"During the summer of 1834 a fine house of worship had

---

* This alludes to a few persons to whom, by special arrangement, pews had been let by the committee.

been erected on Mercer Street, near Waverly Place, and the congregation went immediately into their new home. A call was given to the Rev. Thomas H. Skinner, D.D., LL.D., at the time professor of sacred rhetoric in Andover Theological Seminary. He accepted the call, and on November 11, 1835, was installed as first pastor of the new church. The congregation and membership grew rapidly in numbers and wealth, and at the end of Dr. Skinner's pastorate, February 17, 1848, there were over five hundred members on the roll. Dr. Skinner resigned to take the professorship of sacred rhetoric, pastoral theology, and church government in Union Theological Seminary.

"The Rev. J. C. Stiles, D.D., LL.D., succeeded Dr. Skinner, and was installed June 8, 1848, coming from the Shockoe Hill (now Grace Street) Church, Richmond, Va. Dr. Stiles's health failing him, he was compelled to resign his charge, which he did October 15, 1850. He accepted a general agency for the American Bible Society in the South, and subsequently occupied a pastorate in New Haven, Conn., and then took the lead in organizing the Southern Aid Society to give support to feeble churches in the South. In his latest years he labored as an evangelist in Virginia, Alabama, Florida, Mississippi, Missouri, and Maryland.

"The Rev. Dr. George L. Prentiss became the third pastor and was installed April 30, 1851, resigning on account of ill health May 3, 1858. After two years spent abroad Dr. Prentiss returned, and by earnest work gathered about him a new church, now the Church of the Covenant. He became pastor of this church in 1862, and resigned in 1873 to accept his present position as professor of pastoral theology, etc., in Union Theological Seminary.

"The Rev. Dr. Walter Clarke was installed as Dr. Prentiss's successor in Mercer Street, February 16, 1859, and resigned December 26, 1860. He was succeeded by the Rev. Dr.

Russell Booth, who was pastor when the property passed to the Church of the Strangers.

" The whole number of persons admitted to membership in this church was two thousand and twenty-six, of whom seven hundred and forty-nine made profession of faith, and twelve hundred and seventy-seven were received by certificate.

" In 1869 the Mercer Street Presbyterian Church engaged lots from the Columbia College corporation, on which to erect a church for themselves. The accomplishment of the latter object would throw their church on the market. But the proposed new church was never built. On the sixteenth day of September, 1870, the Presbytery of New York united the Mercer Street Presbyterian Church with the First Presbyterian Church on University Place. By the terms of the union the new church was called the ' Presbyterian Church on University Place,' and the elders and deacons of the former churches became the elders and deacons of the new church. The Rev. Robert Russell Booth, D.D., who had been pastor of the Mercer Street Church since 1861, was duly installed by the presbytery on October 30, 1870, as pastor of the union church.

" In the meantime the Mercer Street Church had offered their property to Dr. Deems for sixty-five thousand dollars, through his friend, the late General James Lorimer Graham, who was a member of the University Place Presbyterian Church. Dr. Deems offered them fifty thousand dollars for the property. Their pastor, the Rev. Dr. Booth, said he would rather Dr. Deems should have it for fifty thousand dollars than any other person for sixty thousand.

" An important providential factor in the history of the Church of the Strangers must now be introduced. One Sunday, during service in the chapel of the university, two ladies were in attendance, who after the service were introduced to Dr. Deems by the Rev. Dr. Charles K. Marshall, of Vicksburg, as ' Mrs. Crawford and her daughter, of Mobile.' These ladies were visiting New York, and became interested in Dr. Deems as a clergyman of their own denomination. The younger of these ladies, in the summer of 1869, became the wife of the late Cornelius Vanderbilt. Mr. Vanderbilt's residence was on the block next adjoining the university, but he never came to the services in that chapel. Mr. Vanderbilt had met the doctor once before the war, in 1860, and was so impressed with what occurred at the interview that he repeated the conversation a few days before he died. This combination of circumstances, and the late acquaintanceship, and a new wife, to whom he was most sincerely devoted, led the commodore to regard the work for the strangers with favor. He urged Dr. Deems to visit him, and often catechized him closely as to his views and plans. He admired the breadth of this new religious society, and believed in the orthodoxy of its pastor.

" The commodore had never been a member of any church; had been a very worldly and even profane man; but he had from his earliest childhood the most unshaken faith in the Bible as the inspired Word of God. He became impatient at any contradiction of this idea; he regarded that man untrustworthy who did not receive the Bible as the Word of God. Toward the close of life, when he was in great agony, he expressed the fear that after his death it might be supposed that he had been influenced on that question by his friend and pastor, and so he said to him: ' Doctor, when I am gone I leave you to do justice to my memory. I want it known that I always believed the Bible, and on that subject you have had no more influence over me than this fan which I hold in my hand.' Although he did become more attentive to religions matters and more devout before his death, yet at this period of our history he believed that there was such a thing as genuine religion, and that it was founded upon a belief in the Bible as the Word of God. Somehow he heard of the movement upon the part of the Mercer Street Presbyterian Church, and made up his mind to put it under the control of Dr. Deems. We cannot do better than to give the doctor's account of the presentation in his own words, as reported in the 'Homiletic Monthly,' of New York, July, 1880, and afterward republished in a London periodical, from which it is here reproduced:

" ' A short time before he started for the East, our reporter called on the Rev. Dr. Deems, to learn from him how he came in possession of the Church of the Strangers. The following is his account:

" ' " Well," said he, " the manual of the church shows how I came to be preaching in New York in 1866. Before the organization of any church and while I was simply preaching to strangers, a lady of high character living in Mobile, when on a visit to New York, always attended our service with her daughter. With them I became acquainted. The daughter was that excellent woman whom Commodore Vanderbilt had the good fortune to make his second wife. I had very slight personal acquaintance with the commodore, and had not seen him in six or seven years, so I supposed that I should probably not again meet my fair hearers. I learned afterward that it had been intended that I should celebrate the marriage, and that it would have been done but for my absence. I also learned, after they had been married some weeks and were living within a block of the place where I was preaching, that there was a feeling that I was neglecting them. I have never gone after rich people nor particularly avoided them, but when a man conspicuous for wealth or position desires to know me he must always seek me. That was the only thing that had kept me from visiting the commodore and his new bride. But so soon as I discovered that it was expected, I called and was very warmly welcomed.

" ' " The commodore paid me special attention; we conversed very freely, and I did not hesitate, when it was proper, to introduce the subject of religion and talk on it—I trust in a natural and proper way. On all the visits the commodore catechized me carefully about my preaching, my past history, and my expectations of the future. He was always answered frankly. One evening in the sitting-room the conversation ran upon clerical beggars. I acknowledged that in early life I had had some reputation in that line, but that I deprecated the whole business. 'Now,' said I, 'here I am. Have been preaching two years almost within earshot of the commodore. The rooms which I have occupied have been overrun with hearers. People have often said to me, "Why don't you see Mr. Lenox or Mr. Stewart or Mr. Astor or Commodore Vanderbilt, and ask them to build you the Church of the Strangers? They ought to do it for the good of the city." And yet,' I added, 'the commodore here will bear me witness that I have never solicited a dollar from him for any object on earth.' Touching his wife, he said, 'Frank, that is so; the doctor never has;' and gave a look at his wife as much as to say that he wished by that observation to raise me in her estimation. The look evidently said that it had raised me in his. And I added: 'And, Mrs. Vanderbilt, so long as there is breath in his body I never shall.' Evidently he did not quite understand my remark, and changed his expression into one of those steely looks of his which were very piercing and very subduing; but I never faltered—turning the whole thing off in a jocose manner by saying: 'For, if he has lived to attain his present age and has not got the sense to see what I need and the grace to send it to me, he will die without the sight!' We all smiled at that and the conversation changed.

"'"On a subsequent visit I met Daniel Drew at the house. It was shortly after one of the great financial battles between Commodore Vanderbilt and Mr. Drew. The lion and the tiger were lying down a little while together. Mr. Drew had repeatedly attended the services I was holding in the university chapel, and had echoed Mrs. Vanderbilt's earnest praises of the usefulness of our little congregation. The commodore catechized me closely as to my views of Christian work, and I answered him to the best of my ability and with frankness. About that time the Mercer Street Presbyterian Church had negotiated for lots up-town belonging to Columbia College, and had put their own edifice upon the market. Its pastor, Dr. Booth, had always seemed friendly to me. My friend, James Lorimer Graham, Esq., conversed with me about purchasing it, and I had authorized him to offer fifty thousand dollars. Somehow this had got to the commodore's ears, but I did not know it and did not intend to ask him for a cent. My impressions of his character at that time were, at least, not favorable. I regarded him as an unscrupulous gatherer of money, a man who aimed at accumulating an immense fortune and had no very pious concern as to the means. The few interviews I had had with him after his marriage had modified my opinions of the man. I discovered fine points of which I had had no suspicion. But still I was a little afraid of him.

" ' " On this particular Monday evening of which I speak he walked to the sitting-room door with me, as his wont was, and as I passed out he said, ' Doctor, come and see me to-morrow night.'

" ' " ' I can't, commodore.'

" ' " ' Why can't you? ' said he, in the tone of a man not accustomed to be refused.

" ' " ' Because,' said I, ' there are a couple of boys from the South here who have come to be clerks, and they have no friends, and I have asked them to my boarding-house to become acquainted with my family, hoping by this social tie to bind them to a virtuous course of living.'

" ' " ' Well, then,' said he, ' come around the next night.'

" ' " ' I can't, commodore,' was my reply.

" ' " ' Why can't you? '

" ' " ' Because every Wednesday night I have a little prayer-meeting in the Bible House, never more than thirteen or fourteen, but almost invariably four or five, being present, and I can't disappoint them.'

" ' " ' Well,' said he, ' come around Thursday night.'

" ' " ' I can't, commodore.'

" ' " ' Why? ' he asked, with a good-natured growl.

" ' " ' Because,' said I, ' I have engaged to marry a couple of very poor people on the West Side of the town, and it would never do to disappoint them. You know how that is yourself ' —alluding to the fact of his recent marriage, and of his not being able to find me to perform his marriage ceremony.

" ' " ' Well,' said he, pleasantly, ' doctor, come when you can.'

" ' " Having pondered over the impressiveness and repetition of his invitations, I concluded I would go on the following Saturday evening to make a call in acknowledgment of his hospitality. 'It was about eight o'clock. There were visitors. I sat about half an hour conversing with the circle, when I arose to go, telling the commodore that on Saturday evening ministers of the gospel ought to be quiet in their studies preparing themselves for the pulpit, and that I had simply called around to thank him for his kind invitations on the preceding Monday. He invited me into a little office adjoining his bedroom, and sat down upon one side of the table and pointed me to a seat on the other. He said, ' Doctor, what is this about that Mercer Street property? '

" ' " ' Well,' said I, ' commodore, only this : it is in the market ; they want sixty-five thousand dollars for it, and I ventured to offer them fifty thousand. It is on leased ground, and I think it is about worth that.'

" ' " ' Well,' said he, ' how much have you got toward your fifty thousand dollars? '

" ' " I felt in my pocket and playfully said, 'Well, sir, as near as I can judge, about seventy-five or eighty cents.'

" ' " ' How do you expect to pay for it, then? '

" ' " ' Well, commodore, this is my thought about it. I have been here preaching some little time. My work seems to prosper. I shall propose to the Mercer Street Presbyterian Church to let me have their building for six months. I shall preach in it those six months. I shall announce to the people of New York that I wish to establish, on an unsectarian basis, a free church for all comers, especially for strangers in the city —a church that shall be evangelical and undenominational; and I shall appeal for the money in large sums and small. Now, commodore, if God wants me to stay in New York and do this work to which my heart seems to be inclined, the money will come. If not, the Mercer Street brethren have only lost the use of their property six months, and it will have been employed in Christian work. But I believe the money will come and the church go on.'

" ' " He looked me straight in the eye and said, ' Doctor, I'll give you the church!'

" ' " I was mad in a minute. I had not been made so angry since I reached New York. I thought that Commodore Vanderbilt desired to obtain that property for some railroad or other business purpose, or for his estate—that he had some deep design, and chose to put me forward, supposing that I was a greenhorn of a parson from the pine forests of North Carolina, and he could use me. I fired up, and leaning upon the table looked him straight in the eye and said, ' Commodore Vanderbilt, you don't know me! There is not any man in America rich enough to have me for a chaplain.' I shall never forget the look he returned. He had been accustomed to be solicited. Here he was, making the largest offer of charity he ever had made, and found a man refusing to accept fifty thousand dollars! It was an amazed and quizzical look; it was the look of a man who had a new sensation and could not tell whether he was enjoying it or not. As soon as he could frame a reply he said, 'Doctor, I don't know what you mean. Me have a chaplain! The Lord knows I've got as little use for a chaplain as any other man you ever saw. I want to give you this church, and give it to you only. Now will you take it?'

" ' " I paused a moment, and felt that perhaps I had made a mistake in the man, and then said, 'Commodore, I should not like to be under so great a pecuniary obligation to any gentleman that, when I had the guns of the gospel directed against the breastworks of any particular sin, and should see his head rising above them, I should be tempted to suspend my fire or change the range of my shot.'

" ' " ' Doctor,' said he, 'I would not give you a cent if I did not believe that you were so independent a man that you would preach the gospel as honestly to one man as to another. Now I believe that and I want to give you the church.'

" ' " After the discharge of the lightning of my anger, I felt that a sort of April shower was coming. My eyes were moistening. It seemed to me a wonderful providence; and you know we always think it is a wonderful providence if it runs with our ideas. I extended my hand and said, 'Commodore, if you give me that church for the Lord Jesus Christ, I'll most thankfully accept it.'

" ' " ' No,' said he, 'doctor, I would not give it to you that way, because that would be professing to you a religious sentiment I do not feel. I want to give you a church; that's all there is. It is one friend doing something for another friend. Now, if you take it that way I'll give it to you.'

" ' " We both rose at the same moment, and I took his hand and I said, 'Commodore, in whatever spirit you give it, I am deeply obliged, but I shall receive it in the name of the Lord Jesus Christ.'

" ' " ' Oh, well,' said he, ' let us go into the sitting-room and see the women.'

" ' " It so happened that the Mercer Street brethren were disappointed in their movement, and I felt in honor compelled to withdraw any claim I might have on what had occurred before, and for a considerable time after they occupied their church. After that long and tiresome suspense, again the church was offered me. I did not know that the commodore had not changed his mind. I had not talked with him on the subject since I announced that I was compelled to give up the church. But when the time came I walked in and said, ' Commodore, this church is again in the market, and I can get it if I renew my proposition to them.'

" ' " Said he, ' Offer them the fifty thousand dollars cash. The property is worth it and always will be worth it, even with the ground-rent. Fix the day for the transfer.'

" ' " Through my friend, the late General James Lorimer Graham, this was done. The commodore went to Saratoga. I communicated to him the day when the papers were to be made. He directed me to call at his office, which I did, and when I entered, his clerk, Mr. Wardell, said, ' Doctor, here is a package containing fifty thousand dollars of money from Commodore Vanderbilt for you.'

" ' " I said to him, ' Do you know what this fifty thousand dollars is for?' ' No, sir, I don't.' ' Didn't the commodore tell you?' ' No, sir.' ' Shall I give you a receipt?' ' No, sir.' ' Why don't you take a receipt?' ' The commodore didn't tell me to take one.'

" ' " And that is the way I got the Church of the Strangers. I desired to have it put in charge of a body of trustees of prominent gentlemen selected from the principal churches in New York; but the commodore refused to do so, saying, ' No; you hammer away at some of those fellows about their sins, and they will turn around and bedevil you so that you will have to quit the church. I am going to give it to you personally.'

" ' " He subsequently made the deeds of settlement so that the pastor should have a life-estate in the property, and that at his death it should fall into the hands of the trustees of the Church of the Strangers appointed according to law. And thus we got the church.

" ' " He lived seven years after that, and never by deed or word or look did he make me feel that he felt that I was under obligation to him. On the contrary, from that day forth he always treated me as one gentleman treats another who has done him a very great favor. It was done in a princely style, and I do believe God paid him and his family a thousandfold in many ways." '

" The events just narrated took place during the summer of 1870. The pastor at once set to work making the necessary repairs. As for several years the congregation which had been occupying the building had been expecting to make some arrangement for removal, the property was neglected and very much had to be done. Ten thousand dollars should have been expended upon it, but the pastor ventured only half that amount and supervised all the repairs. He had so little trained his people to work, having had nothing for them to work upon, that he was compelled to do nearly the whole of this alone while continuing his ministration in the little chapel. Not an officer of the church visited the premises during the repairs. When all was done he went to his friend, Commodore Vanderbilt, and told him that the repairs were all finished and that service would be held on the first Sunday of the next month, October, and that it had cost five thousand dollars to make the repairs. The commodore said, ' Well, doctor, how are you going to pay for it? ' The reply was, ' I do not know, sir;' for the doctor thought probably the commodore would assume the debt. Instead of doing so he said, ' Neither do I.'

It afterward transpired that the commodore did this to try the pastor's 'pluck' and further to satisfy himself that his confidence in the doctor's ability was not misplaced. The pastor arose, saying, 'But I will pay it, commodore,' and left. He went immediately down into Wall Street, and through a friend, Mr. Charles W. Keep, borrowed the money on his own personal credit, and paid for all the material used and all the work done in repairing the building. This load he bore for some time before he could obtain enough, above what was necessary annually for the running of the church, to liquidate the debt, but it was finally accomplished.

"On Sunday, the 28th of August, the Sunday-school had taken possession of its department in the chapel, under the superintendency of Mr. William J. Woodward. The building which the Church of the Strangers was now to occupy is of historical interest. When that portion of the city was almost in the country, and a number of members of the old Brick Church,* which was then under the pastorate of Dr. Gardiner Spring, separated themselves in order to build a new up-town church, they selected this spot. To that congregation and to the old St. Mark's Episcopal Church in the Bowery almost all the principal families of the city belonged. To the new Presbyterian church the Rev. Dr. Thomas H. Skinner, as we have seen, was called as its first pastor.

"The great revival services under the Rev. Dr. Kirk in 1839–40 had taken place within those walls. In what is now the pastor's study, in the chapel facing on Greene Street, were heard the first classes of the Union Theological Seminary, which now has a noble residence at No. 1200 Park Avenue. All the commencements of the theological seminary were held here until 1871. In what is now the parlor of the church there was a Sunday-school, in which men and women who

* This church occupied the block now covered by the Potter and Times buildings.

have since distinguished themselves in church work, in literature, and in the department of teaching received their training.

"We are indebted to Mr. R. R. McBurney, secretary of the Young Men's Christian Association in this city, for the following facts:

"'On the evening of May 28, 1852, a meeting was held in the lecture-room of what is now the Church of the Strangers, which had been called by a few young men, members of evangelical churches in this city, who had previously on several occasions met together to consider the propriety of forming a Young Men's Christian Association. About three hundred young men assembled at that time, who manifested a deep interest in the subject; and it became evident that such an association might be formed with every prospect of usefulness.

"'The chair was occupied by the Rev. G. T. Bedell, D.D., then rector of the Church of the Ascension, Tenth Street and Fifth Avenue, now Protestant Episcopal Bishop of Ohio, who expressed a fervent interest in the cause.

"'The Rev. C. J. Warren also took part in the exercises, and an admirable address was delivered by the late Rev. Isaac Ferris, D.D., then pastor of the Market Street Reformed Dutch Church, which embodied a lucid exhibition of the nature and the probable benefits of the proposed organization.

"'After the address, the names of one hundred and seventy-three young men were enrolled as members, J. W. Benedict, Esq., acting as chairman.

"'At several successive meetings, held in the same place, the proposed constitution was brought forward, and after being fully discussed was finally adopted in nearly its present shape.

"'On the evening of the 30th of June, 1852, the association was permanently organized by the election of its officers.

"'From the pulpit of the church was delivered the first annual sermon before the Young Men's Christian Association, by the Rev. Dr. Ferris, who was afterward chancellor of the University of the City of New York.'

"THE OPENING

"On Sunday, October 2, 1870, the Church of the Strangers was duly opened. The following account of the opening exercises is taken from the three programs issued during the days of their continuance:

"*Sunday, October 2, 1870*

"Morning, 10:30 o'clock. Singing the long-meter doxology, 'Praise God, from whom all blessings flow,' etc. The first morning lesson. The hymn, 'I love thy kingdom, Lord,' No. 33 of 'Hymns for all Christians.' The creed. Prayer, by Joseph Holdich, D.D., American Bible Society. The second morning lesson.

"HYMN WRITTEN FOR THE OCCASION BY PHŒBE CARY

"'Come down, O Lord, and with us live!
  For here, with tender, earnest call,
The gospel thou didst freely give
  We freely offer unto all.

"'Come with such power and saving grace
  That we shall cry, with one accord,
"How sweet and awful is this place,
  This sacred temple of the Lord!"

"'Let friend and stranger, one in thee,
  Feel with such power thy Spirit move
That every man's own speech shall be
  The sweet eternal speech of love.

"'Yea, fill us with the Holy Ghost;
  Let burning hearts and tongues be given;
Make this a day of Pentecost,
  A foretaste of the bliss of heaven!'

"Sermon, by Robert S. Moran, D.D., Methodist Episcopal Church, South. Address, by Abel Stevens, D.D., LL.D., Methodist Episcopal Church.

"At the conclusion of the morning service the pastor in his address, among other things, returned thanks for the many attentions the church had received from its friends, and alluded to the motto in the flowers on the communion-table, 'All for Jesus,' and said that should now be the motto of the Church of the Strangers.

"Afternoon, 2:30 o'clock. Baptism of infants. 3:00 o'clock. The holy communion, conducted by the pastor, assisted by Thomas H. Skinner, LL.D., George L. Prentiss, D.D., pastor of the Church of the Covenant, Robert R. Booth, D.D., pastor of the University Place Presbyterian Church (these three gentlemen having been pastors of the Mercer Street Church); Gardiner Spring, LL.D.; William B. Sprague, D.D.; John P. Durbin (one of the secretaries of the Methodist Missionary Society); A. C. Wedekind, D.D., pastor of St. James's (Lutheran); Rev. R. Koenig, of Pest, Hungary; and other clergymen.

"Evening, 7:30 o'clock. Prayer, by Philip Schaff, D.D., professor in Union Theological Seminary. Sermon, by John Cotton Smith, D.D., rector of the Church of the Ascension (Protestant Episcopal). Address, by Mancius C. Hutton, D.D., pastor of the Washington Square Reformed (Dutch) Church.

"At the conclusion of the evening service Dr. Deems read the following stanzas, which had been sent him during the day:

"'ALL FOR JESUS'

"'Written for the Church of the Strangers by Mrs. M. A. Kidder

"'This holy, peaceful Sabbath day
We bow our inmost hearts and pray
To thee, O Jesus!

And while we give afresh to thee
This Christian church, so broad, so free,
Our voices and our hearts agree,
    'Tis all for Jesus!

" ' This structure with its rocky bands,
This holy temple as it stands,
    Was built for Jesus!
The very floor beneath our feet,
The walls that catch the echoes sweet,
This pulpit, aye, and every seat,
    Belong to Jesus!

" ' The strangers' church! the world's wide home
Where all, yea all, may freely come
    And learn of Jesus!
The rich, the poor, the grave and gay,
The lonely wanderers by the way,
May hear God's Word and sing and pray
    To blessed Jesus!

" ' O generous heart, that gave so much!
O open hands, whose gentle touch
    Was seen by Jesus!
O sisters kind and brothers true,
O loving friends in every pew,
Whate'er we've done, whate'er we do,
    Is all for Jesus!'

" *Monday Evening, October 3d*

" 7 :30 o'clock. Public meeting. Rev. Chancellor Ferris presided. Vice-presidents: Gorham D. Abbott, LL.D., William H. Alexander, Albert T. Bledsoe, LL.D., Nathan Bishop, LL.D., A. T. Briggs, Theophilus P. Brouwer, William C. Churchill, A.M., George W. Clarke, Ph.D., Charles C. Colgate, Peter Cooper, Lyman Denison, Cornelius R. Disosway, Hon. William E. Dodge, Thomas C. Doremus, Daniel Drew, John Elliott, Hon. William M. Evarts, Richard C. Gardner, James Lorimer Graham, Hon. William F. Havemeyer, Thomas A.

Hoyt, Edward S. Jaffray, Morris K. Jesup, John H. Keyser,
Dr. Jared Linsly, R. R. McBurney, Belden Noble, Ex-Gover-
nor Olden of New Jersey, John W. Quincy, John A. Stew-
art, Algernon S. Sullivan, Ex-Governor Throop of New York,
John F. Trow, John Elliott Ward, Horace Webster, LL.D.,
A. R. Wetmore, Stewart L. Woodford.

"Prayer, by George R. Crooks, D.D., editor of the 'Methodist.'

"The meeting was a profoundly interesting one. Dr.
Deems gave a history of the rise and progress of the Church
of the Strangers, and of the work proposed to be accomplished.
He was followed by the Rev. Mr. Koenig, pastor of a similar
church in Pest, Hungary; and by the Hon. William E. Dodge
in a most happy address of indorsement and congratulation;
and by Dr. S. Irenæus Prime, of the New York 'Observer,'
in a most touching and beautiful speech.

" *Tuesday, October 4th*

"The Rev. Dr. Armitage, of the Fifth Avenue Baptist
Church, preached a most impressive sermon.

" *Friday Evening, October 7th*

"7:30 o'clock. Public temperance meeting, under the
direction of the Fidelity Temple of Honor. The Grand
Worthy Chief Templar, Calvin E. Keach, of Rensselaer
County, presided. Prayer by the Rev. Stephen Merritt, Jr.,
chaplain of Fidelity Temple. Addresses by Templar William
S. Stevenson, the Rev. C. F. Deems, D.D., and Hon. B. E.
Hale, of Kings County. Sacred and temperance songs by a
young lady.

" *Sunday, October 9th*

"Morning, 10:20 o'clock. Prayer, by Thomas C. De Witt,
D.D., Collegiate Reformed Church. Sermon, by William E.

Munsey, D.D., Methodist Episcopal Church, South. Address, by the Rev. George J. Mingins, superintendent of city missions.

"Afternoon, 2:30 o'clock. Baptism of adults. 3:00 o'clock. Sunday-school concert, conducted by Philip Phillips. The address by William H. C. Price, Esq., former superintendent of the school.

"Evening, 7:30 o'clock. Sermon, by Leonard Bacon, D.D., Congregational. Address, by the pastor."

CHAPTER VIII

THE Church of the Strangers, now thoroughly rooted, and with "All for Jesus" for its motto, promptly won not only a local, but also a national, even an international, reputation. It was the supreme achievement of Dr. Deems's life, and is worthy the thoughtful study of a'l who are interested in the church of Christ and the salvation of society.

As already stated, the Apostles' Creed is the symbol of the faith of the church. The Advisory Council, made up of seven men, has charge of all spiritual interests; the receiving, dismissing, and disciplining of members, and other spiritual matters, being in their hands. They are elected annually at the December monthly meeting, being nominated at that meeting by the pastor. The members of this council and the superintendent of the Sunday-school are nominated by the pastor, because they are his assistants in his spiritual work. Should the monthly meeting fail to elect a nominee for membership in the Advisory Council, the pastor makes another nomination. All other church officers are nominated by the members of the congregation. The secular and general interests of the church are controlled by a monthly meeting of the church, which elects annually in December a president, vice-president, and clerk of the monthly meeting. Nine trustees have charge of the finances, three being elected annually.

222

THE CHURCH OF THE STRANGERS, INTERIOR.

CHAPTER VIII

THE Church of the Strangers, now thoroughly rooted, and with " All for Jesus " for its motto, promptly won not only a local, but also a national, even an international, reputation. It was the supreme achievement of Dr. Deems's life, and is worthy the thoughtful study of all who are interested in the church of Christ and the salvation of society.

As already stated, the Apostles' Creed is the symbol of the faith of the church. The Advisory Council, made up of seven men, has charge of all spiritual interests; the receiving, dismissing, and disciplining of members, and other spiritual matters, being in their hands. They are elected annually at the December monthly meeting, being nominated at that meeting by the pastor. The members of this council and the superintendent of the Sunday-school are nominated by the pastor, because they are his assistants in his spiritual work. Should the monthly meeting fail to elect a nominee for membership in the Advisory Council, the pastor makes another nomination. All other church officers are nominated by the members of the congregation. The secular and general interests of the church are controlled by a monthly meeting of the church, which elects annually in December a president, vice-president, and clerk of the monthly meeting. Nine trustees have charge of the finances, three being elected annually.

THE CHURCH OF THE STRANGERS, INTERIOR.

CHAPTER VIII

THE Church of the Strangers, now thoroughly rooted, and with " All for Jesus " for its motto, promptly won not only a local, but also a national, even an international, reputation. It was the supreme achievement of Dr. Deems's life, and is worthy the thoughtful study of a l who are interested in the church of Christ and the salvation of society.

As already stated, the Apostles' Creed is the symbol of the faith of the church. The Advisory Council, made up of seven men, has charge of all spiritual interests; the receiving, dismissing, and disciplining of members, and other spiritual matters, being in their hands. They are elected annually at the December monthly meeting, being nominated at that meeting by the pastor. The members of this council and the superintendent of the Sunday-school are nominated by the pastor, because they are his assistants in his spiritual work. Should the monthly meeting fail to elect a nominee for membership in the Advisory Council, the pastor makes another nomination. All other church officers are nominated by the members of the congregation. The secular and general interests of the church are controlled by a monthly meeting of the church, which elects annually in December a president, vice-president, and clerk of the monthly meeting. Nine trustees have charge of the finances, three being elected annually.

The Church of the Strangers, Interior.

The trustees conduct their business through a committee of their members: the president, the treasurer, and the financial secretary, together with two other trustees. This committee is called the Board of Finance.

From the inception of this unique church no pew has ever been rented. All pews and sittings are always free for all worshipers. Funds have been raised by the envelope system of weekly subscriptions, and by the plate collections, which have ever been very generous. The finances of the Church of the Strangers are managed with the most businesslike system, accuracy, and energy.

One of the best features of the church is the Committee on Hospitality, a board of ushers, young men carefully selected and especially instructed to make every stranger feel perfectly at home.

The ritual of the church in its simplicity departs from the ordinary form of service in the non-liturgical churches chiefly in the use of the Apostles' Creed by the congregation after the first hymn of the morning service. A volunteer chorus choir, trained and led by Professor George W. Pettit, leads the congregational singing, which is unusually fine, the hymnbook used being "Hymns for all Christians," prepared by Phœbe Cary and Dr. Deems. The prayers of Dr. Deems in his pulpit will never be forgotten. They impressed the hearer with the thought that the pastor knew all the experiences of every heart before him, and was vividly impressed himself by the presence, power, and love of the Deity whom he devoutly addressed as the hearer and answerer of prayer.

The sacrament of the Lord's Supper is administered on the first Sunday of every month, when new members who have been admitted to the sealing ordinances of baptism and the Lord's Supper are welcomed by the officers and members of the church. The communion and baptismal rituals are practically the same as those of the Methodist Episcopal Church, the members of the Advisory Council first partaking of the elements while seated at a long communion-table, and then assisting the pastor in the distribution of the bread and wine to the people, who are seated in alternate pews. It is a remarkable fact that no communion season, excepting one, has ever passed without at least one new member to be welcomed. Generally there have been more.

Infants are baptized on the third and adults on the fourth Sunday of the month. Under the pulpit platform is a baptistery which is used for those whose consciences call for baptism by immersion, while in front of the pulpit stands the font from which babes are baptized and those adults who do not ask for immersion. Dr. Deems s theory was that the mode of baptism was a matter for settlement by the candidate, his part being the application of water in the name of the blessed Trinity.

Besides the regular Sunday morning and evening services held in the church proper, a stone building with a square tower in the façade, a laborious and fruitful Sunday-school is held in the chapel, a two-story brick building fronting on Greene Street (which at its northern end is called Winthrop Place), the chapel being No. 4. Dr. Deems made it a rule to visit the Sunday-school every Sunday morning and offer prayer, also frequently speaking. This part of the church, equipped as it has ever been with a primary, intermediate, and Bible-class department, has been, and is, one of the brightest and most fruitful sections of the life and work of the Church of the Strangers. In 1883 a Chinese Sunday-school was organized, and is held every Sunday afternoon at 2 : 30, a most gratifying evidence of the missionary life of the church.

At 6 : 45 P.M. every Sunday, under the auspices of the young men of the church, a vesper service is held preparatory to the regular evening service. It is held in the church parlor, a large room under the Sunday-school room, on the ground floor of the chapel building, in which is also held the regular church prayer-meeting every Friday evening, a mothers' meeting every Wednesday afternoon following the first Sunday of the month, and a church sociable every Wednesday evening following the first Sunday of the month.

The Friday evening church prayer-meeting is in charge of a committee, who provide leaders and topics, except for the Friday evening preceding the communion, when the pastor leads a service preparatory to the Lord's Supper. It is an interesting custom of the Church of the Strangers to take up a collection at every meeting, of every sort, held in the chapel on Wednesday evening.

Three organizations, besides those already mentioned, carry on the work of the church: the Sisters of the Stranger, the Missionary Society, and the Young People's Society of Christian Endeavor.

Recognizing that in a city of a million and a half people there must always be a large number of strangers in sickness or some other distress, and recognizing the value of woman's work in the church, Dr. Deems, in January, 1869, organized the Sisters of the Stranger, whose object is to aid worthy strangers in distress in New York City.

The office of this society is in the northeastern corner of the church parlor, where the secretary is to be found at her desk daily from 3 to 5 P.M., to receive, pass judgment upon, and respond to applications for help. God, who so signally blessed every work of his servant's hand, had provided for the work of the secretary of the sisters an ideal woman.

Gifted with an acute mind and a wise and tender heart, Miss Cecile Sturtevant accepted the position of secretary at the founding of the sisterhood, and for five and twenty years she was at her post of duty with exemplary regularity, devotion, and constancy. She was deeply attached to her pastor, and not only with her pen helped him in his large correspondence and the care of his parish books, but also, by adding to his her judgment and knowledge of people and of details of church life, assisted him in carrying successfully the heavy load of his widely extended and peculiar parish. Sister Cecile was to Dr. Deems as a daughter. She survived him less than a year, and was buried from the old church on Friday, August 11, 1894. To the few older members then present this seemed to be next to the last act in the life-history of this unique, useful, and beneficent movement.

The Sisters of the Stranger is still alive and bearing fruit, Mrs. Sara Keables Hunt being secretary, and Miss Rena Sturtevant, a worthy sister of the late Miss Cecile Sturtevant, being treasurer.

Mrs. S. M. Blake was the first president of this society, and Mrs. Charles F. Deems has been the only other president. To give an idea of the fruitfulness of the Sisters of the Stranger we quote the following paragraphs from Mr. Joseph S. Taylor's "History of the Church of the Strangers":

"From the beginning of their work and covering a period of seventeen years, the sisters have disbursed $23,446.11. They have helped 8415 persons, and through them and their families many other persons. Of the 8415 recorded, 4311 have been Americans and 4104 foreigners.

"Throughout all the years of the sisters' work the Church of the Strangers has intrusted to them the disbursement of the communion offertory for the poor. The claims of needy members of the church having first consideration, the balance, if any, has been allowed to go to the general work of the society. Whenever the offertory fell short of what was required by church-members, the sisters have made up the deficiency from their fund. The disposition made of this money is reported to the Advisory Council."

The Dorcas Committee, who meet every Thursday afternoon to cut and sew garments, are a good right arm of the sisters, during the first fifteen years of their labors distributing

thirty-eight hundred new garments and cast-off clothing valued at four thousand dollars.

In the memories of those who knew the noble work of the
sisters will ever be associated the name of Mrs. Frank A.
Vanderbilt, the wife of the first Cornelius Vanderbilt. She
was for years the first directress of the sisters. When, on
May 4, 1885, her death came in the prime of a superb Christian life, a writer in the " Christian Worker " said of her:

" The papers have announced the death of this ' elect lady.'
All over the land she has scattered her benedictions—to
public institutions, private charities, missions, schools, orphans,
widows, aged clergymen, and people in almost every kind of
straitness in mind, body, and estate. She was known to the
whole Church of the Strangers, to whom she fulfilled the
prophecy, ' Queens shall be their nursing mothers.' The Sisters of the Stranger lose an honored and beloved directress.
Her last words to her pastor, the Rev. Dr. Deems, were uttered
brokenly with failing breath: ' I am—going—*not triumphant
—but—trusting.*' Let that be the motto of the bereaved sisterhood: ' Not triumphant, but trusting.' "

The Missionary Society was organized in the Sunday-school
early in the history of the church; but when the church grew
stronger, in January, 1878, the scope of this society was enlarged and it became an honored and useful church organization. The payment, in advance, of one dollar per annum
makes a member, and the payment of five dollars at one time
makes a life-member, while the payment of twenty-five dollars
constitutes the donor a patron. The pastor is the president,
the superintendent of the Sunday-school is the vice-president,
and the executive committee is made up of six women and six
men, who select a secretary and treasurer from their own number. The Chinese Sunday-school, the Gospel Mission, and the
Young People's Society are represented on the executive committee.

A quarterly missionary prayer-meeting was inaugurated in 1884, and this Missionary Society has made itself felt all over the world, in both home and foreign mission fields of various denominations.   In addition to regular contributions to Miss Whately's English school at Cairo, Egypt, to the Anglo-Chinese University at Shanghai, China, and to Bishop Gobat's Memorial School on Mount Zion, Jerusalem, the Missionary Society have rendered substantial aid to the Syrian Protestant College, Beirut, Syria; Bethany Institute, for training women to become missionaries; the McAll Mission, in France; the Seamen's Friend Society (eight libraries for United States Life-saving Service), the New York Medical Mission, the Tombs Mission, the Hebrew Christian Church, the East Side Chapel, and many other home and foreign fields.   No pastor ever realized more keenly than Dr. Deems that a church without the spirit of missions is a church without Christ, a spiritually selfish and dead thing.

One of the fruits of the spirit of missions in the Church of the Strangers is the Gospel Mission, at the corner of South Fifth Avenue and Bleecker Street.   This work was commenced at the corner of Wooster and Bleecker streets on June 18, 1885, having originated in the heart and mind of Mr. Edgar W. Russell, then a member of the Church of the Strangers, now a pastor in the Presbyterian Church.   In planting and rooting this noble work in a part of the city whose most striking features are poverty, filth, and vice, Mr. Russell had the hearty coöperation of his pastor and the substantial aid of the Missionary Society.

Youthful and buoyant in spirits to the end of his life, it almost goes without saying that Dr. Deems from the beginning of his work in New York loved and was loved by his young people; and he kept them actively employed in Christian work in various ways, but the Young People's Society of Christian Endeavor was not organized until January, 1886.

Since that time it has been one of the most efficient arms of the Church of the Strangers. It is organized along the general lines of the model Young People's Society of Christian Endeavor, but shows slight differences in minor matters.

With about six hundred resident members working privately and through the organizations just sketched, the Church of the Strangers has been an interesting spiritual landmark in New York City and a great spiritual power during the past quarter of a century. Its eminent success has been due to a number of contributing causes: its attractive name, its undenominational character (there being on its roll at the time of Dr. Deems's death members from sixteen denominations), its large numbers, its splendid organization, and its homelike and well-appointed buildings.

But all who have known well the Church of the Strangers attribute its splendid success, next to the divine power working through it, to its gifted pastor, Dr. Deems. He was a man of pronounced and original personality. In the pulpit he was wondrously eloquent as an orator, in his pastoral work he was indefatigable, and without apparent effort was equally at home with the pauper and the millionaire, with the scholar and the unlearned. Affectionate with his people in their homes, he was yet perfectly free from hypocritical cordiality. Naturally a leader, his executive qualities had received thorough training while he was engaged in his various educational undertakings, and were used at their best in organizing and carrying forward the work of the Church of the Strangers. Above all, in character he was manly, spiritually minded, earnest, and honest.

But we shall at this point quote the testimony of others than his sons, as given in a chapter in "A Romance of Providence" entitled "'How' and 'Why.'" In order to help the readers of his "History of the Church of the Strangers" to understand the secret of its growth and power, Mr. Taylor, in

1887, addressed to various members of the church the following formula:

" Please write out an account of *how* and *why* you came to
join the Church of the Strangers. Make it as long or as short
as you please, and write in a familiar style. No names will
be published."

The following are selections from the replies received. One
gentleman, a jeweler, said he liked the church: "(1) On account of its simple service; (2) because Dr. Deems preached
Jesus Christ without an 'ism'; (3) because I loved the singing
of the orphan children."* A young man testified: "I was
convinced [by Dr. Deems] of my duty to join some Christian
body, and in making a selection, if one thing more than another
influenced me outside of the personality of the pastor, which
I think is always one of the first considerations, it was the unsectarian principle on which the church is founded." The
father of this young man wrote: "I liked the preaching."
Another, a widow, wrote: "It was the *home feeling* which
pervaded our church. . . . When myself and daughter presented ourselves as candidates for admission to the Church of
the Strangers, and Dr. Deems said to me, 'And what led you
and your daughter to come to us?' I could truly say, 'The
fact, sir, that we have found a home!'" From a trustee:
"We concluded to follow this crowd. We were led into a
church. Opening one of the hymn-books which I found in
the pew, I discovered that we were in the Church of the
Strangers. I said at once, 'Why, this is the church for us;
we are strangers.' I have been a regular attendant of the
church from that day to this;" that is, for fifteen years. A
business man says: "I first heard Dr. Deems preach in the

---

* For many years, until its removal from West Tenth Street far up-
town, the Protestant Half-Orphan Asylum worshiped every Sunday
morning at the Church of the Strangers, almost filling the galleries, and
singing during the offertory.

Hedding Methodist Episcopal Church, East Seventeenth Street. I was so much pleased with him that I determined to attend whatever church he might be called to in this city." An artist says: 'I came to New York in 1870. One Sunday morning my attention was attracted by a placard reading 'The Church of the Strangers' at the entrance to the university building. That appeal made me think. I was a 'stranger,' and I concluded this must be my church. I stepped inside and heard Dr. Deems for the first time. I have not yet recovered from the powerful effects of that sermon." From a publisher: "I knew all the truths of the gospel by heart, and the most brilliant sermon had no effect unless I felt sure the preacher himself was genuinely in earnest. From what source I hardly know, I got the conviction that Dr. Deems was a truly good and earnest man. I went to hear him, and a sermon of his on the Fifty-first Psalm, in which he brought out very forcibly David's desire for purity as well as pardon, was really the deciding point in my life. I did not wait long before I joined the church. I shall always feel for Dr. Deems the respect and affection of a son."

A professional man and an ex-Romanist, after graphically describing his spiritual ignorance, his heart-hunger, the heartlessness of the formality of the church in which he had been reared, and the spiritually destructive effects of the fashionable churches he turned to, says: "At this time my dear wife insisted on my going to hear Dr. Deems preach. I went, and with a slight variation of Cæsar's phrase I was obliged to say, 'I came, I saw, and was conquered!' I found in Dr. Deems an earnestness in expounding the gospel which I had never heard before, and the more I heard him the more I regained my faith. The horizon of the dark and turbulent sea on which I was drifting, ready to give up hope, became clear and bright. The inner man underwent a metamorphosis. I began to feel that some sincerity, after all, remained in this world. I found in the discourses all the logic and rhetoric I wanted, sufficient clearness to enable me to know what the Master wants me to do, and, above all, an earnestness which convinced me that the preacher was intent on saving my soul."

Here let it be noted how the grand secret of his great success in his sacred calling lay in the fact that his talents were sanctified; that above, below, behind, and all through his learning, his gifts for oratory, his cogent logic, his brilliant rhetoric, and, in one word, his intellectuality, were his sincerity, his earnestness, his spirituality, and his intentness on saving souls. Blessed indeed is that minister of God who subordinates and consecrates all his powers to this one end of saving souls! From a young woman: "By his gentle and Christian conduct and conversation he so wrought upon me that I returned the same night to my situation" (she was a governess, friendless and a stranger), "and soon after I began to attend preaching services in the Church of the Strangers. One day I was in great trouble, having just received word that my sister—the only support besides myself of a poor old widowed mother in distant Ireland—was dangerously ill. I went out into Washington Square. As I sat there I saw Dr. Deems passing. Instinctively feeling that from him would come sympathy and help, I rose and met him, saying, 'Doctor, I have a sister who is dying; will you pray for her?' His reply was, 'God bless you, my daughter; I will. Let us pray now.' And raising his hat, he then and there breathed a silent prayer for my sister. Afterward I announced my name and explained the circumstances of the case. And this is *how* I came to the Church of the Strangers. In answer to the question *why* I joined, I can only say, because 'I was a stranger, and ye took me in.'"

A former member of the Advisory Council of the church says: "I looked in the newspapers, and my weakness was accommodated by this announcement: ' Church of the Strangers; strangers welcome; all seats free.' Now I had been a stranger in New York over ten years, and so far as the invitation went, that was the church for me. I went there on the first Sunday in January, 1871. There was nothing there that I could find fault with!" (He had explained that he was a Scotchman.) "The rich and the poor were treated alike. The preacher had wit without flippancy, and boldness and originality without irreverence. He hurt my pride a little, but I forgave him; for I knew it was only a random shot and he could not possibly know me." (Not "a random shot," my good brother; he knew somebody like you and was aiming at him. He always preached from his own pulpit at some particular person in his audience; hence the one invariable directness of his aim and the penetrative quality of his messages. When preaching to a strange audience he preached at himself. Somebody was always hit. He wasted no ammunition shooting in the air with both eyes shut.) "I was attracted. I went every Sunday." Six months thereafter this gentleman gave his heart to God. His whole, candid, and self-searching confession was summed up in his own words: "I had thought myself a philosopher. I saw that I had wrestled like a fool. I had boasted:

' I shall never follow blindly where my reason cannot go;
I shall know by reason only all that mortals need to know.'

Overwhelmed with a sense of my unworthiness and unfitness, I reluctantly went to see Dr. Deems. I had never spoken to him, and by way of introduction I sent him a letter and afterward called upon him. I expected to have my sinful heart cauterized with theological caustic and had braced myself up for the operation; but instead of pain he gave me pleasure, instead of humiliation he gave me sympathy—'the oil of joy for mourning, the garment of praise for the spirit of heaviness.'

With faith small as a grain of mustard-seed I was admitted to the church on the first Sunday in July, 1871."

Yes, he was a gentle and skilful surgeon for moral hurts, a wise physician for spiritual ailments, a true disciple of the divine Healer of souls. Equally apt was he to deal with the forlorn loneliness of a poor friendless girl or the intellectual pride and stubbornness of a rebellious and controversial disputant. These few brief extracts, taken and condensed from those published in the history of the church, will, we trust, give the reader some additional knowledge about, and some deeper insight into, the personality of Dr. Deems. They will also show how his church grew up around him, and how and why, first and last, more than 1475 persons came to be enrolled in the church-membership. But who shall gather up the records and compute the untold good done to those unknown thousands who once or twice or oftener have just dropped into the Church of the Strangers to hear him preach —those who were just passing through the great city or were making their annual visits to purchase merchandise? No one will, for no one can. But they carried away with them to every part of our great land the spiritual blessings which they had received through him. Death may silence forever the golden tongue of eloquence,—and such was his,—but the echoes of this devout and faithful minister of Christ and him crucified will go on sounding in their ears and keeping them true to our most holy faith and transforming their lives; and they will pass on by word and by deed, to the world about them and to their children and their children's children, that blessed and imperishable influence; so that God only knows how many blessings he has bestowed through his faithful and consecrated servant, disciple, and messenger. Verily, such a life is worth living and worthy of being perpetuated in memory for an example to us all who knew him and to those who shall come after us. Past all words of thankfulness do the writers of this memoir confess their gratitude to their heavenly Father for the gift of such an earthly father, and the very natural, if mistaken, regret that they are so inadequate to the fulfilment of the attempt to fitly portray the character, the work, and the influence of the venerated father whose presence is still so vividly and constantly with them.

CHAPTER IX

HAVING taken a general survey of the Church of the Strangers, we may turn back and take up the story of Dr. Deems's life in its more personal bearings and in its other relations.

In the spring of 1867 he rented the cozy little frame house, No. 221 West Thirty-fourth Street, where for one year he and his family, after years of unrest and the discomforts of boarding-house life, once more tasted the sweets of a home. His journal shows that ill health annoyed him frequently during 1866 and 1867; but his indomitable will and the gratifying growth of his church were more than an offset to these trials of the flesh.

On Saturday, September 7th, the first number of "Every Month" appeared, a neat four-paged periodical, edited and published by Mr. S. T. Taylor, and designed to be the organ of the Church of the Strangers. Each number of the paper furnished information about the church and contained a sermon by Dr. Deems, which had been taken down by a reporter.

During the closing months of this year Dr. Deems added to his labors and widened his influence by visiting and doing evangelistic work every Monday afternoon among the prisoners at the Tombs, or city prison, on Center Street.

Extracts from Dr. Deems's Tombs Journal

"September 16th. Last week as I was passing the Tombs the words came so distinctly to my memory, 'I was in prison, and ye came unto me.' At once my other errand was postponed, and I said, 'Yes, Lord; the prisoner shall have fraternal greetings this day from me for that word of thine.' And so I entered, and after talking to some men who were behind the grates I went to the boys' prison; and then I saw the matron of the female prison and talked separately with some of her charge.

"While speaking with one of the women in a corridor at the door of her cell an inmate of another of the cells recognized my voice and came out with much shamefacedness. She had been a servant in the house in which I had boarded, and it seemed like a godsend to her that one who knew her should have come into the prison. She made an *ex-parte* statement of her case. She had been committed for grand larceny. It seemed to me that her fault was not quite so deep as that, although she had manifestly done a wrong. It was right to promise that I should do what I could for her; which promise was afterward kept, as will subsequently appear.

"This gave me a somewhat favorable introduction to the inhabitants of the Tombs, and I promised to conduct divine service for them on Mondays at two o'clock.

"In accordance with that engagement the first service was held to-day in the little chapel of what is called the 'female prison.' What a sight! There were old women and young girls, whites and negroes; some abashed and evidently hiding their faces through shame, others brazen; some frivolous and careless, and others stony, hard, or sullen; some neat and tidy, others slatternly, dirty, and barefooted. After making a very few general remarks in as pleasant a way and in as non-clerical a manner as was proper, but in a tone which, as it is now recollected, conveyed the idea that, while cant is not pleasant, there is to be special acknowledgment of God's presence when we worship, I invited the women to join me in singing a familiar hymn. About as large a proportion complied with this request as is usual in our fashionable congregations; that is to say, very few.

"It was my first address to prisoners. How it was to be done successfully was a question. To assume that they were guilty of the charges made against them would be doing gross injustice to some, as there are always some who are innocent. In any case, it would seem to be taking sides with the strong against the weak, the free against the captive, the prosperous wicked against the unfortunate wicked. So I endeavored as much as in me lay to think and feel as the blessed Teacher must have thought and felt in the midst of sinners.

"But I could not bring myself to this standard as the thought occurred to me that I was a fellow-sinner with these women—not sinning in their ways, not breaking society's laws, but, alas! breaking God's laws.

"And so I fell into a strain of talk much like the following:

"'I have been requested to render weekly service in your chapel and to assist others who are laboring for the good of your souls. Before beginning it seems to me necessary that we have some understanding. If it is expected that I am to ride down-town every Monday from my residence to the Tombs and remove my gloves and patronizingly proceed to give bad women some moral advice in a gentlemanly manner, *I sha'n't do it.*' Eyes twinkled, and glances were exchanged, and some whispers, which were interpreted to mean, 'Old fellow, you would lose your time if you did.' 'Nor will I hector you, nor lecture you, nor harangue you, nor talk to you as though you were much worse than the elegant ladies who sit in the pews of my church on Sunday, or as though I were

better than you. You shall not be prejudged. I'll tell you
how it is : all I know against you is that you are in the Tombs,
and the most innocent person might be here, whereas, alas!
my own heart is known to me, and that humbles me. Look
at me, women; do I look like an honest man that would not
deceive you?' They inspected me a moment, and two or
three nodded their heads as though they thought I was pass-
ably honest.

"'Well, here we are, sinful mortals together, not knowing
one another's names, met to worship God. In worship we
pray. The best prayer the world knows is that which was
taught it by Jesus. The foundation of all religion is in the
first two words, "Our Father." That believed, everything
else follows. Without that all theology, orthodoxy, and worship are nothing. Before we unite in repeating that prayer,
let us see what it means and whether we believe it. If you
repeat it without lying unto God—and I beseech you, do not
utter lies upon your knees—you believe three things, namely:
(1) That God is your *Father*—not your Creator, your Ruler,
your Judge; he is all these, but in prayer you claim the higher,
tenderer relationship of *Father.* Do you believe that? God
chose to have us *born* instead of made, that there might be
fathers and mothers and children, that we might understand
this relationship. There sits a woman holding her little sick
child so closely and tenderly. I appeal to her. God is nearer
kin to her than she to that baby. The babe is flesh of her
flesh, but she is spirit of God's spirit. She is the mother of
her infant's *body;* God is the father and mother of her soul.
Drop all hard thoughts of God.' Here I stated some of these.
'They are all wrong. "God is my Father" answers all the
riddles of my life. Do you believe that God is *your* FATHER?
(2) If you are going to repeat the prayer with me and say
"our," you must believe that God is *my* Father. And then
follows this: (3) You and I are close kindred; you are my

sister, I am your brother. Society would put us far apart; prayer brings us close together. We may have wandered in our ways very far from the Father and far from one another; in this prayer we clasp hands.

" ' O my sisters, I steadfastly believe all these things in my very heart, and desire as many as wish to believe it to come with me to the Father's mercy-seat.'

" This is an outline of about twenty minutes' talk, and many seemed melted and not a few joined in the prayer. At the close several came and made a kind of confession and expressed a desire to reform, and some seemed only solicitous to obtain help to escape conviction, and some seemed totally careless."

Dr. Deems wrought also among the boys and men, becoming deeply interested in and following up several cases. Few things in his life better illustrate his tenderness of heart and versatility of mind than his work in the Tombs prison and his account thereof.

Early in 1868 his aged father, the Rev. George W. Deems, visited him for the last time. No filial affection and thoughtfulness for a father's interests could surpass that which Dr. Deems at this time entertained and exhibited toward his revered father.

It was while he was preaching in the large chapel of the university, and in January, 1868, that the poet sisters Alice and Phœbe Cary first heard Dr. Deems. They became members of his congregation; he was a constant visitor at their home at No. 52 East Twentieth Street, and they were often welcomed by his family circle. At a regular weekly meeting of congenial literati at the Cary home Dr. Deems became acquainted with Horace Greeley, the Rev. Dr. Bellows, and other distinguished people, between some of whom and himself there grew up the warmest friendship.

In his journal for February 29, 1868, he underscores this entry: "To-night my son, Francis Melville Deems, was graduated to the degree of M.D. by Bellevue Hospital Medical College. Commencement in the Academy of Music. Splendid audience." His journal for this year reveals the fact that, busy as he was, he was a large part of the time not physically well.

The greatest literary effort of his life was commenced by Dr. Deems in the fall of 1868. In the Mercantile Library, on Astor Place, he was given an alcove in which he wrought four hours a day on his life of Jesus. It would appear that for a long time he had contemplated writing a life of our Lord from a point of view not taken by others who had dealt with this sacred theme. Of this work we shall have more to say farther on, only remarking at this point that for the ensuing three years he put the best of his time, heart, brains, and toil into this labor of love, for Jesus was always to him an intensely real and beloved person.

About a month after commencing this work Dr. Deems and Miss Phœbe Cary began their joint labors on their collection of hymns, which was published early in 1869 with the title, "Hymns for all Christians." It contains three hundred sacred poems: one hundred hymns, one hundred spiritual songs, and one hundred lyrics. The poet Whittier said that all that are worthy to be called "hymns" are in this collection; and reviewing the book at the time of its publication, the late venerable Rev. Dr. Sprague, of Albany, author of "Annals of the American Pulpit," wrote:

"I have had the pleasure of examining the new collection of hymns compiled by the Rev. Dr. Deems and Miss Phœbe Cary, entitled ' Hymns for all Christians,' and have been highly gratified by the excellent taste and judgment, as well as the truly devout spirit, displayed in this selection. It adds much to the interest of the work that a brief account of the authors

of most of the hymns is prefixed to some one of their respective productions. I cannot doubt that the book will be cordially welcomed by all evangelical Christians as a very important addition to our devotional literature."

"Hymns for all Christians" has been used in the Sunday
services by the Church of the Strangers ever since its publication. Its preparation, as the reader can readily imagine, was
congenial work for the gifted compilers, and was thoroughly
enjoyed by them both.

We learn from his journal that Dr. Deems, in addition to
his other labors, was, during this and the subsequent years of
his life, increasingly in demand as a lecturer. The subjects of
his more popular lectures being: "Husbands and Wives";
"Proverbs—Not Solomon's"; "Trifles"; "Unnatural Culture"; "A Plea for the Money-makers"; and "Ethics and
Poetry of Trade Life." As a lecturer he enchained the attention of his audiences by his wit, wisdom, originality, and
eloquence.

Among his published thoughts few have had a warmer welcome than his Christmas sermon preached in 1868, and appearing as a neat booklet entitled "No Room for Jesus."

From His Journal

"Thursday, December 31, 1868. Another year going out—
going out with me, amid hard work and ten thousand blessings."

The year 1869 was a laborious but happy and significant
year for Dr. Deems. A few extracts from his diary will give
the reader hints as to his work and experiences at this time.

"March 4th. Went to Washington [from Baltimore, where
he had been attending conference] and witnessed the inauguration of General Grant as President of the United States. Great
crowds.

"March 21st. After night sermon a telegram that my brother George is dead."

"March 22d. Went to Baltimore. Spent the evening with my poor father, who is in grief for George."

"March 23d. My half-brother, George W. Deems, buried to-day in a vault in Landowne Park Cemetery, Baltimore. The Rev. Mr. Williams, of Bethany Church, performed the ceremony."

"March 24th. Went with George Day and found the grave of my mother. Have not stood by it in thirty-four years. Am to have the remains removed."

"March 31st. Dr. Gardner and myself looking up lots for a church."

"May 3d. Entered on the use of Room 45, Bible House. The Sisters of the Stranger are to take it, and my study will be there."

"May 10th. *The Pacific Railroad completed to-day.*"

"May 18th. In the afternoon organizing the Sisters of the Stranger."

"June 15th. Went to Boston [where he attended the great Peace Jubilee, or musical festival, projected by Gilmore, and heard sublime vocal and instrumental music, including the singing of Parepa-Rosa]."

"September 5th. The largest congregation in the morning I have ever had. Am enthusiastic."

"October 21st. Worked all the morning at the book. In the afternoon read an hour to Alice Cary. Spent the evening with Commodore and Mrs. Vanderbilt."

"December 31st. May God have mercy upon me and forgive all the shortcomings of this year gone. Another year to answer for! Another year to be grateful for!"

The entries in his journal during 1870 are brief, but suggestive. There are frequent references to his work on his book, "Jesus."

"April 18th. At night called to see Alice Cary, who seems to be sinking. She kept me busy singing the hymns of her childhood: 'Oh, how happy are they!' 'Jesus, lover of my soul!'"

"June 9th. Returned from Baltimore. Have been watching by my father. It was feared he would not be able to survive until I reached him; but he has grown better."

"June 24th. To-day Commodore Vanderbilt authorized me to agree to give fifty thousand dollars for the Mercer Street Church. *Laus Deo!*"

"July 3d. While at the supper-table at Mr. James Lorimer Graham's a telegram came announcing that my father was dead. Preached a short sermon and took the train for Baltimore. Father died to-day at half-past one."

"July 5th. Father buried to-day. The Rev. Dr. Huston and the Rev. Dr. Thomas B. Sargent made addresses. Father was interred in Mount Olivet Cemetery."

"September 25th. At the Young Men's Christian Association to meet the foreign delegates to the Evangelical Alliance."

"Sunday, October 2d. Church of the Strangers reopened in the Mercer Street Church."

"October 7th. At the Evangelical Alliance heard Bickersteth, of 'Yesterday, To-day, and Forever.' Spoke to him. A kindly man."

"October 16th. My first sermon in the new Church of the Strangers."

Dr. Deems wrote quite complete autobiographical notes for the year 1871, the following extracts being the most interesting:

"On the 9th of January I left New York and went to Wilmington, N. C., to perform the marriage rite for a dear friend. This journey enabled me to visit my friends in places where I had formerly been pastor, in Goldsboro, Duplin County, and Wilmington. It so happened that the quarterly meeting of the Front Street Methodist Church was held on the following Sunday, and so I had an opportunity of preaching to many of my old friends. On the 18th I lectured in Goldsboro, spent a day in Baltimore, and on Saturday, the 21st, find this record in my journal: 'Returned to New York and the Russian baths.'

"The following extract from my monthly report to my church will show what lay on my heart at this period of my work:

"'My indebtedness for the repairs now stands at $3135.08, being only $167 less than last month, of which $100 was collected by Mr. James E. Halsey. If I had any property to sell I would liquidate this debt at once; but I have not. My policy of life-insurance is staked for it. I fear you think there is some one who will lift what you do not pay. There is no reason, let me assure you, for that supposition. If I live I must bear this burden and pay it off out of what savings the denial of my family can make. If I die the Church of the Strangers has a very good building, in capital repair, and my family are embarrassed. I regret to say this, but five months of burden-bearing have pressed it out of me.'

"On the 4th of February I attended the funeral of the Rev. Dr. Skinner, the first pastor of the Presbyterian church that worshiped in the building we now occupy, and who died a distinguished professor in the Union Theological Seminary.

"On the 7th of February of this year a remarkable circumstance took place. An awful accident occurred on the Hudson River Railroad near the town of New Hamburg, between Poughkeepsie and Fishkill. When the report of that accident came to the city it was told that my wife and myself were among the victims. The excitement created by it made quite an event in my history. It gave me weeks of answering letters and telegrams, and afforded me the curious sensation of enjoying posthumous fame in some measure.

"On Sunday, the 12th of February, I had a sore bereavement: my dear friend, Alice Cary, departed this life a few minutes before five o'clock. Her life had been to me a great comfort. Although more intimate with Phœbe, because her health was so much the stouter and she was more frequently at the church, my intercourse with Alice was always very pleasant; and for weeks and months before her departure I had frequently visited her sick-room and endeavored to soothe and comfort her. She was a rare woman, large of physique but delicate of spirit, a woman of taste and culture and of purest religious sentiment.

"On Tuesday, the 14th, she was buried from our church. The service was appointed at one o'clock. A severe snow-storm, which fell all that day, prevented very many from coming, but the attendance was very large. The service opened with an organ voluntary from the 'Messiah,' followed by the anthem, 'Vital spark of heavenly flame.' I read the church service and delivered a brief address, which is thus reported in the next morning paper.

"'"I have not thought of a single word to say to you to-day, and I do not know that it is necessary to say one word more than is set down in the church service. Most of us knew and loved Alice Cary, and to those who did not know her my words would fail in describing the sweetness and gentleness of her disposition and temper." The speaker then described the patience with which she had borne her last sickness, and told how he had been by her side when the pain was so intense that the prints of her finger-nails would be left in the palm of his hand as he was holding hers; but she never made a complaint. "She was a parishioner," said he, "who came very close to my heart in her suffering and sorrow. I saw how good and true she was, and the interest she had in all the work I had in hand.

"'"And now she has gone from our mortal sight, but not

from the eyes of our souls. She is gone from her pain, as she desired to die, in sleep, and after a deep slumber she has passed into the morning of immortality. The last time I saw her I took down her works and alighted on this passage, so full of consonance with the anthems just sung by the choir, and almost like a prophecy of the manner in which she passed away:

> " ' " ' My soul is full of whispered sorrows,
> My blindness is my sight;
> The shadows that I feared so long
> Are all alive with light.'

" ' " There was one thing in Alice Cary of which we would better remind ourselves now, because many of us are working people, and people who work very much with our brains; and I see a number of young people who have come, out of tenderness to her memory, to the church to-day; and there may be among them literary people just commencing their career; and they say, ' Would I could write so beautifully and so easily as she did!' It was not easily done. She did nothing easily, but in all this that we read she was an earnest worker; she was faithful, painstaking, careful of improving herself, up to the last moment of her life. Yesterday I looked into the drawer, and the last piece of manuscript she wrote turned up, and I said to Phœbe, ' That is copied;' and she said, ' No, that is Alice's writing.' It was so exceedingly plain it looked like print in large type, though she wrote a very wretched hand. But her sister told me that when she came to be so weak that she could not write much any longer, she began to practise like a little girl to learn to form all her letters anew. She worked to the very last not only with the brains, but the fingers.

" ' " When Phœbe wrote me last Sunday that she was alone and that Alice was gone, I could not help telling my people, and there was a sob heard that went through the congregation. It was from an old lady, a friend of hers, who often told me about her and spoke of her nobility of soul. Alice Cary once thought of making a cap for her, and she said, ' I will make a cap for Mrs. Brown;' but her fingers ached so and her arm became so tired she had to drop it; and the needle is sticking in that unfinished cap now, just as she left it. She would have finished it, but they had finished her own crown in glory, and she could not stay away from her coronation. And we will keep that cap with care; and I think Jesus will remind her of it and say, ' Child, inasmuch as you did it to one of the least, you did it unto me.' Should I speak for hours I could only tell you how I loved her. She came to me in the winter of my fortunes, when I had very few friends, and I loved her and will revere her memory forever—forever." '

" On the following Thursday I delivered an address at the dinner of the alumni of Dickinson College, held at Delmonico's, and on the following day I lectured at Port Chester, N. Y., and made a very pleasant visit to Summerfield House, at that time occupied by the family of Mr..Blackstock, who had married one of Summerfield's sisters. A single sister was still living with them. I saw many mementos of the wonderful young preacher who had pronounced his benediction on my earliest life.

" I find in my journal of Sunday, the 19th, the following entry: ' Commodore Vanderbilt and Daniel Drew sat in one pew.' I find also this entry on the Sunday following: ' Heard Dr. McCosh lecture. (Memorandum.—Never *hear* him again, but *read* him.)'

" The 2d of April was the first Sunday that sickness kept me from my pulpit since I commenced to preach in New York. During that week I suffered very much from my old catarrhal affection, which in the South had given me such distress in my eyes and ears.

" On the 20th of May my son, Dr. Frank M. Deems, left for Europe to pursue his studies in hospitals and colleges there.

"On the 27th of June in this year I affiliated with Crescent Lodge, No. 402, Freemasons, meeting then in Union Square. For years I enjoyed the association of the members of this lodge, acting all the time as their chaplain, except one year, when they elected me Senior Warden.

"In the summer of this year my family took board at a farm-house a mile and a half back from Eagle Rock on the Orange Mountain, in New Jersey. It was a simple, quiet, enjoyable place, not difficult of access, away from any place of fashion-able resort, where they lived in great quiet and had much en-joyment. Whenever it was practicable I spent a few days with them.

"On the 1st of August I heard of the death of Phœbe Cary. From the time of Alice's death she commenced to de-cline. Her health had been perfect; she scarcely knew any-thing of aches and pains; there was not a gray hair on her head; but she aged, grew pale and wrinkled and gray; every-thing lost power to interest her. A few Sundays after Alice died Phœbe was in church, and at the close of the service came to Mrs. Deems and said, 'I feel so lonely; let me sit with you in your pew during church service.' She came into my study and laid her head upon my shoulder and wept violently. This was so utterly unlike her that it almost unmanned me. I had been accustomed in the weakness brought on by my severe struggles to look to Phœbe for reserves of strength. I cheered her as well as I could, visiting her in her sick-room before her removal to Newport, and by all playfulness and badinage and every method I could command endeavored to assuage her grief and divert her attention; but it was a case of spiritual Siamese twinship: neither could survive the other. Their de-parture has left me in great loneliness; they have been to me two sweet, good, helpful sisters.

"The congregations of the church during the summer were very large. I had greatly feared that I should not be able to fill so large a church as that into which we had removed; but week after week has given me a pleasant disappointment, and Sunday after Sunday of the summer and fall of this year the congregations filled every available portion of the church.

"On the 26th of October I assisted at laying the corner-stone of the Franklin monument in Printing-house Square. On this occasion occurred a little incident which subsequently got into the papers and gave me a wide-spread reputation for punctuality. My watch had gone wrong and I had been delayed by a slow street-car; when I reached the Astor House I found I had but a minute and a half in which I must gain Mr. Greeley's office on the corner of Nassau and Spruce streets, and every approach seemed blocked. I forced my way as rapidly as I could up Nassau Street; but the company were in waiting. It wanted just one minute to twelve; the master of ceremonies said, 'We are all here except Dr. Deems, who is to offer the prayer.' Mr. Greeley said, 'He is a punctual man, but lives at some distance; give him a few minutes.' Dr. Irenæus Prime, the editor of the New York 'Observer,' said, 'Gentlemen, if he is not here at the precise moment we may as well send for the coroner.' As he said that the City Hall clock commenced to strike twelve and I opened the door: twelve was the appointed hour. I did not understand Dr. Prime's quizzical look when he turned to the company and said, 'Gentlemen, I told you so.'

"In November I left for Charlotte, N. C., to attend the session of the conference there, and I returned to my home bearing many and pleasant reminiscences of my Southern trip.

"My Christmas dinner was taken, with my whole family, at Commodore Vanderbilt's, and we had a most enjoyable time."

CHAPTER X

ON the last day of February, 1872, as we learn from Dr. Deems's journal, the first volume of his book, "Jesus," was on the publisher's counter. This was the consummation of three years of devoted toil, and is a monument to the scholarship, industry, genius, and spirituality of its author. In fact, it ranks as the greatest literary work of his life. It is a large octavo volume of over seven hundred pages, illustrated with an ideal head of Jesus after Guercino's "Ecce Homo," and sixty-five engravings on wood, drawn by the celebrated traveler-artist, A. L. Rawson. In the preface to the first edition Dr. Deems disclaimed the idea that he was writing a life of *Christ*, and declared his work to be the *facts* in the life of the person *Jesus*. He closes the last chapter with this language:

"Who is this Jesus?

"I have told his story as simply and conscientiously as possible, and have honestly endeavored to apprehend and to represent the consciousness of Jesus at each moment of his career. The work of the historian is completed. Each reader has now the responsibility of saying who he is. All agree that he was a man. The finest intellects of eighteen centuries have believed that he was the greatest and best man that ever lived. All who have so believed have become better men therefor. We have seen that he never performed an act or spoke a word

251

which would have been unbecoming in the Creator of the universe if the Creator should ever clothe himself with human flesh. Millions of men—kings and poets and historians and philosophers and busy merchants and rude mechanics and purest women and simple children—have believed that he is God. And all who have devoutly believed this and lived by this as a truth have become exemplary for all that is beautiful in holiness.

"What is he who can so live and so die as to produce such intellectual and moral results?

"Reader, you must answer."

The book received glowing encomiums from the press both in America and Europe. Professor Francis W. Upham, author of "The Wise Men" and "Thoughts on the Holy Gospels," said that he spent a winter of retirement in Europe in reading all the lives of Jesus that had ever been published in the English language, and that, in his opinion, the work by Dr. Deems outranks them all; and the late Dr. Henry Smith, of the Union Theological Seminary, used to speak of Dr. Deems's volume "Jesus" as "that great book."

This undertaking brought to completion, he turned his attention more closely to his church work, raising an endowment fund whose interest should annually pay to the Sailors' Snug Harbor Association the rent for the ground on which the Church of the Strangers stands.

Dr. Deems took no summer vacations. The name and nature of his work, and the temperament of the man, precluded that indulgence. Yet he never censured his brother ministers who did take a season of rest in summer, although he always contended that there was something grievously wrong somewhere when multitudes of Christian pulpits in New York were silent at a season of the year when unusual numbers of visitors were in the city and Satan unusually active. Dr. Deems's friends believe that he shortened his life by his incessant toil. During 1872 his family again sought a retreat from the city on Orange Mountain, where they were visited between Sundays by the busy pastor, who ever brought gladness with him, and who entered into the out-of-door games and recreations with that zest and push which made him so successful in his serious undertakings.

In the fall of 1872, at the Church of the Strangers, Dr. Deems married his elder daughter, Minnie, to Mr. Marion J. Verdery, of Augusta, Ga. Of another interesting incident of his life during the closing months of this year he thus writes in his journal under date of October 22d: "Spent the day on an excursion up the Hudson River with the English historian, Mr. Froude, and the philanthropist, Miss Emily Faithful. Delightful time! At night was at Dr. John G. Holland's at a reception given to George MacDonald, the novelist. A great crowd. Called in at Crescent Lodge."

Sometime during 1873 Dr. Deems was enabled to use his influence to assist in the founding of a noble institution of learning in the South. The next best thing to doing something great and praiseworthy one's self is to get somebody else who can to do it. Dr. Deems, as we have seen, was always deeply interested in the cause of education; also he loved the South. He had won the complete confidence of the elder Cornelius Vanderbilt, and, aware that efforts were on foot to establish a college in Tennessee under the auspices of the Methodist Episcopal Church, South, Dr. Deems contributed his full share toward the influences which led Commodore Vanderbilt to found Vanderbilt University at Nashville, Tenn. To this great institution Mr. Vanderbilt gave one million dollars.

It was in the spring of 1873 that Dr. Deems bought and moved into the house No. 429 West Twenty-second Street, where he continued to reside for fifteen years. At last he was able to have that which up to this time his soul had yearned for in vain, a comfortable and permanent home. It is true that it was over a mile from his church, but this fact he considered an advantage, as it would make his home a retreat. His study was in the church, where he attended to all his business. The house was kept as free as possible from all reminders of his regular work, that it might afford him an asylum from his flood of cares. With all the intensity of his nature he enjoyed his home and his family while living on Twenty-second Street.

It would be impossible to tell what Dr. Deems was in his home in more truthful or more eloquent language than that used by his son-in-law, Mr. Marion J. Verdery, when, in the closing address at Dr. Deems's funeral, in 1893, he said, among other things:

"Out in the busy world, where he spent so much of his life, he was the incarnation of activity and industry. Dashing at work with an energy suggestive of military genius, he accomplished more in a day than many men do in a week. Work was not second but first nature to him. I do not believe he ever wilfully wasted an hour in his life. He counted time by seconds, and contended that every tick of a man's watch meant a breath of his life, and therefore was precious. This marvelous energy, illumined by the highest order of intellectuality, and directed by a spirit wholly consecrated to the service of God, inspired his life of vast usefulness and made Dr. Deems the great and good man that he was. Thus you all knew him out in the world!

"At home, oh, what a sweet privilege to have known him there! I cannot trust myself to talk much about it. Words seem too harsh to wrap our tenderest thoughts in. If I could show you through my heart's eyes a thousand pictures that hang on memory's wall, and let them be my hearthstone tribute, love would be content with the offering, and the sweetness of home be idealized.

"He never came in from work too tired to be tender. He

never became so engrossed by his interest in outside affairs that he lost relish for domestic affiliations. His wit was never so dulled by use in public places that it ceased to sparkle in the family circle. His humor did not exhaust itself in great crowds with the hope of applause; he made his rarest fun and told his best stories at the fireside.

"When serious he delighted to fold us all in his abiding love and enrich us with his blessings. When joyous he suffused the whole house with the sunshine of his soul and made his gladness contagious.

"With his grandchildren he was playfellow, even after he wrote 'My Septuagint'; with his children he was always boon companion; and to his sweetheart bride of fifty years he was courtly knight and loyal lover down to their golden wedding-day.

"His whole life was a love-letter to mankind, with its sweetest, tenderest, and holiest passages dedicated to his family."

At this time Dr. Deems was living in the fullness of his physical, intellectual, and spiritual vigor. Much as he loved his home, he almost literally lived the last twenty years of his life in public. Few men in New York were doing as many different things, and doing them as well, as he. We need not tax the reader with details; much must be left unsaid; but the language of the Apostle Paul was applicable to Dr. Deems, "in labors more abundant." Nothing, however, was allowed to detract from his distinctive work for Christ and souls. At the February communion in 1874 as many persons were added to the Church of the Strangers as composed the whole congregation when the pastor preached his first sermon in the chapel of the university. The names of over five hundred communicants were on the church roll.

For the first time in his New York pastorate Dr. Deems, yielding to the demands of his overtaxed body and mind and the urgent advice of his church and family, on January 5, 1875, went to Florida, where he spent four weeks with congenial people and under the restful influences of the balmy air and historic and romantic associations of old St. Augustine.

On his return from the South his people gave him a royal welcome in the church, which was decorated and thronged with people. The Rev. Dr. R. S. Moran, who had supplied the pulpit in Dr. Deems's absence, made the address of welcome in a most happy strain. One who was present says:

"The response of Dr. Deems was equally felicitous. He commenced by saying, 'I am glad I am home.' (Applause.) A voice in the audience exclaimed, 'So are we!' This brought down the house. The doctor then proceeded somewhat in the following terms: 'It is really worth going away to be so welcomed back. If I had known that it was so good a thing to be so received I should have gone oftener. But perhaps if I had my reception would have been less enthusiastic. I knew you were to meet me to-night, but such a demonstration of affection surely had not entered my mind. This really looks like a wedding scene, and I feel as if I were a party to a bridal with the dear Church of the Strangers.

"'It is not the least element in the pleasure to-night that these nuptials should have for officiating priest my excellent friend, the Rev. Dr. Moran. One of the many ways in which you have shown me kindness is that quick manner you have of immediately taking any friend of mine to be your friend; and it is very gratifying to me that you have so keenly appreciated the admirable and devoted services of my dear brother in my absence. But never did I hear officiating parson talk to any party as Dr. Moran has talked to me. I do not know how to be equal with him. But now and here I give him warning that if ever a good providence afford me an opportunity of marrying him to a church or to a woman, I will pay him with interest.' (Applause.)

"Dr. Deems continued: 'It is not needful that I tell you that I love this church. Our relations are peculiar. Perhaps nothing similar exists in this city. I did not come to you; you did not call me. You had no organization. You did not offer me a salary and ask me to a church. You had no existence originally. I began to preach, and you came to me, each one, so that I know your church-membership from the beginning. You did not furnish me a church building. God's good providence gave me the sweet privilege of doing that for you. This makes our relations peculiar. It makes the burden harder for me and gives me more need of love. It would be too bad to stay in this church without affection for the pastor, because you cannot send him away.

"'But sometime I shall go away to come back no more. I shall go to the Father's house. I shall go before many of you. I am older than a majority of the members of this church. As I have stood at the door of this church and welcomed you, until the little church has grown to be one of the greatest congregations in the city, so may I stand beside the Saviour at the gates when you enter after me, and to each have the blessed privilege of exclaiming, in the words of the legend which you have spread in evergreens across the chapel to-night, "Welcome home, welcome home!"'

"After another song by the children the pastor was conducted to the Sunday-school room, whither he was followed by the people, all eager to clasp his hand. This room was also hung with evergreens and garnished with flowers.

"To render the entertainment more social, a bountiful collation was provided, and words of cheer were exchanged between sips of fragrant coffee. All were happy. Hand-shaking and good-wishing were general."

On Monday, October 4, 1875, Dr. Deems delivered the opening address at the dedication and inauguration of Vanderbilt University, commenting upon which the Nashville "American" said at the time:

"Probably no one feature incident to the inauguration of

Vanderbilt University attracted more attention than the masterly address delivered by the Rev. Dr. Deems, of New York, a full report of which is published elsewhere. Elaborate in conception and detail, it treats of the subjects discussed in a way to claim the closest attention throughout. The burden of the address bears on the relations between science and religion, and many a subtle thrust is given by the learned speaker at those he aptly terms weak religionists and weak scientists. There is no real conflict, he contends, between science and religion. It is only guesses on both sides which collide, and the result is an explosion of bubbles, not bombs. We do not know of any more valuable contribution to the current discussion on one of the profoundest of topics than the present address—a production which cannot fail to elicit the most favorable comment in all quarters and add no little to the already great fame of its distinguished author."

At the close of this address the speaker was handed a telegram from the generous founder of the university, which he read to the audience: "Peace and good will to all men." With characteristic aptness and impressiveness, Dr. Deems turned, and, looking toward a full-length portrait of the commodore, with deep feeling replied, "'Cornelius, thy prayer is heard, and thine alms are had in remembrance in the sight of God.'" The dramatic interest of this scene can be imagined better than described. Dr. Deems ever took a profound and practical interest in Vanderbilt University, where, on the occasions of his subsequent visits, he was uniformly given a most hearty welcome.

From His Journal

"December 4th [1875]. This is my fifty-fifth birthday. I have finished another year. I reconsecrate myself to the work of the ministry of our Lord Jesus Christ, greatly humbled at the little I have already accomplished."

To the North Carolina Annual Conference of the Methodist Episcopal Church, South, which met at Wilmington, December 1, 1875, Dr. Deems sent the following letter:

" CHURCH OF THE STRANGERS,
" NEW YORK, November 29, 1875.

" *To Bishop McTyeire.*

"REV. AND DEAR BROTHER: Thirty-four years ago I became a member of the North Carolina Conference. In the more than a third of a century which has elapsed, until last year I never missed a session and never failed to be present at the opening, except in a solitary instance, when I was unavoidably detained on the road. During that time I have served the conference and the church as circuit-rider, stationed preacher, presiding elder, professor, secretary of the conference, delegate to the General Conference, and president of the Annual Conference. I have never asked for any office, appointment, or accommodation, but have gone, at any pecuniary, personal, and domestic sacrifice, wherever and whenever sent.

" In the providence of God, without my own seeking, I am the pastor of the Church of the Strangers, an evangelical independent church in this city. The history of my connection with it is well known to many. I came to New York in 1865 to attend to certain Southern interests, supporting myself and family by literary labor while engaged in the effort. On account of the prejudices naturally engendered by the then recent Civil War that project failed, and I was ready to return to North Carolina or accept the presidency of a Southern college then tendered me. The bishops of the Southern Methodist Church unanimously recommended me to stay in New York and take care of a congregation which had begun to gather around me, composed mostly of strangers of different denominations. That recommendation was communicated to me by Bishop Pierce, and you, Bishop McTyeire, wrote me, as it were, prophetically, 'You went to New York for one purpose: our God is keeping you there for another.' The congregation grew and consolidated into a church, and every month that church has grown, until now it is regarded by many as one of the most important centers of religious influence in America. The Southern Methodist Church has appointed me to this pastorate from year to year, and the Church of the Strangers, although it is independent and a great majority of the members have never been Methodists, has not been unwilling to receive me under that appointment.

"For several reasons I have not sought to make any altera-tion in my ecclesiastical status. I am not given to change, but cling to old friends and old associations. Moreover, a num-ber of leading laymen and ministers of the Southern Methodist Church have urged me to continue my membership therein. Furthermore, I supposed it was the unanimous wish of the bishops that I should remain; and I was doing a work which honored the church and brought no burden to it. Since I have been pastor here I have not drawn one dollar, so far as I know, from the Southern Methodist Church, or any member thereof, for the support of the Church of the Strangers, while my pastorate in this church—I write what is notorious—has been the providential occasion of thousands upon thousands of dollars being sent not only to Southern Methodists and their institutions, but also to other evangelical churches in the South.

"Perhaps it was in view of all these things that the General Conference of 1870 passed a resolution covering any case like mine that might arise. That resolution was rescinded by the General Conference in 1874 and another in a modified form was adopted. I have this to say: that I had nothing to do, by request, suggestion, or otherwise, with any of these proceed-ings; I have never desired any action to be taken by the An-nual or General Conference exceptionally in my favor.

"Notwithstanding all this, there are members of the North

Carolina Conference who seem to believe that I ought to abandon the Church of the Strangers or withdraw from the conference. Their agitation of the case subjects me to the constant annoyance of being misapprehended by good men and misrepresented by others.

" I believe I am as much called of God to the office of pastor of the Church of the Strangers as you can believe that you are called to the office of bishop in the Southern Methodist Church. It seems to me that I should as much be leaving the lead of the Master in quitting my present work as you could think that you would be abandoning your line of duty by returning to *your* Annual Conference.

" So long as I felt that the North Carolina Conference desired to retain me I made no motion to withdraw. In the membership of that conference I expected to close at once my ministry and my life. But I do not believe that the Master desires me to stand in a position in which I am made by others an occasion of concern to the authorities of the church, and of trouble to the brethren who love me, simply that I may indulge one of my sentiments, however excellent that sentiment may be. In view of all these things, through you I respectfully ask the conference to grant me a location. I should have done this in person if the session of the conference had not fallen at a time when the temporal and spiritual interests of the church render my presence here more than usually needed.

" This motion on my part is made without consultation with any member of the North Carolina Conference or any officers of the Church of the Strangers. It is done in the fear of God and in charity toward all my brethren of the North Carolina Conference. I love North Carolina. The most of my public ministry was in that State. All my children were born there. My two dead sons lie in its soil; my first-born, my young hero-martyr, sleeps in the cemetery in Wilmington. God has given me many spiritual children out of the population of North

Carolina. They will bear me witness that by the space of twenty-four years I preached the gospel from town to town and from house to house, coveting no man's silver or gold, but generally partly and sometimes wholly maintaining myself, that I might serve the people in the ministry of the Word. I left the State no richer than I was when I entered it, except in memories and in friends. My clerical brethren will bear me witness that I have belonged to no clique, have opposed no measure captiously, and set myself against no good man for his injury. · At the same time I have not through self-seeking failed to oppose frankly every measure which I believed to be hurtful to the church and every man whom I regarded as an ecclesiastical demagogue.

"It is a comfort to know that I have enjoyed the affection and confidence of the most able and beloved of the ministers, the Brocks, the Leighs, the Bumpasses, the Doubs, the Nicholsons, the Pells, the Reids, the Barringers, and others now in glory, as well as those living who deserve to be named in the same category. If, through want of thought on my part or any frailty of my temper or character, I have given a moment's pain to any brother, I most humbly beg that he will treat it as we all pray the Lord Jesus to treat all our sins.

"And now, desiring this letter to be read in open conference, I pray that the Head of the church may pour upon you and all other officers, ministers, and members of the Southern Methodist Church the abundant blessing of his heavenly grace. Pray for me, that I may finish my course with joy and this ministry which I have received of our Lord Jesus Christ.

"Affectionately and faithfully your brother,

"CHARLES F. DEEMS."

After fraternal remarks by Bishop H. N. McTyeire, the presiding bishop, and other members of the conference, Dr. Deems was by vote "located" at the Church of the Strangers in New York City, and a committee was appointed to draft appropriate resolutions.

On the fifth day of the session the committee reported as follows, and their report was adopted:

"WHEREAS, Dr. Deems, who has been for thirty-four years a member of the North Carolina Conference (believing it to be his duty), has asked for and has been granted a location; and WHEREAS, He has been eminently useful and successful during his connection with our conference, in his eloquent pulpit ministrations, in his ardent work as a competent instructor in our institutions of learning, and in wielding his vast influence over the public mind to promote the cause of Christ; therefore

"*Resolved*, That we can but deplore the act that severs him from us; but as, in the providence of God, his lot is cast in a field of labor where we believe his brilliant talents and active energy will accomplish grander results for the good of souls, we acquiesce in his decision.

"*Resolved*, That we duly appreciate his valuable services while among us, and pray that the benedictions of the great Head of the church may be upon him in his present important and inviting field of labor.

"Respectfully submitted,
"W. H. BOBBITT,
"J. H. WHEELER,
"IRA T. WYCHE."

Dr. Deems, by this action of the North Carolina Conference and by not uniting with any Quarterly Conference or church in the North, practically suffered his connection with the Methodist Episcopal Church, South, to lapse, and technically was not a member of any church or denomination. Practically he was a member of the Church of the Strangers, somewhat as a pastor of a Congregational church is at the same time a member of that church. And now, however anomalous his ecclesiastical position might be and seem, it was in reality very clear and simple. He was left free to be the pastor of the Church of the Strangers as long as he pleased, and as such was responsible to God and to public opinion; but answerable to no ecclesiastical body on earth except his own congregation, and to them he was responsible only to a limited extent. If his people did not like him or his doctrine they could argue the matter with him, and if that did not restore harmony they could leave him and the church, and he would have had empty seats.

It was indeed an exceptional position which Dr. Deems held; but the reader of the Preface of this volume will remember that therein it was claimed that Dr. Deems's character and career were exceptional, and that fact was given as one of the reasons for the publication of this memoir. How well he discharged his peculiar duties and how little he abused his unlimited power, let the history of that independent body of Christians answer. The concord that reigned among its heterogeneous elements and the harmony of its practical working are all tributes to and proofs of his ability, his rectitude, and his conscientious fidelity to Christ and the gospel.

And this concord between pastor and people, and fruitful activity of both people and preacher, were kept up to the very end, as appears from Dr. Deems's report to the monthly meeting of the church held in December, 1892, the month near whose close he was stricken down. That report concludes as follows:

"During the year I have delivered 184 discourses, administered the sacrament of the Lord's Supper 11 times, celebrated the rite of matrimony 36 times, baptized 22 persons, attended the funerals of 19 persons, and paid 652 visits. During the year we have added 55 members; on confession of faith, 40, by letter, 15.

"There have been received into the church during the past twenty-five years 1809 persons; 940 on confession of faith and 869 by letter. There have been taken from the roll by removals, death, etc., 1264. Total on roll at close of 1892, 545.

"Affectionately and faithfully your pastor,

"CHARLES F. DEEMS."

Early in 1876, having to go to Richmond, Va., to lecture, and to Weldon, N. C., to dedicate a church, he went on farther South to the home of his daughter, Mrs. Marion J. Verdery, in Augusta, Ga. This entry is in his journal for Tuesday, the 15th of February: "With my dear daughter and her precious babe, whom I now see for the first time." He remained in Augusta eight days, and described the visit as "a little job of dry-nursing." He spent the most of the time with his new grandchild, who became an endeared pet.

On the 22d he baptized his baby granddaughter and on the 23d started for New York. Upon reaching home he found the Moody and Sankey meetings in full operation. Occasionally he took part in them, but he had so much pastoral work that he could not be a constant attendant. His estimate of these "evangelistic" exercises, as they were called, was not quite so high as that of some of the other New York clergy. He thought that in some directions they did good in stimulating the church-members, but that they did very little toward reaching "outsiders." He also thought that they had a dissipating effect upon the members of the church, creating in them roving habits and making them so used to excitement that it required a long time after the evangelists left to bring these people into regular working order in their own churches. He did not, however, feel himself at liberty to utter any opposition to the work. It might be of God and his judgment might be at fault, so he would not oppose it; but he never entered into it very heartily.

Before Dr. Deems went South Mr. Frank Leslie, the well-known publisher of a number of periodicals, had sent for him to consult him in regard to the publication of a "Sunday Magazine" somewhat on the basis of an English periodical bearing that name, and with such modifications as Dr. Deems's experience would give to it in adapting it especially to the American religious public. At first the proposition did not strike the doctor as desirable. Although he saw in it a vast field of constantly increasing usefulness, he was afraid that he should not be able to sustain the magazine and discharge his church duties in a befitting manner. Nevertheless he consented to take into consideration the proposition which Mr. Leslie made.

He saw certain objections to undertaking this work, and others of more or less weight were suggested to him. But, on the other hand, he saw so many ways in which the "Sunday Magazine" might be used for the good of men and the glory of God that he finally concluded to take the post of its editor, but to take it on his own terms. These he proposed to Mr. Leslie, supposing them so stringent that that gentleman would perhaps retire. But he did not; on the contrary, he gave the doctor the complete control, agreed to supply him all assistance needful to keep the periodical from interfering with his pastoral work, and also to improve the tone of his issues. In accordance with this the most offensive, because it was the most sensational, of Mr. Leslie's periodicals was drawn from his list of publications and suppressed. Improvements began to be made in every department, and Dr. Deems fell to work to prepare for the new "Sunday Magazine," which, owing to several causes, did not appear until the beginning of the next year, although the bargain had been made on the 16th of March, 1876.

Commodore Vanderbilt had been growing feebler in health since the previous Thanksgiving day, when he took a cold while riding in Central Park. He had been only a few times to his office after that day. On the 22d of April Dr. Deems had a talk with the commodore in regard to the founding of some public institution in this city, which should be extended and continued in its beneficence, and thus be the consecration of a portion of his property to the Lord. The commodore requested Dr. Deems to draw up a plan for such an institution which should require at least a half-million of dollars. With his usual alertness, he at once fell to work, thinking over the plan on Saturday night and giving Monday and Tuesday to writing out a rough draft. The commodore had been confined to his house, but not to his bed, for some weeks. On Wednesday morning, April 26th, Dr. Deems had his plan ready, waited on his old friend with it, and found him in bed in great pain and not able to consider anything. His heart fell. He was afraid that it was too late. As the commodore had done so handsome a thing for the South, he was very anxious that he should do some very great act of beneficence which would make his name a precious savor also in the North. Nothing seemed to Dr. Deems so poetical and beautiful as that the commodore should erect, on some conspicuous and happy site, an institution to care for those who had become disabled in railroad service; and yet there seemed to him almost insurmountable difficulties in making this a diffusive benevolence.

For more than eight months the commodore was confined to his bed, and from the 26th of April, 1876, to the 4th of January, 1877, Dr. Deems visited him every day except eight. Those eight days were divided between three visits to the country. The commodore would not let him leave his side, often keeping him for hours. His sufferings were prodigious, and Dr. Deems represented himself as being often thrown into profuse perspiration by simply witnessing the agony of the great sufferer. Through all those months the attachment between the two men increased. The pastor was devoted to his parishioner, and the parishioner grew more and more to love his pastor. Sometimes he would send for him, and when he arrived would say to him with tears, "Doctor, I have sent for you to tell you how I love you." In his funeral sermon and in other publications Dr. Deems has set forth his estimate of the character of Commodore Vanderbilt. The two men had the greatest possible regard for each other.

All the summer long Dr. Deems remained in the city. He had several important engagements which he was compelled to cancel because of Commodore Vanderbilt's illness. One was to deliver an address at Emory and Henry College, Virginia, and another to repeat his lecture on "The Bible and Science" at the Chautauqua Assembly in the western part of New York. But he had learned to submit to what seemed to be the demands of Providence.

Several times during this season it was supposed that Commodore Vanderbilt would die, and yet he rallied marvelously. Just after one of these spells he insisted that Dr. Deems should go to the Centennial Exposition, which he did, spending parts of three days in Philadelphia at the great exposition in company with Mrs. Deems and a few friends.

On the 22d of October Dr. Deems was one of the pall-bearers at the funeral of his old preceptor, the Rev. Dr. Durbin, to whom he was much attached, and of whom he has spoken in his autobiographical sketch as one of his teachers at Dickinson College.

On the 1st of December he took part in the third anniversary of the First Reformed Episcopal Church, of which the Rev. Dr. Sabine was pastor. He had always taken a great interest in this new ecclesiastical movement, because he recollected that he would have entered the ministry of the Protestant Episcopal Church but for the dogma of apostolic succession. He was also interested in it because it had been set on foot by Bishop George D. Cummins, who had been his college-mate and personal friend through many years.

On the 4th of December he made this record in his journal: "Entered upon my fifty-seventh year." He was not given to recording sentimental reflections. He closed one year of his life and entered upon another with as much cheerfulness as though there were no end to life, and with such elasticity as if he had but one more year to work.

CHAPTER XI

INCREASING ACTIVITY, 1877–79

" Oh, to be ready, ready,
    Yielding my Saviour my all,
And waiting with loving patience
    For the Master's gracious call!
Soothing the poor in their sorrow,
    Helping the rich in their woe,
Seeking to find new treasures
    On suffering saints to bestow.

" Oh, to be ready, ready,
    Hidden from every delight,
And hearing no voices of praises,
    While toiling alone in the night!
Lonely, unmourned, and forsaken,
    And cast from the hearts of all men,
Walking the fiery furnace
    Or sleeping with beasts in their den.

" Oh, to be ready, ready,
    Following the lead of my Lord,
While armed with salvation's helmet
    And the Spirit's flaming sword!
Meeting the foe with high courage
    And fighting the good fight of faith;
Shouting in triumph while dying,
    And soaring to life out of death."

A GREAT snow wrapped the city in a thick white mantle on January 1, 1877. From his journal we learn that on this date Dr. Deems received visitors most of the day, and that he also "composed the hymn, 'Oh, to be ready!'" He appears to have felt the chill of death in the air.

From His Journal

"January 4th. Commodore Vanderbilt died this morning at 10:51."
"January 7th, Sunday. Commodore Vanderbilt's obsequies at the Church of the Strangers."
"January 8th. Oh, how lonely without the commodore!"

On the day of Commodore Vanderbilt's death Dr. Deems reached the bedside of his dying friend at nine o'clock in the morning, where he found gathered the family and four physicians, and where he remained until the end. The commodore to the last was conscious and spoke to his loved ones calm words of parting. His wife's sister, Mrs. Robert L. Crawford, led the little group in singing his favorite hymns, "Nearer, my God, to thee," "Show pity, Lord," and "Come, ye sinners, poor and needy." With a bright countenance falteringly he joined in the singing. He asked Dr. Deems to pray, and tried to follow the prayer and repeat the benediction. At the close of the prayer he took Dr. Deems's hand and said, "That's a good prayer. I shall never give up trust in Jesus; how could I let that go!" At 10:51 A.M., peacefully and apparently painlessly, the commodore fell asleep.

Sunday morning, January 7th, Dr. Deems conducted the funeral services for his faithful friend at the Church of the Strangers, whose capacity was unequal to holding the multitudes who sought entrance. In accordance with the expressed wishes of Mr. Vanderbilt, these services were marked by simplicity.

In the funeral address Dr. Deems said, among other things:
"My brethren, it would seem to be a happy thing that the

custom of the pastor of this church at funerals should be in such perfect accord with the explicit wishes of our deceased friend. It is almost never appropriate to speak about a dead man at his obsequies. No man would desire to allude to any of his human frailties and faults, and no man can make the dead man's friends love him more than they do when they surround his remains. And so when he charged that at his funeral not many words should be said, and that those words should be said deliberately, and that there should be no attempt to set forth any supposed virtue he might possess, the request was in accordance with my own feelings. . . .

" I think it will be a soft pillow for my dying hour that I have one remembrance—which I may venture to state even here—of our beloved friend. One day he took my hand and looked me in the face; the tears started to his eyes and he said, ' Dear doctor, you never crowded your religion on me, but you have been faithful to me.' ' Yes,' I said, ' commodore, I have held back nothing of the counsel of God which I thought needful to say to you for your salvation.' And shall I here, in the presence of this people and in the presence of his precious remains, fail to be faithful to his memory and to you? What gave him his comfort at last? That there was not a civilized nation on the face of the earth that did not know his name? That there was not a king or an emperor or other ruler of men upon earth that did not know his name? That the luster of his deeds shone like sunlight among the nations? What gave him his comfort at the last? That he could count up millions to be left to his children? No! It was this: that Jesus Christ, by the grace of God, had tasted death for him; that there was in the Godhead not simply his Creator, but his Redeemer, and that, coming as a little child, he could lay his head in the lap of Jesus and feel that he had a Saviour there. . . .

" There were two things our beloved friend lacked. One

was the advantages of early scholastic culture; another was intimate religious associations through his middle life and the main part of his career; and those two wants of his life, as he has solemnly said to me, were the only great regrets he had. But remember that, while Cornelius Vanderbilt had not the advantages of the schools, that great lack was compensated for in a large measure by the extraordinary intellectual endowments with which God had gifted him. And then, and above all, remember this: that what saved him was the fact that never in any part of his life did he for one single instant doubt that this sacred Book was the Word of God and the rule of faith and practice. That was his sheet-anchor, and his love for his mother was his sheet-cable. I must now say what he charged me to say if ever I spoke of him in public: 'Say to all men that you did not have the slightest influence in the world in persuading me to believe in the Bible; that you could not, nor all the angels or ministers; for I have never had a minute when I did not believe it was the Word of God, whether I kept it or not.' Have you that faith? If he had gone through life without that faith and come to this great battle, this eight months' campaign, fighting for life,—fighting on the outskirts, fighting in the intrenchments, fighting in the citadel to the last,—if he had come without that wonderful faith in the Word of God, who could have helped him? . . .

" If one grain of love is worth ten thousand tons of admiration, then Cornelius Vanderbilt died rich. This I say as one who, with the solicitude of a pastor and a friend, watched all his spiritual motions through the last year of his life, and say it as if he were alive and that lid were open and he had those eagle eyes turned on me: I will say I believe that this man at the last had true repentance toward God, had simple, child-like faith in the Lord Jesus Christ as his personal and divine Saviour, and did yield himself to the operations of the Holy Ghost; and that, having thus yielded, and in such repentance, in such faith, and in such submission died, we may confidently trust that he who is able to save to the uttermost did fulfil his promises to our beloved friend, and that he is numbered with the saints in glory everlasting. Let us not attach undue value to the things of this world, but let us not underrate ourselves. That man lying there never owned one single dime; he never possessed one single foot of ground in his own right. He was bound to hold these things as a steward of God. That is the state of the case with us, and we must give an account at the last, as he has gone to render his account of his stewardship, to the only One who has a right to judge him, Jesus Christ our Lord." *

Shadowed though its opening was for Dr. Deems, the year 1877 was one full of labors in the pulpit, the pastorate, on the platform, and in the editor's chair as he wrought on the "Sunday Magazine." Not the least interesting experiences of the year were his visits to the University of North Carolina, at Chapel Hill, and Randolph-Macon College, at Boydton, Va. These visits occurred in June. At the former he preached the baccalaureate sermon, on Acts xxvi. 25, while at the latter he delivered the annual address before the two literary societies. On Thursday, June 7th, the University of North Carolina conferred on Dr. Deems the honorary degree of LL.D., which he not unsuccessfully strove to wear with becoming grace and dignity.

From His Journal

"September 26th. Mrs. Deems finished reading 'Macaulay's Life' after prayer-meeting. What a fortunate and superb career! He died only two years older than I am now. How much more work of a certain kind he accomplished! Such

* The whole of this address and Dr. Deems's prayer on this occasion may be found in the "Metropolitan Pulpit," vol. i., p. 65 (New York: Funk & Wagnalls Co.).

men make the rest of us seem small. It is so sad to close such a book; we came to feel as if the man were our personal friend." "October 23d. Went to Asbury, N. J. Had not been there for thirty-two years. Married there. Mrs. Deems with me. Stayed with Mr. McElrath, who had been Horace Greeley's partner."

A Letter from Dr. Deems

"NOLO EPISCOPARI

"NEW YORK, February 14, 1878.
"*Rev. J. J. Lafferty.*

"DEAR BROTHER: In the 'Richmond Christian Advocate' I see that Judge Simmons has mentioned my name in the 'Central Methodist' among the names of three persons who might, in his opinion, be elected bishops by the next General Conference of the Methodist Episcopal Church, South. It is a gratifying compliment to be mentioned in such a connection, but, of course, I am out of the question. The providence of God seems to have assigned me my diocese. It fills my hands and head and heart and time. It is one in which I have probably been able to do more for all branches of the church than if I had been a bishop in any one of them. The Southern Methodist Church has been singularly happy in the choice of its chief pastors, all of whom are my personal friends; and I trust that grace may be vouchsafed to save the General Conference from ever electing any man who, for selfish reasons, desires and seeks the office.

"Affectionately and faithfully yours,
"CHARLES F. DEEMS."

From His Autobiographical Notes for 1878

"In February of this year I had a visit from Bishop Pierce, of Georgia, who had been invited to preach a sermon on the anniversary of the leading Methodist church in Newark, N. J., in whose dedication he had taken part many years ago. I invited him to come to New York and remain with us as long as agreeable to himself. His health was poor. My family became very much attached to him.

"On the 6th of March I took recess from labor and went South with Mrs. Deems. We stopped in Baltimore and were the guests of our beloved cousin, Mrs. Martha A. Flack. The Baltimore Conference of the Methodist Episcopal Church, South, was in session. On Thursday I addressed the conference, and on Sunday, by the request of Bishop McTyeire, I preached the sermon at the ordination of the elders and assisted the bishop in the ordination of the deacons. Three days of the succeeding week were spent amid the hospitalities of our excellent friends, the Faisons, in North Carolina, and on Saturday, the 16th, we reached Charleston. Arriving early in the morning we found Bishop Wightman awaiting us. He had written insisting that I should be his guest. We remained until the following Tuesday, and by special request I preached in the Trinity Methodist Episcopal Church. We were very much interested in Charleston, and this was the first visit my wife had ever made to this noble old city. Bishop Wightman and Mr. George W. Williams and their wives were indefatigable in showing us attentions. I was particularly interested in the orphanage, in the Home for Confederate Widows, and in the seminary for young ladies, of which Miss Kelly was principal.

"From Charleston we went to Florida, spending most of the time in St. Augustine, where we met our dear friend, Mrs. Noble. There is not much to record of this quiet old town, which I had visited before. It is a most attractive place to me. It would be delightful if I could live there all winter. I have very little to record of this visitation. We went on the water and to all the surrounding places of interest, and filled up our leisure time with Miss Phelps's new book, 'Avis,' which I exceedingly disliked on account of its morale.

"After St. Augustine we made the tour of the Oklawaha, whose wonderfully weird scenery by night was quite a novel enchantment. We had the misfortune to come upon the Silver Spring in a shower of rain; but nevertheless it was a very interesting sight. On the 6th of April, on our return, we reached Augusta, where, with our daughter, her husband, and her precious babe, we spent more than a week—a delightful week, in which the babe grew more and more into my heart.

"On the 18th of April we reached New York, having spent a day with our friends in Goldsboro, N. C. On this trip I had preached in St. Paul's Methodist Church in Baltimore, in Trinity Methodist Church in Charleston, in the Presbyterian church in St. Augustine, and in the First Presbyterian Church and St. John's Methodist Church in Augusta. This Southern trip, which I took for rest and to relieve me from the great pressure of my work, did not prove very helpful to me. It seemed to develop the rheumatism, which I suppose I inherit from my father. I had occasional slight visitations of this malady up to June, when I went to Emory and Henry College to deliver the address before the two literary societies. On my way thither my suffering increased. I suffered very greatly while there, but was very much interested in the college and enjoyed the kind attention of President Wiley.

"On my way I stopped a day in Lynchburg especially to see my old friend, the Rev. John Bayley, who had been the minister in Randolph-Macon circuit when I was professor in college. I was interested also in seeing this beautiful country in a visit to Abingdon, where the Martha Washington College is situated, and to Saltville and Glade Springs, where I received the kindest attentions. I bore up under my pain until I could reach home, but the strain upon me and the effort in preaching two sermons upon my return prostrated me, and during the succeeding week I gave up and was under medical treatment. Nevertheless on the following Sunday I was at my post, and although suffering more or less during the summer I fulfilled all my public duties, among them a sermon and an address before the great Chautauqua Assembly.

"In the summer of this year I received a letter inviting me to become a member of the Victoria Institute, which is the philosophical society of Great Britain, of which the Earl of Shaftesbury is president. Nothing else of special note occurred until the 18th of December, when I united my son, Dr. Frank M. Deems, in matrimony with Miss Grace Brotherton, by which I believe he got from the Lord a good wife and I an excellent daughter. The year of the church closed in great peace and harmony. All our financial obligations were met, an admirable board of officers was elected, and while, owing to the fluctuation of the New York population, many had left us, we closed the year with more upon our roll than we had when we began."

Dr. Deems's pulpit and pastoral work and his editorial labors on the "Sunday Magazine" were the objects of unremitting attention and faithful efforts throughout the year 1879. The only recreation he indulged in, if recreation it may be called, consisted in several visits to various parts of the land to preach, lecture, or make addresses.

The fact that he did not break down under labors to which an apparently stronger man would have succumbed was due largely to his talent for sleep and his observance of Saturday as his physical Sabbath.

In an article in the "Homiletic Review" for October, 1889, while giving his views on the subject of "Ministers Breaking Down in Health," Dr. Deems wrote:

"I have pretty strictly observed the Sabbath law during the last score of years, namely, of sequestering one day, Saturday, in each week from all kinds of professional business, making it a day on which on no account would I read a sermon, a treatise on theology, or anything that has to do with my profession—a day in which I sleep, bathe, doze, browse, and do nothing in the most promiscuous manner.

"Some pastors may believe in touching up their sermon on Saturday in order to be ready for the next day's service. When I go to bed on Saturday night, I do not know what I am to preach about the next day; I have clean forgotten. But on this Thursday afternoon in which I am being interviewed both my sermons are in a drawer of my desk as ready as I can make them for my use next Sunday morning.

"When I come in on Saturday evening [after a Russian bath and a meeting of the genial Philothean Club of ministers.—EDS.] my wife reads to me until bedtime, and ordinarily the reading of that evening consists of stories. Among men I prefer Walter Scott as a pure and unadulterated story-teller; among women, on the other side George Eliot, and upon this side Amelia Barr."

In February, 1879, he keenly enjoyed a visit to Boston and its vicinity, where he had been invited to deliver one of the addresses at one of Joseph Cook's famous conversations, and where he met many charming people. The entry in his diary for February 12th reads: "Went with A. Bronson Alcott to Concord. Paid a visit to Ralph Waldo Emerson; to the library; to 'Sleepy Hollow'; to Hawthorne's and Thoreau's graves. Back to Boston. Heard Phillips Brooks; had an interview with him after service."

On June 22d of this year Dr. Deems preached the university sermon at Union College. From Schenectady, passing through New York, he went to Carlisle, Pa., to attend the commencement of his alma mater, Dickinson College, where he made an address before the literary societies and delivered the alumni oration, of which the following account appeared in the Harrisburg "Patriot":

"CARLISLE, June 25th.

"The trustees, alumni, and the literary societies have all had their respective meetings to-day. This evening the Rev. Charles F. Deems, D.D., LL.D., of the Church of the Strangers, New York City, delivered the alumni oration. He called it 'Forty Years Ago.'

"The speaker began by a description of affairs at Dickinson College forty years ago, when his class was graduated. He characterized the faculty—President Durbin, Professor Caldwell, Dr. John McClintock, the Rev. Robert Emory, and Professor Allen, now president of Girard College. He reviewed the class of '39, giving what he knew of the history of its members, and complimenting the Rev. Dr. Crooks and the late Rev. Thomas Vernon Moore. The condition of Carlisle and of the State was then spoken of. Joe Ritner was then governor and had just vetoed a railroad bill. In connection with this fact the story of Slaymaker's bull was told. On a railway line then recently opened lived a gentleman named Slaymaker. His bull heard the oncoming train, and planting himself on the track, pawing, bellowing, and preparing to gore the new and terrible comer, he struck the engine, which was not going at a killing rate, but returned the attack with enough force to throw the bull over the fence. Three successive days this was done, when the bull gave up the contest in final discouragement. At a public meeting soon after, this toast was given: 'Here's to Joe Ritner and Slaymaker's bull—both opposed to railroads.'

"The general condition of the country, the slavery discussion, and the financial distress were described. From college life Dr. Deems passed on to note the state of things in New York City at the time. He described the city as he saw it then, the principal ministers, and the excitement of the Methodists over their centenary. The newspapers were talked of, and sketches were given of Bryant, Francis Hall, Willis, and Gaylord Clark. Some interesting reminiscences were furnished of what was then in the daily papers. For instance, the 'Commercial Advertiser' of June 22, 1839, had in it a letter from Boston dated four days before, signed 'H. G.,' a signature which afterward became of world-wide fame. In the 'Evening Post' of the 24th of June the latest English news was dated May 20th, and five steamships were announced to sail for Europe during that whole year. On the 28th the same paper glorified an 'expeditious passage to Buffalo,' which was described in detail by river, rail, canal, and steamboat, and was triumphantly announced as occupying only two days and three nights for the 'immense journey.'

"Some notable occurrences of the year 1839 were then reviewed. Daguerre had just announced to the world the process of taking pictures. The Queen of England had courted and married Prince Albert. Penny postage was proposed in Great Britain while a boy at an American college was paying a quarter of a dollar for every letter he sent to his sweetheart.

"Dr. Deems, it is well known, is a Southerner, and was in the Confederacy during the whole of the late unpleasantness. What he said on that subject may be worth recording in full. He said:

"'Almost midway across the path of forty years fell the gigantic shadow of the Civil War. Men from this college fought on both sides. It would not be wise at this time to say anything which could quicken any root of bitterness not yet thoroughly dead. Yet scholarly men, when nearly a score of years have passed away, ought to be able to talk of such far-off events with rational dispassionateness; and I think you will concede that it would not be an unreasonable claim upon my part if I should suppose myself capable of making fair judgments in the premises.

" ' If to me were committed the task of instructing the muse of history how to set forth the relative position of the parties in that unhappy conflict which tore our country, I should put the statement thus: the North loved the Union and constitutional liberty; the South loved constitutional liberty and the Union. The North saw no way to preserve liberty except by the maintenance of the Union, and would not allow its regard for the Constitution to stand in the way of the Union; the South saw no way of maintaining constitutional liberty inside the Union, and would not let its regard for the Union stand in the way of constitutional liberty. If any at the South supposed that the Northern people were willing to infringe the Constitution wantonly they did the North a grievous wrong. It lacerated the hearts of many noble men in the North when the conviction was forced upon them that it was expedient for a season to put the Constitution in abeyance for the sake of the vast ulterior good which should come from the preservation of the Union. If any at the North supposed that the Southern people had no love for the Union they did the South a grievous wrong. Thousands of Southerners stood by and saw the spade that turned up the first sod to begin a grave for the Union, and wept heartbrokenly such bitter, manly tears as a man might weep who stands by the tomb that opens to receive a cherished child whom he had given up to death rather than dishonor.

" ' When the conflict began the pertinacity of the South naturally intensified the love for the Union at the North, while the pertinacity of the North decreased the regard for the Union at the South. From the history of the times might be brought abundant testimony to confirm these statements. No more conspicuous and honest representative of the North existed during the war than Abraham Lincoln; and this is the text of a telegram of the 22d of August, 1862, sent by him to Horace Greeley: " If there be those who would not save the Union unless they could at the same time save slavery, I do not agree with them. If there be those who would not save the Union unless they could at the same time destroy slavery, I do not agree with them. My paramount object is to save the Union, and not either to save or to destroy slavery. If I could save the Union without freeing a slave, I would do it, and if I could save it by freeing some and leaving others alone, I would also do that. What I do about slavery and the colored race, I do because I believe it helps to save the Union; and what I forbear, I forbear because I do not believe it would help to save the Union. I shall do less whenever I shall believe what I am doing hurts the cause, and I shall do more whenever I believe doing more will help the cause."

" ' This is a perspicuous, exhaustive, and manly utterance, and I suppose may be taken to represent the sentiment of the Northern mind. On the other side, Robert E. Lee thus wrote his sisters in April, 1861 : " The whole South is in a state of revolution, into which Virginia, after a long struggle, has been drawn; and though I recognize no necessity for this state of things, and would have forborne and pleaded to the end for redress of grievances, real or supposed, yet in my own person I had to meet the question whether I should take part against my native State. With all my devotion to the Union and the feelings of loyalty and duty of an American citizen, I have not been able to make up my mind to raise my hand against my relatives, my children, my home. I have therefore resigned my commission in the army, and, save in defense of my native State, with the sincere hope that my poor services may never be needed. I hope I may never be called on to draw my sword."

" ' The bitterest thing for the whole country, in the dread series of horrors which marked our Civil War, was the assassination of Abraham Lincoln. Will a personal reminiscence be admissible? I shall never forget the day of the terrible tidings. General Joe Johnston had been falling back before the advancing columns of Sherman. I had left a portion of my family in Raleigh, N. C., in the house of my friend, the Hon. D. M. Barringer, and had gone on to Greensboro, having been formerly president of a college there. Negotiations were being pushed between Generals Sherman and Johnston, and hourly consultations were taking place between gentlemen collected in the town by the exigencies of the war. Two of the best friends I ever had were Governor Morehead and the Hon. John A. Gilmer, member of Congress from that district. The latter was one of the most intense lovers of the Union that the country ever produced. It is said that in his interviews with President Lincoln before the secession of North Carolina the presentation of his views would often be accompanied with tears. These two gentlemen walked with me toward the railway, and while we were conversing an aid, I think, of General Johnston brought the intelligence that Mr. Lincoln had been assassinated. Not one of us could believe that such an atrocity had occurred, and I remember that I openly disavowed my belief in the statement; and when asked by my friends how I could account for the origin of such a rumor, I presented the view that some of the Federal troops, desiring to break through military restraint, had started the story in order to excuse the perpetration of outrages which they desired to commit and which, I feared, General Sherman could not restrain.* I am satisfied that the most trustworthy Southern men do believe that the loss of Mr. Lincoln was one of the greatest disasters that ever befell the South and the whole country.'

" From this sad theme the speaker passed on to speak of

* This was his view immediately upon hearing the news, but we learn from his journal that he was among the first to accept the tidings as " true and dreadful."

the religious movements of that era: the revival in 1858, which began to lead to the present unity of the churches in Christian work, the rise of the Evangelical Alliance, the increase of fraternity, and the inception of the Reformed Episcopal Church under the leadership of Bishop Cummins, the speaker's old college-mate.

" Dr. Deems concluded by reviewing hastily the additions that had been made to human knowledge and comfort by the inventions and discoveries of the past forty years. In '39 there were no railways to speak of, no gas-works, no telegraphic communication, except between Baltimore and Washington, no grain elevators, no street-cars, no sleeping-cars, no photographs, no celluloid collars and cuffs. What may we not expect forty years hence? "

In August, 1879, by invitation, he went to Kentucky to attend, near Paris, the Deering camp-meeting, and to preach. On this occasion he was made happy not only by making many new friends, but also by reunions with such old friends as the Rev. Dr. Charles Taylor, of Covington, Mr. Hiram Shaw, of Lexington, who had been his traveling companion in Europe in 1860, and the genial Bishop Kavanaugh.

But Dr. Deems was at this period overtaxing his physical and mental powers of endurance, and began to suffer accordingly. He therefore decided to give up his work on the "Sunday Magazine," which he did, resigning the editorship September 1st. Moreover, he was persuaded to lay aside his work for several months and go abroad for rest.

Before starting on his long journey, at the suggestion of his people he heartily gave his attention to placing in the Church of the Strangers a bronze tablet as a grateful memorial of the late Cornelius Vanderbilt. The expense of this tablet was paid by a fund created by individual subscriptions of the people, no subscription exceeding one dollar. Messrs. W. Gibson's

Sons, of New York City, were the artists, and this effort of their skill has been pronounced by the best critics to be of the highest order of merit. The memorial was viewed by the press on Saturday, December 6th, and was unveiled Sunday, December 7th. It consists of a handsome black marble slab, embedded in the west wall of the church, to the south of the pulpit, and measures four feet in width by two feet and four inches in height. The bronze tablet itself is one foot and a half high by three feet wide, and is richly and artistically designed and ornamented in the Romanesque style. . Around the border is engraved the Scripture text, " He was worthy: for he hath built us a synagogue." Within, in ornamental letters and surrounded by artistic designs and symbols, are engraved these words: " Erected to the glory of God and in memory of Cornelius Vanderbilt by the Church of the Strangers." In this inscription the most prominent position and the most striking lettering are given to the name of the Deity, that the idea might be conveyed that while gratitude is expressed to man the chief glory is given to God. This tablet, as well as the motive from which it sprang into existence, has received from right-minded people only words of highest commendation.

At the December monthly meeting of the congregation, which was also the annual meeting, all the reports were so encouraging as to set Dr. Deems's mind at rest as he started off for a six months' absence. The church owed not one cent, many new members had been added during the year, and a spirit of unity and industry prevailed.

Another gratifying thing both to Dr. Deems and his son, the Rev. Edward M. Deems, was the action of the church authorities in inviting the latter to serve as acting pastor during the absence of his father from January 1 to July 1, 1880.* No

---

* Mr. Deems had been pastor of the First Presbyterian Church, Longmont, Colo., for two years, and had recently returned from a four months' tour in Europe.

pastor could have left his church for a prolonged absence under circumstances more favorable to freedom from anxiety.

About the last thing Dr. Deems did before starting on his travels was to establish the Deems Fund in the University of North Carolina. He thus wrote of this matter some years later:

"The history of this fund is this. My father was a Methodist minister on a limited salary. He found it difficult, with all the economy which I exercised, to meet all my expenses at college, although I believe there is not an alumnus of Dickinson College who spent less in the four years of his undergraduate course than I did. I lacked not quite twenty dollars of paying up every bill I owed when the time of my graduation came. I borrowed it of the president, the Rev. Dr. Durbin, and in less than a year I had repaid the loan. There was a sense of independence in this that has always been a great gratification to me. It suggested, also, that I in my turn might be able to do something for some one else going through college under straitened circumstances.

"In the year 1879 I began to carry out my design. My former pupil, the Hon. Kemp P. Battle, had become president of the University of North Carolina. While I was a young professor there my first child, Theodore Disosway Deems, was born. He fell in the Confederate service under Stonewall Jackson. As a memorial to him and as carrying forward my project, in December of 1879 I forwarded one hundred dollars to President Battle, to be loaned to students at easy per cent. and on easy time, the amounts when repaid to be reloaned. I had contributed six hundred dollars in this way when, one day, I was invited by Mr. William H. Vanderbilt to call at his house, then at the corner of Fifth Avenue and Fortieth Street, to give him some advice in regard to a matter upon which he had been studying and upon which I happened to have, as he believed, the information he needed. He knew something about my students' loan fund, and asked me particularly as to its details.   It was a short story, which I told him frankly.

"'Why, doctor, I will give you ten thousand dollars for that!' he said.

"'You will?' said I.   'Scholar and gentleman!'

"That was all that was said.   Next day a check came for the amount; and when I wrote to Mr. Vanderbilt to ask for directions for its disbursement, his reply was that he wanted it to go just where my donations had gone and in the same way, his only request being that I should make it do the most good possible to the most boys."

At length all preparations were completed, and on Tuesday morning, December 30th, attended by troops of friends, Dr. Deems entered the cabin of the "Germanic" of the White Star Line.   Under a shower of flowers and farewells he started on his pilgrimage to Egypt, Sinai, and Palestine, full of joyful anticipations of the realization of one of the sweetest dreams of his life—to see earth's most sacred places, with which already he had become so familiar by his studies for the pulpit and his preparation for writing the life of Jesus.

CHAPTER XII

DR. DEEMS'S voyage across the Atlantic was uneventful, but most restful. He thus writes of his one Sunday on the ocean:

"The first Sunday in January, 1880, was spent on the sea in the good ship 'Germanic' of the White Star Line. A minister of the gospel of the Son of God is never 'off duty'; his whole life must preach when his tongue is silent. Ten days of confinement to the same party, in a limited space, with the routine of ship life, put a clergyman under very close inspection. It is of no use to put on anything, and he cannot stand off from his fellow-passengers. If love for God and love for men and an intense conviction of the truth of the gospel pervade his whole spiritual constitution, his presence will be a blessing; for these will come out in all his actions and speech, whether he pray or play; but if these be absent, all priestly airs will pass for nothing. Few things are so searching as a sea voyage. Happy is the minister who feels when he lands that he has been servant to no other than his divine Master. If this be not the case, it would seem to have been better that he should have been dropped into the river at the dock before starting, even if no Jonah whale were there to give him a warm bath.

289

"We had but one Sunday on our voyage.   On Saturday the purser politely invited me to officiate next morning.   I make it a point to accept every invitation to preach when there seems to be a fitting occasion and no other minister is present.   A pulpit was rigged at the end of one of the long tables, and nearly all the saloon passengers were present.   Of course I conformed to the Sunday custom of the ship and read the morning prayers of the Church of England, omitting such portions as are specifically appropriate only in Great Britain, not, however, omitting the 'prayer for the queen's majesty,' modifying it after this fashion : ' Most heartily we beseech thee with thy favor to behold the [our] Most Gracious Sovereign Lady, Queen Victoria, and thy servant, the President of the United States, and to replenish them,' etc.   There was a supply of prayer-books and the responses were hearty.

"The text of the sermon was Genesis xii. 2 : 'And thou shalt be a blessing.'   I had no sermon on this text, except such as had suggested itself to me in reading this chapter in my state-room the day before.

"I regretted to discover that the second-class passengers had not been invited to the saloon, together with such of the ship's crew as were off duty, and resolved to make a stipulation for their presence if a similar invitation should be given me.   No service seems complete without a collection.   As a thank-offering I 'took up a collection' for the Liverpool Orphan Asylum, and a neat sum was contributed.   No doubt there will be some light-minded party to suggest that it was the 'ruling passion,' and perhaps throw up to me, as an English lady already has done, the story of the two sailors on the wreck.   In the afternoon I read the life of Archbishop Whately, written by his daughter.   In several places I was reminded of the great injustice which may be done to men under the charge of plagiarism; for in this book were thoughts which I had frequently uttered and supposed them to be original.

On the Sunday immediately preceding my departure I had made a statement in the morning sermon which evidently startled the congregation, so much so that I felt compelled to repeat it with explanatory phrases. In this book I found the identical sentence, word for word, recorded as a saying of the archbishop very many years ago. Of the existence of the volume I had no knowledge until I found it in the ship's library. It was pleasant to know that I had ever thought as such a man as Whately had thought; but it was not pleasant to reflect that some microscopic critic might see a report of the sermon, might also see this memoir, and then might scribble for some newspaper the charge that the pastor of the Church of the Strangers had, before preaching it, become 'saturated' with the great Archbishop of Dublin!" *

From the London "Christian Age"

"The Rev. Dr. C. F. Deems, pastor of the Church of the Strangers, New York, arrived in London on the 10th of January, and gave us a call. The doctor is of medium height, quick in speech, affable in manner, employs few but well-selected words. Dr. Deems presides over a large church with a membership of six hundred persons, and has a congregation of twelve hundred. He is *en route* to the Holy Land. During the week he spent in London he has received the most cordial receptions. Among these we may note his breakfast with the Rt. Rev. Bishop of Rangoon, at the Religious Tract Society's premises. Here his address was acknowledged by the committee's unanimous vote of thanks, one of the committee adding, 'Dr. Deems joins wit to wisdom.' By a special invitation, he visited the Presbyterian College in Queen's Square. The London Presbytery was in session, and he was requested to

* "Homiletic Review," vol. iv., p. 353.

remain as a 'visiting member.' This led to a pleasant inter-view with Dr. Oswald Dykes and Dr. Donald Fraser, who invited Dr. Deems to attend their annual social meeting in the Regent's Square Church. The doctor has been solicited to arrange for the publication of a volume of his sermons after his return from the East. During his short stay in London the doctor managed to hear Cardinal Manning, the Rev. Newman Hall, and Dr. Joseph Parker."

From the "Anglo-American Times" of January 30th

"The Rev. Dr. Charles F. Deems, of New York, spent in Paris three days last week *en route* to Egypt. He will go up the Nile as far as the first cataract, after which he will make a tour through the Holy Land, thence to Constantinople and Athens, and return to Paris for a brief visit. Dr. Charles F. Deems is the popular pastor of the Church of the Strangers. When passing through London *en route* for Palestine he stayed with his friend Mr. Hoge at Bexley, Kent. The day before his departure for France, while engaged with the family in quiet conversation in the drawing-room, all were startled by a piercing scream. Mrs. Hoge, who once lost a little child by an accident, was almost palsied with fright. The doctor ran through the hall, down the stairs, and made his way to the kitchen, where he found Mr. Hoge's little three-year-old boy, who had been left alone for a moment by his nurse, enveloped in flames. Stripping off his coat with great presence of mind, the doctor wrapped it around the little fellow and thus smo-thered the flame and saved the child. Dr. Deems said he knew very well his letter of credit and excursion tickets to and from the first cataract were in the side pocket of his coat, but he never faltered a moment on this account. The fire was ex-tinguished before it had gained much headway."

To His Wife

" PARIS, HÔTEL DE LONDRES, January 19, 1880.

" Yesterday afternoon I hit on a service at Notre Dame. How exceedingly grand the structure! and what music! In striving to get out, as my luck would have it, I wandered into the sacristy of the chapter among all the 'bigwigs.' I begged pardon, explained that I was 'an American ecclesiastic,' and they actually welcomed me and begged me to go all over the apartments! Thence I took a cab to go to Father Hyacinthe's. What a change from that grand Notre Dame, where he used to thunder, to this modest chapel of the Gallican Catholic Church!

" The service was over two hours in length, the sermon more than one. He had not expected to preach. The lesson for the day was 'The Marriage in Cana,' and he preached on the subject. Under the ban for being a married priest, you should have seen the vigor he put into his discourse. Some passages were very fine. He is about as tall as F—— and as big as Mr. Beecher.

" After service I expressed a wish to speak with him and was shown up narrow stairs to his vestry. There sat Mère Hyacinthe, his spouse, holding her court until he came from the altar. Every one stood around her. She is a noble-looking woman. At last she signed to me. I was beginning to make a little speech in French, handing her my card. The moment she saw the name she arose and said, 'Come, sit by me, and let me have the honor of holding that hand.' The crowd fell back. She held me by the right hand and said, 'I have heard you preach, and shall never forget you. Oh, you cannot tell how many times I have prayed for l'Église des Étrangers.' And many more sayings quite as kind. Then she took me into the inner room, where we talked with the père. When he found who I was he said, 'O, oui, oui; vous êtes comme nous.' 'Oui, monsieur, but a good deal more Protestant.' After pleasant talk, in which each of us explained his ecclesiastical position to the other, the Loysons begged me at the Holy Sepulcher to pray for the unity of all Christians."

To His Wife

"ISLAND CORFU, GREECE, Sunday, January 25, 1880.

"I am to-day heartily homesick. . . . This afternoon must be given to letters. I sometimes fear that letters will drive me to the madhouse. . . . From Paris we had a bitterly cold ride. Left Monday night. Tuesday night at Turin. Wednesday at Bologna. Then twenty-seven hours shut up in one of those infernal machines, which lock you in with no redress, whoever may be your companions. In crossing Mont Cenis it was horribly cold. And all along the snow was from four inches to two feet in depth. Not oftener than every half-century such a snow. But oh, how beautiful, how splendid, the scenery! How often I cried, 'See, ma, see!' and I heard you 'oh'-ing all the way along. Bologna was always interesting to me, and this was a fine visit, but so cold. We reached Brindisi to dine, and took the steamer to this island, passing along the Albanian coast, seeing the high mountains covered with snow.

"This morning I worshiped with the British Consulate Church in the old Parliament House. This population is an odd mixture. On landing I saw the most ferocious faces. The Albanians stalk about with a tool-chest of weapons in front of them and greatcoats hanging on their backs. The modern Greek is spoken here. I copy some names of shops for Ned; his Greek will enable him to make out the businesses."

In his journal Dr. Deems writes: "On Sunday afternoon [January 25, 1880] I came upon a church with the following thrilling inscription: 'ΝΑΟΣ ΤΗΣ Υ. Θ. Φ. ΞΕΝΩΝ' ('Church of the Strangers')."

To His Wife

"CAIRO, EGYPT, February 1, 1880.

"We were in Corfu last week. Then came in the steamers, and we put out that evening for Alexandria—'Skanderéa,' as the Arabs so musically name it. Read Acts xxvii. and you will know what a sea this is when the Euroclydon is upon it. Paul never had my sympathies so much. But we lost nothing but a day. Another steamer lost some passengers. Nearly all our company were deadly sick. I took every meal. If any report of any little accident reach you, it amounted to nothing—only a bruise on the leg, which did not keep me from 'doing' Alexandria to such an extent as to excite the envy of the English co-voyagers.* We reached Alexandria Thursday afternoon. . . . This afternoon I started to find the school of Miss Whately, the archbishop's daughter. The Rev. Mr. Binnie, whose church the Duke of Argyll attended in London, expressed a desire to go along. By perseverance we found it and found two sisters, one who wrote his lordship's life, and one who has founded, and mainly from her own means sustained, these schools. We have a little book of hers. They gave us a warm reception. My familiarity with the works of the family seemed to take them by storm. When we rose to go Mr. Binnie suggested that I should lead in prayer, which I did fervently. Miss Jane, the biographer, gave me two of her books.

"February 2d, 5 : 30 P.M. I have stood on top the highest pyramid, penetrated its farthest recess, stood before the Sphinx,

* It would seem that Dr. Deems, during the storm, came near losing his life by falling on the hurricane-deck, the entangling of his foot in the shield of the rudder-chain being all that saved him from being thrown overboard.

penetrated the recesses of the temple of the Sphinx, hunted on hands and knees in tombs, scraped away the sand from the hieroglyphics, and am back! Before washing out of my eyes the dust of the Pharaohs and their wives I must close this letter to catch the mail. It was most stupendous! Next to getting married, the greatest sensation I have had was at the pyramids."

From His Journal

"Monday, February 2d. To the pyramids. The sheik. The ascent. My helpers, Mohammed and Ali. My sickness. The nuisance of bakshish. The Sphinx. Driving away the Ishmaelites. I asked one of the Arabs, 'Where is Abou ben Adhem?' Of course he had not read the poem, but he answered promptly, 'Oh, that man been dead long ago.' 'Where's his tribe?' 'No tribe.' 'Then did Leigh Hunt pray in vain!' All Greek to him."

To His Granddaughter, Katherine Verdery

"ON THE NILE, IN EGYPT, AFRICA,
" Wednesday, February 4, 1880.

"'Gramper'* is, oh, so far away from his darlings, and so homesick! It is after two o'clock and he has had luncheon, and his babies probably have not had their breakfast. And what sights gramper has seen! Yesterday he saw a building which has stood as long before Abraham was born as the time between the birth of the Babe of Bethlehem and the birth of my darling 'A. K.' When you grow older your dear mama can make you understand this. There he went down into a tomb far underground and saw a stone coffin so large that your whole family could take breakfast in it, and it was a hundred times as old as gramper.

* The child's expression for " grandpa."

"Tell papa and mama that last Monday gramper went to the top of the largest pyramid. It is almost seven times as high as the watch-tower in your street, and the steps almost a yard high. Two Arabs, Mohammed and Ali, pulled gramper up. It was awful; the agony given the poor rheumatic arm seemed more than could be borne, and once gramper sat down to faint. To faint and to fall *there* was an awful death. He could look down to the island where little Moses' bulrush ark stranded, and out to the obelisk that Joseph looked at when married, and when the dim death-sickness fell upon him he saw all his darlings sleeping in their New York and Augusta beds, and so he ruled himself back from the brink of unconsciousness and lived.

"Little and big Arabs run all about this great pile of stones and will do anything for money. The sheik of the pyramids had somehow learned that special attention was to be paid to A. K.'s gramper. How she got there I do not know, but a little Arab girl squatted by me with a goblet of cold water. 'Water, docta, water?' (They all knew me on landing as 'the doctor,' and thought I owned all the English people and carriages, and America too.) 'Yes,' I said. Ali took my handkerchief, sopped it in water, slid it up to my temple, and patted my back. Mohammed rubbed my legs and said caressingly, 'Take your time, doctor.' (They all know a few English phrases.) 'Take your time, doctor,' echoed Ali. Gramper felt life coming back. Silent thankfulness came first; then fun, that said quietly and brokenly, 'Yes, boys; I must take time or eternity will take me.' Then I put all weakness aside and said, 'Up;' and we went on the top, safe, if not sound, my breathing as good as that of a healthy babe; my lungs were the admiration of the company. Then I was all right. Oh, such sights! Oh, such air! I had never breathed anything like that. After staying as long as I wanted and making my observations, the air had so invigorated me that I stood on the cope and looked down, a little dizzy, as if I stood on a chair. I walked the whole way down, supported by the hands of my Arabs, *face foremost*, as sound of mind and clear of head as ever in my life. *It was worth more than it had cost.* But to-day I am so sore that I can hardly put my clothes on.

"Now we are coming into a warmer climate and I trust I shall lose my rheumatism. It is beautiful on the Nile to-day. The sky is perfectly clear; the dome above our head is of the deepest possible blue, and all the horizon an exquisitely delicate pearl color. Little birds come on board, one kind being what they call in England water-wagtail. The Arab name is *ashoor*. They are regular little Turks; each little man bird has several wives, and they whip them well if they don't behave themselves. They all have the crescent mark on their breasts.

"Gramper has had every attention paid him. At Alexandria he was entertained one night by an English merchant. He rode from the station to the mansion on a little donkey named 'Bulbul.' On the way he saw two children in a basket riding on another donkey. He shouted out to them, and soon after they came into the court, and then ran into the dining-room, and one of them rushed into gramper's arms. The black-eyed, rosy-cheeked little Hebe was named Gracie Alderson. She pushed back the hair from gramper's forehead and kissed it and said, 'Have you any little girl?' whereupon gramper proceeded to deliver a discourse on 'Lambly Lamb' and 'Dovely Dove.' The family were so kind to me! The children rode over to the Cairo station to bid me good-by.

"I do not know whether you can read this letter, the boat jars me so. Nor do I know where it is to be posted. As I cannot write much, you must send this to 'grammer.' Dear grammer, how I long to see her!"

To His Wife

"ASSOUAN, UPPER EGYPT, February 16, 1880.

"Oh, how I longed for you to-day at Philæ! The beauty of the island and the grandeur of its surroundings, seen in the splendor of an Egyptian day which gazed down upon the glorious ruins of the last temple built to the old faith, was something to live in the memory forever. We went to it through a desert, some of the party on camels, some on donkeys.

"In some portions not a spear of green growth was to be seen. We then came down to the first cataract, which we had flanked. Down under the ledge of sandstone which forms the plateau on the bend of the river, from which travelers look down upon the Nubians shooting the cataract, I gathered and send you these little flowers, a smile from a frowning brow."

"SUEZ, EGYPT, February 28, 1880.

"Every Monday I have written you, but next Monday I shall be two days' journey from any post-office, and this is my last writing for three weeks. My camels have gone around the head of the Red Sea, and this afternoon I go down by boat and land near the fount, or well, of Moses. There I mount for a few hours' ride to break me in to camels. I shall be on them every day for three weeks, except the three days I propose to spend at Sinai. It now occurs to me how wise the arrangement was to lead the Israelites through this great and terrible wilderness as a preparation for the giving of the law. It is like going up many steps to a high altar. Yesterday I left Cairo and came to this place by rail, doubling the direct distance by sweeping around the land of Goshen, where the Israelites dwelt. If, now, on that elevation down there near the arm of the Red Sea were Sinai, I should not be able to approach it with much awe, but eight days of travel above the measured tread of the solemn camel, wrapped in one's thoughts, and nine nights of sleep in a tent amid the stillness of a region where no bird chirps and no insect flies, must be the best possible preparation for going to the mount that may be touched, where Moses battled with God. Oh, that the Mount of the Law may give me the most solemn preparation to receive the benediction of Calvary!

"I have for dragoman the best recommended man in Cairo. He says the camels are good. We take kitchen, meats, fruit, water, everything, with us. I have shortened my trip and shall not go up through the peninsula to Hebron, but return to Suez and thence to Port Said, to Jaffa, Jerusalem, etc. Will give reason when we meet. I have three companions; one is a clergyman. For my own edification I should prefer to go alone and have three weeks of silence and of thought. But if anything should happen it is better to have companions who speak one's own tongue. Everything now promises a good and pleasant trip. You need not worry. About the day this reaches you I shall be on the canal going to Port Said and all extraordinary danger will be past. The serious part of my whole trip lies between my writing and your reception of this letter. The heavenly Father will be with me. Into his hands, for judgment and mercy, I give my soul."

"SINAI, IN ARABIA, March 9, 1880.

"It would make your head swim if you could see the dizzy heights to which I have carried you in my heart. I write this from the venerable Convent of St. Catherine, more than twelve centuries old. It is a very peculiar place, the description of which is ample in my note-book and cannot be repeated here. It is inhabited by forty monks, presided over by a bishop. They are of the Greek Church, exceedingly dirty and polite.

They have been very attentive to me. One gay and festive little brother calls me ' Episcopus Demetrius.'

" My health has been good. The water here is delicious; the traditional sacred places are innumerable. I have taken water from the well from which Moses drew to water the flocks of his father Jethro. The valley to the north of the convent bears the Arabic name of Jethro, and two mountains bear the names of sisters-in-law of Moses. Yesterday was a marked day. I went up to the spot where they say the law was given. It was a tremendous pull. The view from the right is most grand, far beyond all I had conceived. Then I climbed another great mountain, from which Dr. Robinson believes the law was promulgated. ' In all my life,' as A. H. C. said, have I never seen so perfect a day. The sky was fleckless and blue to a depth of blueness which is indescribable, and the air was delicious to the lungs. From Ras Sassafa the view of the plain in which it is supposed the Israelites were encamped, surrounded as it was by mountains, was a surpassing beauty. And you were with me all the while. In the solemn solitude of the mountain-top I lay on my face before God. Heaven was awfully near there. I prayed for you and for each of my children by name.

" There is no certainty as to which was the exact Sinai. Dean Stanley leans to a mountain which he did not ascend. This morning I hired a Bedouin guide and ascended one side, and, against his protest, descended on the other. He would not at first consent to go to the extreme summit, but while he was meditating I gave him the slip, and, creeping cautiously around and up, sometimes on my stomach, I gained the height, from which I shouted to him to come up and help me down. Getting to a height is one thing, coming down another. But I did come down with swollen feet and torn hands. I know of no one else among the writers on Bible lands who has done it. My dinner was ready, bread, water, cold chicken, cheese, walnuts, raisins, and coffee.   He has spread a table in the wilderness for his child.

"Tell A. K. that we had a baby camel in our caravan, and as she was a girl camel I called her Princess Louise.

"Suez, March 17th. Since the other two pages were written I have followed the supposed route of the children of Israel, reversing it by coming down from Sinai to near their crossing-place.   I have risen very early, slept in a tent, and seen all I could.   To-day was hard and hot, but we have had it punishingly cold.   I am burnt and have grayed and thinned.   It has been twenty days of great exertion."

"DAVID STREET, JERUSALEM, March 29, 1880.

"For an hour my conscience has been pulling at me.   My Monday letter has not been written.   I have been passing about looking at this and at that.   A thousand things are to be seen, and the Bishop of Jerusalem has invited me to a party at his house to-night, and I have promised his lordship to be present and so cannot write after dark.   But you must know that I am still holding up, and so I rush in to write, even if it be a short letter, before I write up the notes of the day.   Sight-seeing is very wearing.   Your time you know is limited, and it may rain.   You will never come back and so you want to see everything.   Your enthusiasm carries you forward until you ache at the close of the day's labor.   I have been here five days, including Sunday, and have done much. There is so much going up and down, as this morning over the Mosque of Omar, and down, down, through rough subterranean structures, and this afternoon over the Armenian Convent and up David's Tower.   I hold out very well for an old man.   The first day I could do little, as a horse in our caravan had kicked my foot the day before.   That passed off, and then yesterday I fell in our hotel, striking myself against the stone step, and am much bruised.   Nevertheless you see how much I have accomplished. I shall not resume the saddle for a day or two, and trust I shall be much better—all right, indeed.

"To-day I called on the Armenian patriarch. This convent is the largest in Jerusalem, and rich. The patriarch maintains much state, but received me most cordially. He can speak neither French nor English. The young man who accompanied me is a friend of the F——s. He knows no English! Now fancy the scene and the struggle. The archbishop would not allow me to kiss his hand, thus acknowledging my orders and my dignity. He knew something of America, and so we began. I frankly gave him my views on the Catholicity of Christianity, and the departure from Christianity by those who are so fond of calling themselves Catholic. That I made my companion understand, and he repeated it to the patriarch in splendid style. I could comprehend his French and know that he was doing it well. It is delightful to be reported *above* the level of one's own rhetoric. The patriarch showed me a very old copy of the gospels (written in A.D. 602), and had the sweetmeats and coffee brought in then, as he smilingly said, treating me 'like a Turk.' He expressed a desire to have a portrait of me. I had no photograph, but promised to send him one when I reached America. I was modest enough to ask for only his autograph. He gave me a fine photograph with his autograph beneath it. He then presented me with a peculiar rosary. It is made of the seed of olive, of a tree which grows adjoining the prison of Christ, or house of Annas. Of course it is not the tree which stood there in the days of our Lord, but the patriarch holds it as a legitimate descendant. He gathers the fruit from the tree, which is carefully guarded by a wall seven feet high, as I was shown, and makes the seed into rosaries, to be given to royal visitors and to *other* 'persons of high distinction'; wherefore he most graciously presented *me* with one. I accepted it very

gratefully as a present from the patriarch, and told him that I
would take it to America and present it to my daughter who
is to be married in July. He learned that I had two daughters
and so insisted on my taking one for the other daughter. So
you see how kindly the way is open before us.

"Yesterday the American consul came and escorted me to
church and took me home to luncheon with him. He occupies
the house which the F——s lived in.

"The interest of this city is past measure. I have been
afraid to begin to speak of it. There is no end. I have been
twice to the Mount of Olives, once going to Bethany. Every
night the full Easter moon rises over the house of Martha, and
comes shining down on the road which Jesus followed as he
came on Palm Sunday, and the place where he wept over
Jerusalem. David's Tower is in front of my hotel door. Every
spot is crowded with thrilling historical recollections.

"Tuesday, March 30, 1880. Was at the bishop's reception
last night. His lordship devoted a good deal of his time to
me, but the affair would have been dull but for a sprightly old
English spinster, a Friend, Miss F——, who is very charming.
It is delightful to be nice when old. Let us be so."

"DAMASCUS, SYRIA, Monday, April 19, 1880.

"I write you from the oldest city known upon earth. It
seems strange, when you have dreamed of anything for fifty
years, to see the reality. This is a wonderful place of about
one hundred and twenty-five thousand inhabitants, the greenest
garden you ever saw, set in the desert. It is very Oriental.
I can hardly write you now for the sights and sounds under
my window. There are all sorts of colors, from the preter-
naturally black Nubian to the beautiful girls of Circassian
blood, white skins, red cheeks, and black eyes. The cries of
the seller are sometimes very funny. A fellow carries bouquets
for sale and cries out, 'Sâlik hamatak' (that sounded much

like A. K.)—'Appease your mother-in-law.' A seller of roasted peas cries out, 'The mother of two fires,' meaning that they are well roasted. A seller of cucumbers begs you, 'O father of a family, buy a load.' As my family is at such a distance, I decline to purchase. But here's a man who desires to dispose of some cresses, and to assure you that they are so fresh, 'If an old woman eats them she will be young again next morning.' Don't you wish you had some? But I cannot go into particulars. I only wish you could see the greenery produced by the Barada as it flows through this city.

"My health is good. I have had my escapes, but I *have* escaped. Sometimes I am dreadfully tired. I am crowding so much into such little time."

"ATHENS, GREECE, May 13, 1880.

"I feel that my tour is drawing to a close. For fifty years I have longed to see Athens, yet when I arrived my enthusiasm was all dead. I had been stuffed with sights from Alexandria to Constantinople until I could endure no more. But every day this city grows upon me. It will be forever a spot toward which the minds and hearts of scholars must turn. There are a thousand broken beauties here which recall a thousand recollections of poetry, eloquence, heroism, and all the glories which have made Greece famous. To-day I stood on the site of the old Areopagus where Paul made his famous address. Strange enough, my guide was named Dionysius. (See Acts xvii.) Thence I ascended the Acropolis and spent two hours around the Parthenon. There is so much to be seen there that I must go back for a few more hours.

"Yesterday afternoon, after riding to Eleusis, the site of the old and famous temple of Ceres, where the Eleusinian mysteries were celebrated, I preached in this city; so you see I have not been entirely idle. I have told you, I believe, about my itinerant Church of the Strangers in the. Holy Land. The

English ladies were so delighted with it that I have a little service in one of their rooms after dinner each evening. We dine from 7:30 to 9:15 P.M. The newest Athens is beautiful, clean, and white, but a little too glaring. You could wish that some of these white marble houses had a soberer tint. Great taste is exhibited in many of the houses, the royal palace being, however, the most uninteresting I ever saw, with the plainest barracks front. This is too bad for Athens. The weather is very warm and I fear that I am writing quite stupidly, but I wish to catch a mail this afternoon, so I write without taking a nap.

"I am ready to go home. For almost a week I have been a little homesick. I begin to long for my regular work and feel as though I could bear to hear our door-bell a little. Is not that a very healthy sign?

"My program is from Athens to Trieste, starting from here Saturday, the 15th inst. A day in Venice, a night in Turin, a day in Paris, a day in Canterbury, then to London. Start for America June 17th. Oh, will it not be good to be at home again!"

This program Dr. Deems carried out, sailing from Liverpool on Thursday, June 17, 1880, in the "Celtic." One entry in his journal is of importance, as it gives an account of an event which really gave birth in Dr. Deems's mind to the idea of the "American Institute of Christian Philosophy," of which he became the founder a few months later.

From His Journal

"Tuesday, June 8th. In the evening attended the annual meeting of the Victoria Institute, the philosophical society of Great Britain. The Rt. Rev. Bishop Cotterill, of Edinburgh, made the annual address. Before the address several gentlemen were called upon for speeches. I made the last, and it

was well received with many cheers. The Earl of Shaftesbury presided."

Dr. Deems's address is thus referred to in the printed records
of the Victoria Institute:

" Dr. Deems (who on rising to speak was at once requested
by the Earl of Shaftesbury to come on to the raised dais by the
president's chair) began his speech by urging the great value
of the work of the society, which now numbered its supporters
in every part of the globe, and he trusted that those who could,
whether in America or any other part of the world, would
strengthen its hands by joining as members. He then spoke
of the high value of the people's edition of its more popular
papers as enabling the society to place the results of its labors
in the hands of the masses. 'And now,' said Dr. Deems, 'I
hope I shall, as an American, not frighten an English audience
by being thought to do a very strange thing; I don't know,
but the fact is, I am going to talk about your president.'
(Cheers.) 'You know, in America we old people remember
hearing about Lord Shaftesbury—our Lord Shaftesbury—when
we were boys, children, and now we still hear about him, his
name being associated with everything noble and for the good
of man; and when I left New York the only man I was told
to be sure and see was Lord Shaftesbury. And I expected to
see an old, decrepit man, leaning on another for support; but
when he walked into this room his step was firm and his eye
as bright as that of any one. And long may he live to glad-
den our hearts and to do the Master's work, to which he has
devoted his life.' (Great cheering.) It would be impossible
to describe the masterly speech and manner of Dr. Deems.
Suffice it to say that there was no speech that pleased so much;
there was that directness and simplicity about it which is now
making American oratory so increasingly popular in England."

CHAPTER XIII

EARLY Sunday morning, July 27th, the "Celtic" was moored at the New York pier of the White Star Line. As Dr. Deems descended the gang-plank he was met with open arms by his two sons and a reception committee appointed by the monthly meeting, the governing body of the Church of the Strangers. He had expected to go immediately into his pulpit, but was informed by the committee that he had two days for rest with his family.

On Tuesday evening a reception was given him at the church. He was first taken into the main auditorium and shown the apse behind the pulpit, which, through the generosity of a lady in his church, had been repaired and tastefully decorated during the pastor's absence. He expressed the greatest delight at this long-needed improvement. Then he was escorted into the lecture-room, which he found packed with happy people, who received him with cheers. Over the raised platform his eyes rested on the conspicuous words made by gas-jets, "Welcome home."

T. E. F. Randolph, Esq., the president of the monthly meeting, presided; Professor George W. Pettit, leader of the choir, led the music; and Mr. George W. Taylor, of the Advisory Council, led in prayer. After appropriate remarks by Mr. Randolph, Mr. Joseph J. Little, the president of the board of trustees, made the address of welcome, which was most tender and interesting, and was closed by Mr. Little presenting Dr. Deems with a generous purse from the congregation. Dr. Deems's reply was as follows:

"Mr. Chairman, my dear Brother Little, Sisters and Brethren: I am taken at a delightful disadvantage by this display of kindness on the part of the officers and members of our beloved church. No hint had been given me that I should be expected to say or do anything to-night beyond grasping again the warm hands which dropped from mine on that cold December night when we parted.

"There has been a little mysteriousness about movements since my arrival. Our steamer reached the pier at seven o'clock last Sunday morning, and I was met by a committee of church officers, who conducted me to my home. A thorough rest of ten days during an exceptionally tranquil voyage had set me up, and I told them that I should be at church. They exchanged glances of distress, and undertook to tell me that I was too tired! and to advise me to remain with my family!! Of course I expected to 'remain with my family,' but couldn't I just as well remain with them in church? The friendly officers did not take into account the rare pleasure it is for a pastor to sit in a pew, in a pew beside his wife; nor did they seem to think that naturally, as a Christian, I longed to hear the gospel, and, as a pastor, longed to see my own church sanctuary. But you know what an obedient pastor I have always been, and so I succumbed! This evening I learned what it meant. When you met me at the church door and under the lights there was displayed to me the newly and beautifully ornamented apse, with the appropriate inscription and decorations with which it was adorned, I saw that you were kindly keeping this as a surprise to increase the delights which you are heaping upon my reception.

"And now in this crowded chapel you have spoken by the

lips of the president of your board of trustees such manly, kind, and Christian words of greeting as go to my very heart and awaken a most cordial response of reciprocation.

" As to the long tour which I have accomplished I shall have other occasions on which to address you. But one thing you will be glad to know, and that is that I have spent six months of total freedom from the cares which for over thirteen years have pressed upon my spirit. It is my good fortune to have the happy faculty of being altogether in the place where I am; so when I went away I left entirely. For my church, for my family, for all with whom I was connected, I made the most complete arrangements within my power. I knew the officers of the church. I knew you. I knew my son whom you had called to be your temporary pastor. I knew the great Head of the church. I knew that I could do nothing more for you before my return, and that if I suffered myself to be fretted by solicitude the whole intent of my separation from all I most loved would be defeated.

" My friends, if I had gone pleasure-seeking, if I had become tired of my work and disgusted with the Christian ministry, if I had fled like Jonah from some divinely imposed but disagreeable mission, I could not have had this freedom from care. But knowing in the depths of my heart that my tour was undertaken in the interests of this church and for the increase of the usefulness of my future ministry, I had no misgivings and no anxiety. Does not this church belong to the Lord? Do not I belong to the Lord? Will he not care for his own as much when we are separated as when we are together? I had served the church thirteen years. The first eight years and five months were without a Sunday of vacation. A few weeks two or three times in the latter years had been spent out of the city. Such continuance in labor in the same sphere, such frequency of preaching in the same pulpit, summer and winter, was calculated to beget sameness and dullness and running in ruts. It seemed to me necessary for my mental health that I should have a total change of scene. So I went into a desert place apart.

" If the first motion to go was personal, I should have been exceedingly obtuse not to have soon seen that our Lord had designs concerning *you* and the Church of the Strangers in this temporary separation. Our history is peculiar. Your pastor was not 'called,' as his brethren have been, to the pastorate of an organized church. You have gathered around me, and the providence of God has raised you up an independent Christian body, an ecclesiasticized evangelical alliance to represent the charities and unities of Protestant Christianity. From time to time it has been predicted that the experiment would be a failure. We are far down-town. *There is no church building in this city in so obscure a place as this.* No street-cars nor omnibuses pass in front of us. We are on the last block of a street which is not long and is occupied by business houses. We are not even on a corner. Such is now the position of our beautiful church, which when it was erected was the cathedral of Presbyterianism in America. You must come in front of it to see it.

" Now, whether such an organized Christian society as ours, unconnected with any of the sects, could sustain itself down-town is a question which has exercised many persons. For myself, it does not seem a matter of paramount importance. If the Lord has no need of this church, I am sure that I have not; if he has, he will take care of his own. But very often it was not only insinuated, but asserted, that this church was kept alive by the exertions of the pastor, and sometimes that has been put forth as a compliment to me. We have tested that question. I have not written you a line of direction or advice about the economies of the church during my absence, and under God you have carried the church along quite as well as I have ever been able to do. So in the future I shall be relieved of any anxiety on that subject, and also from similar prophecies.

"If I have had no anxiety about the church, dear friends, I have not suspended my affection for you. My eyes have been running over this crowded chapel to-night, and their report is that there are no faces present, except those of a few visitors, which I have not seen with the eyes of my heart while riding Egyptian donkeys, Arabian camels, or Syrian horses— faces that have risen up before me as I have gazed on the skies which hang over the lands made holy by the residence of prophets and apostles and of the Son of God. Now my happiness is to see those faces once more 'in the flesh.'

"I have no promises to make. I have formed no new resolutions. But I trust that all that I have seen in distant lands, and all my experiences, may come out in my future ministry so as to be profitable to us all. My heart is filled with delight at your unity and coöperation, your faith and zeal, your hope and charity. Some have left us and gone up to other mansions of the Father's house. You will follow them. When the hour of your departure comes, may you find on that other shore, as I found on landing, friends to cluster lovingly about you, and amid the illumination of the upper temple see glowing with the light of love for *you* the words which you have emblazoned above my head: 'Welcome home.'

"Mr. Chairman, my dear brother who has addressed me, dear brothers and sisters all, I thank you from my heart of hearts for your warm and generous acts and words. You know how I feel better than I can tell you."

The Hon. George W. Clarke, of the Advisory Council, then delivered an address, in which he expressed the sentiments of the church toward Dr. Deems's son, the Rev. Edward M. Deems, who had been acting pastor during his father's absence. A generous purse accompanied the address, and Mr. Deems's address in response closed the speechmaking. In the beautifully decorated church parlor refreshments were served, and the evening was spent in a most delightful social reunion. On the following Sunday the church was thronged with people, and there was held one of the most tender and impressive of communion services.

With rejuvenated powers of body and mind, and with a mental and spiritual horizon widened by his travels, Dr. Deems took up his labors in the pulpit, parish, and elsewhere. He frequently said that he tried to do some special extra work during each decade of his life. This extra professional work during the decade ending with 1880 was his book " Jesus." And now he took up what proved to be the special fruit of the last active decade of his life. The American Institute of Christian Philosophy stands beside the Church of the Strangers and the book " Jesus " as one of the three greatest achievements of his beneficent life.

Those who would know the complete story of the institute must get it from the eleven stately volumes in which áre bound the numbers of " Christian Thought," which for ten years was the institute's organ.

When Dr. Deems attended the annual meeting of the Victoria Institute in London in 1880, and saw what a power it was as a creator of speech and literature that was calculated to be an antidote to the false philosophic literature of the day, the question was suggested to his mind, " Why not have such a society in the United States, where infidel philosophy finds a growing circle of readers? " One of his characteristics was promptly to turn thought into action and organization. He accordingly arranged for a course of lectures at Warwick Woodlands, on the shores of Greenwood Lake, New Jersey, and secured the attendance of a sufficient number of scholarly men to test the desirability and practicability of organizing in our country an institute similar in its aims and work to the Victoria Institute of Great Britain.

In 1891 the institute issued the following paper, which, having been revised by Dr. Deems himself, is practically his account of the rise and progress of this interesting society.

"WHAT IS THE AMERICAN INSTITUTE OF CHRISTIAN PHILOSOPHY?

"Recently a very intelligent manufacturer asked whether there is any organized movement to antagonize materialism and other forms of false philosophy. There is, and the following is an account of its origin and progress:

"To ascertain whether there was enough interest in the subject to justify an attempt to form a society specially devoted to the creation and distribution of a literature illustrating the relations between science and religion, in the summer of 1881, at Warwick Woodlands, on Greenwood Lake, in New Jersey, there was delivered a course of lectures, beginning on the 12th and closing on the 22d of July. The following were the lecturers: the Rev. Dr. Deems, of the Church of the Strangers; President Noah Porter, of Yale College; Professor Borden P. Bowne, of Boston University; Professor Stephen Alexander and Professor Charles A. Young, of Princeton; the Rev. Dr. A. H. Bradford, of Montclair; Professor Alexander Winchell, of the University of Michigan; the Rev. Dr. Lyman Abbott, of the 'Christian Union'; the Rev. Dr. J. H. McIlvaine, of Newark, N. J.; Professor B. N. Martin, of the University of New York; and Professor John Bascom, of the University of Wisconsin; in the order of their names.

"The whole expense of this course, which was liberally maintained, was borne by Mr. William O. McDowell, of New York.

"*Organized in* 1881

"It was so successful that on the 21st of July a meeting was called for the purpose of organizing the American Institute of Christian Philosophy. At its organization the Rev. Dr. Deems was elected provisional president, the Rev. Dr. Bradford provisional secretary, and Mr. William O. McDowell provisional treasurer. President McCosh, of Princeton, and President Battle, of North Carolina, Bishop Cheney, of Illinois, and Bishop McTyeire, of Tennessee, Professor Bascom, of Wisconsin, and General G. W. Custis Lee, of Virginia, were the first vice-presidents. The first monthly meeting was held at Warwick Woodlands on the 28th of August, 1881. The second was held on the 29th of September, 1881, in the parlor of the Church of the Strangers, 4 Winthrop Place, New York. The officers of that church generously provided an office and a place of meeting for the institute from the second monthly meeting until November, 1889, when the meetings were held for a few months in Association Hall, Twenty-third Street and Fourth Avenue. Since June, 1890, they have been held in Hamilton Hall, Columbia College. The number of members to-day exceeds five hundred, including many of the most distinguished thinkers in Europe and America.

" *Papers and Lectures*

" During the first ten years monthly meetings have been held regularly except in the summer months. At those meetings there have been seventy-seven papers read. Two sermons have been delivered before the institute in New York, one by the late Rt. Rev. Bishop Harris, of the diocese of Michigan, on January 18, 1885, in St. Thomas's Church, Fifth Avenue, and another by the Rev. James R. Day, D.D., on February 21, 1886, in the Madison Avenue Methodist Episcopal Church. Two courses of lectures were delivered in the Broadway Tabernacle Church in the winters of 1882–83 and 1883–84.

" *Bishop Potter*

" At the delivery of Bishop Harris's sermon Bishop Potter presided, and followed the sermon with remarks expressing his interest in the institute and its work and his hearty coöperation with it. He thanked the preacher for his admirable address, and said that the Institute of Christian Philosophy had been organized to get at those fundamental truths which more especially concerned society and men. Its members were not confined to any denomination, but embraced, in addition to various bishops of the Episcopal Church, eminent scholars and professors throughout the country. In speaking of what the institute is doing, the bishop said that its publications had already been sought for by some of the scholars in Japan, who were now especially turning their thoughts to the Christian religion as the religion of the country.

" Summer Schools

" The institute has held fifteen summer schools, the first and second at Warwick Woodlands, the third at Atlantic Highlands, the fourth, sixth, and eighth at Richfield Springs, the eleventh at Round Lake, the seventh at Asbury Park and Key East, and the others at Avon-by-the-Sea, N. J. At these schools one hundred and seventy-seven lectures have been delivered, also four sermons.

" Colleges Represented

" These one hundred and seventy-seven lectures have been prepared with great care, and many of them by our foremost thinkers. The lecturers have represented the following colleges, namely, Bowdoin, City of New York, Columbia, Dickinson, Emory, Hamilton, Lafayette, Rutgers, Smith, St. Stephen's, Trinity, and Tufts, and the following universities, namely, Boston, Cornell, Harvard, New York, North Carolina, Pennsylvania, Princeton, Texas, Vanderbilt, Virginia, Wisconsin, and Yale. In addition to the presidents and professors from these colleges, other gentlemen of other learned professions and intellectual men in business circles have contributed to the literature called forth by the institute, among them the distinguished explorer, Hormuzd Rassam, of England, and the acute thinker, Ram Chandra Bose, of India.

" Chancellor MacCracken

" These valuable productions of the institute have been issued periodically and now constitute eight large octavo volumes, of which Dr. MacCracken, vice-chancellor of the University of the City of New York and professor of philosophy, says, ' The lectures and magazines it [the institute] gives each year are themselves almost a faculty of graduate philosophy for the whole country.' The lectures and other papers and the transactions are issued in a bimonthly called ' Christian Thought,' a copy of which is sent to all members. It has also a large list of subscribers among those who are not members of the institute.

" An Endowment Fund Needed

" Attention is called to the fact that its officers serve the institute without salary. There are no honorary members. There are no expenses for rent. No other institute can be managed more economically. All the income from membership fees and other sources is employed in meeting the expenses of the monthly meetings and summer schools, which produce the papers and lectures, and in printing and distributing this literature. There are schools and colleges and mission stations making appeals, to which the institute cannot respond. An endowment fund has been begun, which now amounts to over fifteen thousand dollars. It is wisely invested. The gift of one hundred dollars to this fund makes the giver a life-member, and he thereafter receives all the publications. One thousand dollars will establish a lectureship to bear the donor's name, and he may annually nominate the person he wishes to deliver the lecture. Thus will be created a fountain of blessing which will continue to flow when those living now shall have passed from the work on earth. It is desired to make this fund sufficiently large and productive to meet all expenses of the institute, so that every donation, together with the regular membership fees, may be devoted to the distribution of our literature in all lands.

" Results Already Accomplished

" The work of this institute cannot be computed in figures. It has made a noble stand against materialism and all other forms of false philosophy. It has presented an array of talent which shows the world that all the brains are not on the side of those who scorn or neglect our holy faith, but that the very best intellects of the world, the most competent judges among men, are on the side of the truth as it is in Jesus. It has strengthened the faith and courage of the young men of colleges, among whom its publications have been distributed. A physician who cures many patients can make a resounding reputation, while almost none but the most thoughtful place proper value on sanitary prevention. Thus the institute has not attracted the attention of the masses, and has none of the aid which comes to other institutions by reason of the conspicuousness of results. It must therefore appeal for its support more to the few who are able to value the solidity of a foundation than to the many who casually admire the beautiful outlines of a structure and the brilliant frescos on its ceilings.

" Who May Become Members

" The institute invites to its membership men and women, learned and unlearned, who wish by their names and fees to aid in its good work. One need not say he resides too far from the seat of the institute to take part in its meetings, and therefore he does not become a member. He will receive the publications containing all its papers and lectures, and by his fee help to procure them for his brother who cannot afford such a luxury. The institute is in receipt of frequent letters from home missionaries, pastors of churches at home and abroad, and professors in colleges, whose stipend is so small as to compel them reluctantly to forego or to drop membership. If some one would send one hundred dollars twenty such names could be reinstated. That a man cannot contribute to the production of its literature is no more reason for that man's not becoming a member of the institute than the fact that he cannot produce such writings as the prophecies of Isaiah or the epistles of Paul is a reason for his not becoming a member of the American Bible Society. The annual fee of five dollars helps to stem the tide of infidelity. For further information address Mr. Charles M. Davis, Secretary, 4 Winthrop Place, New York."

From the time that he had been professor of logic in the University of North Carolina and professor of natural science in Randolph-Macon College, Virginia, Dr. Deems had taken a growing interest in science and philosophy; and from the day of his conversion his interest in Christ and Christianity had been increasing. So it was with a large measure of experience and ability, as well as with glowing zeal, that Dr. Deems nurtured the American Institute of Christian Philosophy, a society whose supreme aim was to proclaim and enforce the truth that, however much conflict there may be between false science and dogmatic theology, there is perfect harmony between real science and the religion of Christ and the Bible.

The executive work of the institute and the correspondence involved in making out the annual program of lecturers, to say nothing of the work of editing " Christian Thought," added much to his regular labors, and were pecuniarily expensive rather than remunerative to him. But it was a labor of love with him, and he received much practical help from his faithful amanuensis, Miss Cecile Sturtevant, and from the Rev.

Amory H. Bradford, D.D., Secretary Charles M. Davis, Associate Secretary the Rev. John B. Devins, and others. During Dr. Deems's illness the Rev. J. B. Devins had the entire charge of editing " Christian Thought," and otherwise relieved the president of anxiety in regard to the institute.

Through the efforts of Dr. Deems and the generosity of Mr. Cornelius Vanderbilt and others, an endowment fund for the institute was started, which at the time of Dr. Deems's death amounted to over fifteen thousand dollars. The last two summer schools during his life were held at Prohibition Park, Staten Island. During the last summer school, held in August, 1893, Dr. Deems, for the first time since the institute was founded, was absent; but in spirit he was present. As his son Edward was about to start for the grounds, Dr. Deems with extreme difficulty managed to send this message:

" Tell the officers and members of the American Institute of Christian Philosophy at the summer school that in spirit I will be with them promptly at every meeting of the session; that I am working for them daily by striving to secure members for the institute and subscribers for ' Christian Thought,' and by sending out the circulars which tell of the objects and work of this institute. My hands, in the providence of God, are tied. Tell them," he said distinctly, " tell the officers and members to select another president, an active president, and to work more; tell officers and members to *work more.*"

When the good president passed away it was realized how difficult a task it would be to fill his place. The Rev. Dr. Amory H. Bradford was persuaded to accept the presidency for one year. Then Henry M. MacCracken, D.D., LL.D., chancellor of the University of New York, was made president. The summer schools of 1894 and 1895 were held at Chautauqua Lake. But the future of the institute became more and more problematic. About this time, however, a letter from Dr. Deems, found among his effects after his decease, was brought to light and materially helped the officers of the institute to shape its future course. This letter was directed to Charles M. Davis, so many years the institute's faithful secretary, Dr. Alexander Mackay-Smith, Cornelius Vanderbilt, and the Rev. Edward M. Deems. It reads as follows:

"My Friends and Brothers: I prepare a paper which you will not see until my eyes are closed in death. The fact that it is addressed to you shows my confidence in your brotherly affection, discreet judgment, and Christian faith.

"More than most other men, you know what has been in my heart in all the work I have bestowed upon the American Institute of Christian Philosophy. I know nothing in this world can run on in the same courses forever. It may become expedient that the machinery for doing our work may have to be altered, that the time may come when something must be substituted for the monthly meetings and the annual summer schools of the institute. It may be that a course of lectures delivered each year by some able man may be the institute's contribution to our most holy faith. I have seen the folly of the attempt of men to stretch their hands from out their graves to push back the inevitable or to preserve unaltered something which, however good for its time, could not be useful for all time.

"I simply want to say that if you survive me I do not wish for a single moment that any sentimental regard for plans which I have formed and prosecuted shall keep you from making such alterations in the work of the institute as shall be adapted to the time. My sole desire is that any moneys which I have collected and any prestige which I have created for the institute shall be wisely used to promote the knowledge of 'the truth as it is in Jesus,' in ways best adapted to that end, from time to time.

"Perhaps this letter is an impertinent assumption. It will

stand, however, as a slight testimonial of my great respect and unfeigned affection for you, who have been my helpers in this department of my work for the divine Master.

"CHARLES F. DEEMS."

No one can read this document, written in April, 1892, eight months before he was paralyzed, without being struck by the sweetness of spirit and breadth and profundity of judgment of its author. Helped to a decision by this letter, the institute took steps which resulted in the fifteen-thousand-dollar endowment fund being given to the University of the City of New York, to establish a " Deems Lectureship of Philosophy." And this lectureship is the fruit of Dr. Deems's prayers and toils as founder and president of the American Institute of Christian Philosophy.

CHAPTER XIV

THE story of the twelve years of Dr. Deems's life from 1880 to 1892 may be summed up in one word, *work*. "Never hasting, never resting," Goethe's motto, would have been a most appropriate motto for Dr. Deems at this period. His legitimate work as a preacher and pastor received the most and the best of his time, brains, and toil; what was left of time and energy he gave to his duties as president of the American Institute of Christian Philosophy, editor of "Christian Thought," trustee of the American Tract Society, member of the council of the University of the City of New York, member of the executive committee of the Evangelical Alliance in the United States, lecturer, writer for periodicals, and author of several books. He lived before and for the public, an entry in his journal for January 28, 1886, being significant: "In the house all the evening. Wonderful!"

His native wit and keen sense of the ludicrous, combined with a hopeful disposition and a childlike trust in God, saved him from breaking down earlier than he did under the strain to which he subjected himself. The Rev. Dr. Howard Crosby and he, in conversation one day, agreed that the reason why they stood up under the strain of the intense life of a New York City pastor, while others broke down or died, was that they worked without worry; that it is worry, not work, that kills most active men.

Speaking of Dr. Crosby, whom Dr. Deems admired and loved, suggests one of the sunny features of these last years of the latter's life; we refer to the Philothean Club, a circle of ministers, who met at the homes of the members every Saturday afternoon, and, after business and the discussion of a paper, enjoyed a feast of reason and a flow of soul around the dinner-table. Strong friendships were here formed and old friendships were strengthened. Nor is this to be wondered at when it is remembered that among the members of " Philo " were such men as Crosby, Robinson, Watkins, Bridgman, Page, Sabine, Warren, Mandeville, Payson, Martyn, Schauffler, Virgin, Bevan, Roe, Gregg, and Sanders. The meetings of Philo were used as a clearing-house for the ludicrous experiences and the good jests and jokes of its members. It was after one of these meetings that Dr. Deems came home and said that Dr. Crosby had slandered him by accusing him of "taking up collections at funerals." Doubtless Dr. Deems had a ready reply, for he was gifted in repartee.

We recall a few of his bright sayings with which, for himself and others, he used to beguile life's way of its tedium.

A lady who was brought through a season of great despondency and grief by his sympathy, prayers, counsel, and practical aid said to him a few years afterward, " Doctor, do you remember how I used to wish I was dead? " With a look very different from the words, he flashed back, " Yes, and everybody else wished so too."

At a marriage ceremony which he was conducting the rats in the ceiling kept up a most annoying accompaniment. When some one spoke of it afterward he said, " Yes, I noticed the marriage was being ratified on earth."

Once, after being absent from the city, an intimate friend called on him, and was received with these words: " Now come, tell me where you have been these ten days." " Well, doctor," was the reply, " I have been to Stonington, and it rained every day while I was there!" "Ah," said he, his eyes twinkling with fun, "that was your reign in Stonington!"

In the midst of an eloquent temperance speech he was once interrupted by some one putting the question, "But suppose we can't elect the best man?" The answer was flashed back without a second's hesitation, "I am not required to elect, but to vote for, the best man."

As a raconteur few men of his day could surpass him, and his journal shows in what demand he was as an after-dinner speaker at alumni, club, and other banquets. When he told a story it was evident that no one enjoyed it more than he. His lively imagination and inventive talent led him to embellish and improve on the stories he had read or heard; and when his family or friends would twit him on having changed his story he would invariably reply, "It is one of the fundamental rules for telling a story never to tell it in the same way twice."

It was largely on account of his cheerfulness and wit that he made friends so quickly with children and young people, and, indeed, with everybody whom he met who was not impervious to sunshine. In the New York Hotel, where with his good wife he lived from March 30, 1889, until he was stricken with paralysis, December 27, 1892, it was a common saying that everybody loved Dr. Deems, from the boot-black in the basement up to the proprietor.

His love for young people found, shortly after his return from the Holy Land, a worthy object. On February 2, 1881, a wave of youthful devotion started in Maine and rolled westward. He saw it coming, and when it reached him mounted its crest and rode it until the Everlasting Arm reached down and under him and lifted him to glory ineffable and unending. Dr. Deems loved and was beloved by the Young People's Society of Christian Endeavor. The young people of his parish and of the land appreciated his affection for them and his aid to their cause. Many more invitations than he could respond to were extended to him to address societies and local and national conventions of the Young People's Society of Christian Endeavor.

Dr. Deems derived especial pleasure from his visit to the international convention of the Young People's Society of Christian Endeavor held at Minneapolis, Minn. With a train-load of delegates, he was delayed nearly two days *en route*. In the entry in his journal for July 9, 1891, he writes: "Great delay. We should be in Minneapolis, and here we are a day away. But the company are behaving beautifully and we are a happy band of Christians." At the railway station at Durand the Endeavorers alighted from the train and joined enthusiastically in an open-air meeting that was being held by the Salvation Army. Being called upon to address the meeting, Dr. Deems gave all his powers free play and made the scene one long to be remembered as a little foretaste of heaven.

With his passion for improving opportunities and organizing forces, Dr. Deems led in the formation on the train of what is known among Christian Endeavorers as the "Soo Tribe," because organized while traveling on the "Soo" (Sault Ste. Marie) route to Minneapolis. The Soos were wonderfully drawn together and to their "chief" by the experiences of this memorable trip, and still maintain a happy *esprit de corps*.

When the great Young People's Society of Christian Endeavor international convention was held in New York City, July 7, 1892, Dr. Deems was greatly gratified by being chosen to deliver the address of welcome on behalf of the pastors of New York City. In his address, after giving in complimentary terms his estimate of the body of men he represented, he expressed his opinion of the institution represented by the magnificent assemblage in Madison Square Garden, which numbered between fifteen and twenty thousand people. Dr. Deems's opinion of the Young People's Society of Christian

Endeavor as expressed on this occasion lies in this sentence uttered by him: "The spirit of this society, more than any other found on earth in this nineteenth century, reminds one of Christ's Christianity." Dr. Deems wrote for the Endeavorers the following stirring hymn, which was sung at this convention by the vast chorus of youthful voices to the tune of "The Star-spangled Banner." There is something wonderfully stirring in this shout of the spiritual warrior within a few months of his being stricken down in the midst of the battle.

"THE BANNER OF JESUS

"See, see, comrades! see, floating high in the air,
    The love-woven, blood-sprinkled banner of Jesus!
The symbol of hope, beating down all despair,
    From sin and its thraldom triumphantly frees us.
        By the hand that was pierced
        It was lifted at first,
When the bars of the grave by our Captain were burst.

Refrain:

"That blood-sprinkled banner must yet be unfurled
O'er the homes of all men and the thrones of the world.

"Shout, shout, comrades! shout, that our Captain and Lord
    That standard of hope first intrusted to woman;
And Mary, dear saint, in obeying his word
    Flung out its wide folds over all that is human:
        So there came to embrace
        That sweet ensign of grace
All the true and the great, all the best of our race.

"March, march, comrades! march, all the young, all the old,
    The army of Christ and of Christian Endeavor;
With heroes our souls having now been enrolled,
    Our banner we'll follow for ever and ever.
        For our march shall not cease
        Till the gospel of peace
Shall our race in all lands from its tyrant release."

While lending a helping hand to other good causes during the last and best years of his life, Dr. Deems never lost sight of nor neglected that cause which, as we have seen, drew out his first public efforts as a writer for the press—the cause of temperance. Temperance never had a more loyal friend than Dr. Deems. When the angel of death came in November, 1893, and announced to him that at the close of the seventy-third year of his life God had promoted him to the higher experiences and activities of heaven, it found him, by tongue and pen, by preaching, praying, voting, and every other means, doing all that he could to destroy that remorseless enemy of society, the liquor traffic, and thus to glorify God by saving souls from the drunkard's ruinous career and destiny.

Devotion to the cause of temperance, although more conspicuous in his riper years of life, was no late fancy nor passing whim. His first survey of human society, taken as it was through the atmosphere of a Christian home, made his heart ache over men's sufferings from strong drink, and made his whole soul indignant at that fatuity of human society and government which tolerates in Christendom, in the nineteenth century, a habit and a traffic so inimical to God and so bitterly hostile to all the interests of mankind.

Referring to Dr. Deems's autobiographical notes, the reader may see that while only thirteen years of age he delivered at Elk Ridge, and elsewhere in Maryland, temperance addresses. Let the children who may read these pages learn how early one may begin to help in this good work; and let parents, as they note how this child was *formed* to temperance ideas and habits by his parents, learn how much more hope of success lies, for the friends of temperance, in *formation* than in *reformation*. Grateful to godly parents for what they had done for him in this direction, Dr. Deems to the end of his career, while favoring the reformation of drunkards by every possible means, yet emphasized the formation of temperance ideas and habits, and for this formation trusted in part to education at home and at school, but chiefly to the regenerating and sanctifying power of the Lord Jesus Christ.

Referring again to his autobiographical notes, the reader may find that in 1852, in the vigor of his young manhood, he was still an enthusiastic but practical worker for the temperance cause; for in that year he started and edited the "Ballot-box," one of the first organs, if not the very first organ, of those who believe in legislation as a help to the solution of the liquor problem. In 1852, also, Dr. Deems inaugurated a movement which resulted in a memorial going to the legislature of North Carolina on the subject of the legal prohibition of the liquor traffic, signed by over fifteen thousand people. Now, when we remember that it was not until two years later, namely, in 1854, that in the State of Maine prohibitory laws against the liquor traffic went into effect, we see that Dr. Deems is worthy to be remembered as one of the *pioneers* of the legal prohibition movement. And the longer he lived and studied this problem, and the more closely he came in touch with the practical effects of alcoholic stimulants, the deeper grew his convictions, the more frequent and eloquent his appeals, and the more persistent and practical his efforts, to abolish, first, indeed, by moral suasion, but also by legal suasion, that most successful enemy of God and human hearts and homes, the accursed liquor business.

During the last ten years of his life Dr. Deems, from being an independent voter, became a voter with the Prohibition party. But he did not regard that party as perfect or worthy of a blind following, frequently saying, "I will, other things being equal, vote with any party which has in its platform a plank favoring the prohibition of the manufacture and sale of liquor for use as a beverage." Dr. Deems, in joining the Prohibition party, gave in an article written for the "Voice" this reason for taking the step: "Heretofore I have belonged to no party, voting for Republican or Democrat according to the character of the candidates when I have voted at all. Now I am a Prohibitionist simply and solely because I see no other way of destroying the saloons which are destroying our people —no other way except by a revolution and bloodshed, and this I deprecate; but the saloons *must be swept away.*"

Of course Dr. Deems's wisdom and eloquence made him to be much in demand as a temperance orator, and his journal is full of records of temperance addresses delivered in various parts of the Union during the last ten years of his life. In an address on temperance which he delivered on several occasions he dealt with the liquor question, first, as of universal interest; secondly, as a question of political economy transcending in importance civil-service reform, ballot protection, the tariff, and other great questions receiving at the time attention in America; thirdly, with reference to the character of the men engaged as being unchristian, dishonest (because dealing in adulterated goods), and defiers of the law; and fourthly, he put the question, *What is to be done?* Then he gave the two answers: (1) Regulate and restrict the liquor traffic by high-license laws. (2) Prohibit the traffic. The latter course he favored as the true course, whether it succeeded or not, because it has these advantages: (1) It will withhold sanction of a wicked traffic. (2) It will discountenance that traffic. (3) It will educate the people. (4) It will give moral dignity to the nation. The objections raised are equally applicable to the decalogue, which never has been enforced. The address was closed substantially as follows:

"There was once an old Roman senator who was accustomed to conclude every speech he made in the senate with these words: 'Carthago delenda est!'— 'Carthage must be destroyed!' He knew that so long as Carthage existed Rome would have woe. For the new party I would have the watchword, 'Caupona delenda est!'—'The saloon must be destroyed!' and I would set aside every other issue until the country did see the saloon destroyed."

On the evening of October 3, 1887, there assembled in the Church of the Strangers a notable gathering. It had been called together by the officers of the church, and its object was to celebrate the close of twenty-one years of pastorate of Dr. Deems. The Rev. Dr. Thomas Armitage, D.D., LL.D. (Baptist), presided, and the vice-presidents were his honor the mayor, Abram S. Hewitt, Esq., William E. Dodge, Esq., Ex. Norton, Esq., R. R. McBurney, Esq., Hon. Stewart L. Woodford, Hon. Thomas F. Bayard, John H. Inman, Esq., Hon. O. B. Potter, Hon. Roger A. Pryor, Hon. Algernon S. Sullivan, Cornelius Vanderbilt, Esq., General Clinton B. Fisk, James Talcott, Esq. The vice-presidents were either present and spoke in the course of the evening, or else sent letters of warmest congratulation and commendation for Dr. Deems and his work. Addresses breathing the sincere spirit of brotherly love and expressive of appreciation of Dr. Deems's gifts and labors were made by the Rev. Drs. Armitage (Baptist), Philip Schaff (Presbyterian), Mackay-Smith (Protestant Episcopal), William M. Taylor (Congregationalist), John M. Reid (Methodist Episcopal), William Ormiston (Reformed Dutch), Wilbur F. Watkins (Protestant Episcopal), Howard Crosby (Presbyterian), and Gustav Gottheil (rabbi, Temple Emanu-El). At the opening of the services the Scriptures were read by Vice-Chancellor Henry M. MacCracken (now chancellor), of the University of New York, and prayer was offered by the Rev. John Hall, D.D., pastor of the Fifth Avenue Presbyterian Church. The names of those who took part in this service are an eloquent tribute both to Dr. Deems's catholicity of spirit and to his ability and success as a pastor and preacher.

A felicitous reply by Dr. Deems followed, in which, with evident emotion, he thanked his brethren, and toward the close of which he said: "Now, all I can say in conclusion is that you have put me under bonds to be good, and I will strive to be. Having tried to be modest for two or three hours,—and modesty is only one characteristic of goodness,—and having found it so hard, I am afraid that I shall find it extremely difficult to come up to the standard set to-night. I will endeavor to do my best. I do not suppose that I shall be any taller next Sunday when I come to this pulpit. Certainly I shall not stand on a stool, as has been suggested by a gifted brother. I am not in the habit of standing on anything to make me taller."

Busy as he was during his last years in the pulpit and pastorate and on the platform, Dr. Deems found time for much literary work, as he wrote for periodicals and published three new books.

In January, 1881, appeared the first number of the "Christian Worker," an eight-page illustrated religious paper. It was and still is the organ of the Church of the Strangers. Mrs. Sara Keables Hunt, a devoted and valued member of the Church of the Strangers, was appointed editor, and still holds that position, which she has filled with ability, making the "Christian Worker" one of the best fruits of the church. In it appeared not only Dr. Deems's monthly report of his work as pastor, but also many articles from his pen.

As president of the American Institute of Christian Philosophy and editor of "Christian Thought" he wrote a number of articles along the line of the harmony of science and religion. Several books written by Dr. Deems were published during this period. "The Deems Birthday Book," arranged by Sara Keables Hunt, contains about five hundred brief extracts culled from the best of Dr. Deems's writings. It was published in 1882. In 1885 a new edition of his sermons was published. In 1887 "A Romance of Providence, being a History of the Church of the Strangers," appeared. It was edited by Mr.

Joseph S. Taylor, but involved no inconsiderable amount of work on Dr. Deems's part. "The Gospel of Common Sense as Contained in the Canonical Epistle of James," a volume of three hundred and twenty-two pages, was published in 1888. This work was followed up in 1891 by a companion book entitled, "The Gospel of Spiritual Insight, being Studies in the Gospel of John." Both these works received high encomiums from the press of America and Great Britain.

"Chips and Chunks for Every Fireside," a handsome illustrated volume of six hundred and forty pages, was published as a subscription book in 1890. It contained not so much new matter as a careful selection and orderly arrangement of articles, essays, and booklets, not including sermons, which Dr. Deems had in preceding years given to the public. It was meant to be, as the author puts it in his preface, "a book for homes."

The introduction to "Chips and Chunks" was written by Dr. Chauncey M. Depew, and we insert it here as being an estimate of Dr. Deems by an able, practical, and successful business man:

"In dictating an introduction to this work I am actuated by two motives—personal friendship for the author and admiration for his book.

"The work has been lying upon my desk for several weeks, and I have taken it up at various times, dipping into it here and there, as a busy man naturally would. I have been impressed with the wide range of Dr. Deems's studies, the breadth of his sympathies, and his wise way of putting things.

"The doctor has been a man of great activity and a multifarious author; but while with most authors their utterances are purely ephemeral, the doctor manages to put into every article from his pen something worth preserving. It is well known that Dr. Deems had the confidence of Commodore Vanderbilt, whose practical judgment was probably keener and more accurate than that of any other man who ever lived in this country, and upon the doctor's advice the commodore spent hundreds of thousands of dollars for beneficent objects.

"The qualities which impressed Dr. Deems upon Commodore Vanderbilt and also upon his son, William H., are everywhere evident in this book—honesty of purpose, a clear conception of the object in view, lucidity of statement, and wisdom of suggestion. I am sure that this work will be found of value in the home circle, both to the old and to the young.

"CHAUNCEY M. DEPEW."

In March, 1892, the "Evening World" offered a prize of twenty dollars in gold for the best article on "How to Manage a Wife." Dr. Deems appeared as happy as a boy prize-winner at school when he was informed that he had won the prize. His article was as follows:

"Manage? What is that? Does it mean to control? We manage a horse. We use our superior human intellect to control and guide his superior physical strength so as to obtain the best results. But a wife is not a horse. When two persons are well married the wife is as superior to her husband in many respects as he is superior to her in others. If happiness is to be the result of the union the first business of the husband is to manage himself so as to keep himself always the wife's respectful friend, always her tender lover, always her equal partner, always her superior protector. This will necessarily stimulate his wife to be always his admiring friend, always his affectionate sweetheart, always his thrifty housewife, always his confiding ward. And this will so react upon the husband that his love for his wife will grow so as to make it easy for him, with all his faults, to bear with all the infirmities of his 'one and only' wife.

"A JOINER."

In the spring of 1892 Dr. Deems copyrighted the last book
he ever published, "My Septuagint." In this volume of two
hundred and eight pages, daintily bound in white and gold,
Dr. Deems writes this brief preface: "The name of this book
suggested itself to my mind because what it contains has been
written since the *seventieth* anniversary of my birthday. That
is all." The volume is inscribed, "To the memory of the
seventy men, all departed this life, personal contact with whom
now seems to have been most influential for good in the formation of my character and the furtherance of my career." Then
follow the names—a notable list of good and-great men who
lived in America and Europe. "At Seventy-one," "The
Present Outlook in Theology," "George Washington," "Address of Welcome to the Young People's Society of Christian
Endeavor," and "Mr. Markham's Dream" (a temperance
allegory) are the titles of some of the chapters. Several new
hymns appeared in the volume. One we insert as being
prophetic:

"THE LIGHT IS AT THE END

"At the thought of love eternal
Time began its course in night;
'Twas the evening and the morning,
First the darkness, then the light.
Let us not grow weary watching
In the shadows God may send;
Darkness cannot last forever,
And the light is at the end.
Refrain:
Go bravely through the darkness,
For the light is at the end.

"On the paths we now are walking
Our great Master's feet have trod;
And each weary, faltering footstep
Brings us nearer to our God.

> Then in passing through the valley,
> When the shadows o'er us bend,
> Let us keep our courage steady,
> For the light is at the end.

> " We shall soon be called to travel
> Through the vale of death's dark shade;
> But we know who will be with us,
> And we shall not be afraid.
> We shall cheer the way with music,
> Walking with our Saviour-Friend,
> Leaning on his staff, and gazing
> At the light that's at the end."

Probably the most interesting chapter in " My Septuagint" is the first, in which Dr. Deems wrote, among other things: " I sit in my study and talk to my heart and dictate these lines, and feel that I am approaching the experience of the Apostle Paul: ' For me to live is Christ, and to die is gain.' . . . Being assured of the immortality of my spirit because of my spiritual alliance with him, I have ceased to pray to be delivered from sudden death, which may be a blessing." It was but a few short months after penning these words that, one day, in his study—it was December 16, 1892—his pen dropped from the hand which had guided it so patiently, so industriously, so effectively, for so many years.

He did not appear to be alarmed, but his family and friends were. It was hoped, however, that it was only "writers' cramp" and that a season of rest would make all right. Everything was done to shield and save him. But he insisted on preaching once on Sunday, December 18th. In the morning the Rev. Dr. Heidt preached, and in the evening, sitting in the pulpit chair, a picture never to be forgotten by those who saw him, Dr. Deems preached to his people from Colossians iii. 16: " Let the word of Christ dwell in you richly in all wisdom." It was his last word to men from the pulpit.*

* See Appendix I.

In view of the paralytic stroke which fell upon him ten days later, how pathetic the following letter to his people, read from the pulpit and published in the " Christian Worker "!

" (Dictated.)

" Christmas, 1892.

" My dear People : I seem to have reached another station where I must rest. Such is the verdict of my consulting physicians, and they lay great emphasis on the *must*.

" I am glad that I was permitted last Sunday night to talk to you awhile on that blessed passage of Holy Scripture, ' Let the word of Christ dwell in you richly in all wisdom.' I leave that with you while I go away to rest awhile.

" I rejoice to know that already such beloved servants of God as Dr. Schauffler, Professor Hamilton, Edward M. Deems, and John Paul Egbert have consented to serve you. You will serve the interest of our beloved Church of the Strangers in proportion as you love it. I have no more to ask.

" I know that you will remember me in your prayers; and you know that I will return to my pulpit just as soon as I believe it right to give myself the dear delight of preaching to you the gospel of our blessed God, to whom be glory for ever and ever. Amen!

" Affectionately yours,

" Charles F. Deems."

And this paragraph, with which he closes his monthly report to his church:

" This report was kindly written for me by another hand from my notes and journal. Since Friday, 16th inst., I have been unable to sign my name. I have left the church affairs in the hands of its dear officers, who have been always so faithful. I go aside awhile to rest. My soul is in perfect peace, because I know whom I have believed, and am persuaded that he is able to keep that which I have committed unto him until that day.

"Affectionately and faithfully your pastor,

"Charles F. Deems."

CHAPTER XV

DR. Deems's life during the year 1892 was intense, laborious, and fruitful. Looking back upon him in his work at this time, he reminds us of a man in a race, who, as he realizes that he is near the goal, by a supreme effort brings to the front all his latent powers. His records show that from January to December, 1892, he delivered in the form of sermons, lectures, or addresses one hundred and eighty-nine discourses. This involved visiting seven different States in various sections of the Union. Into each and all of these discourses he flung glowing enthusiasm, blended with the wisdom which comes from long study of books and men. An illustration of the strain to which he subjected himself in 1892 is his visit to Silver Lake Assembly, in western New York, where he delivered to vast congregations eight powerful discourses within four days.

While engaged in public speaking he kept up also his work as pastor, president of the American Institute of Christian Philosophy, and member or officer of various societies, committees, and institutions. In February his mind was greatly exercised by the question of the wisdom of removing the Church of the Strangers to some more favorable position. It was finally decided to drop the consideration of that matter for a time. In March his lifelong and beloved friend, Robert

339

S. Moran, D.D., died, and Dr. Deems was one of the speakers at his funeral in Wilmington, N. C. In August General James Lorimer Graham died, and in October Mrs. Graham passed away. By the death of these three friends, the best of about his own age he had in all the world, he was indeed bereft.

In July, 1892, the eleventh annual international convention of the Young People's Society of Christian Endeavor was held in Madison Square Garden, New York City, and Dr. Deems made a host of friends by his eloquent address of welcome.

On August 15th, while traveling with his wife in Canada, his nerves were subjected to a great shock by a thrilling experience on the St. Lawrence River. Mrs. Deems, in a letter written to her daughter, Mrs. Egbert, said:

" Your father and mother have made the narrowest escape of their lives, having just missed being dashed to pieces in the rapids. We left Alexandria Bay on the new steamer, ' Columbian,' a week ago last Monday, bound for Montreal, which we expected to reach that evening about seven o'clock. We had a perfect day, and everything went well until, between three and four o'clock in the afternoon, the rope connecting with the steering-gear suddenly broke, and then the hand steering-gear, the only other hope of saving the steamer, also broke. And all this happened while we were in the midst of the Cedar Rapids. But a merciful Providence directed us to a small island, where we were stranded on the rocks around it, about thirty feet from the island.

" As the steamer crashed upon the rocks I thought we were gone; and as father met me his exclamation was, ' Well, ma, let us thank God that we are *together*, whatever befalls!' and he looked so as though he thought our doom was imminent that I could think of nothing but a watery grave. But our brave crew went to work vigorously, and word was gotten to a small village not far off in Canada, Vaudreuil, and the boatmen came rowing over the rapids to the relief of the passengers.

"Trees were then cut down off this thickly wooded little island and with wonderful ingenuity contrived into a bridge from the steamer to the island. Then the steamer was securely moored by means of many strong ropes, for had we drifted off there seemed no hope but that we would have been plunged right into the most fearful of the rapids. Well, they succeeded in taking about half the passengers over before dark, having to row them from island to island over that swift current, the passengers (about one hundred of them) walking across the three islands before reaching the mainland of Canada. Father and I remained on the stranded steamer, preferring, with one hundred others, to remain on board until the next morning, after having been assured that there was no possibility of being carried off the rocks in the night.

" A religious service of thanksgiving was held on the boat at night, and it was a most interesting occasion. The next morning, Tuesday, all who had remained on the steamer were carried off; but I can assure you, dear daughter, that it was not without fear and trembling that your timid little mother committed herself to the rushing water in the small boat. But a merciful Father was better to us than all our fears, and we reached Montreal in safety at 2 P.M."

The remaining months of 1892 were marked by experiences and labors similar to those referred to already, only, if possible, they were even more intense and fruitful.

Is it to be wondered at that Dr. Deems's powers of endurance at last broke down under the strain? Although for ten days after his last sermon, delivered Sunday evening, December 18th, and referred to in the preceding chapter, Dr. Deems was able to go to his meals at the New York Hotel and attend to a little business, such as dictating letters, church reports, etc., yet his right side continued to lose feeling and motion. The crisis finally came Wednesday evening, December 28th. He and his wife were sitting quietly in their room at the hotel, reading and talking, when suddenly he lost all power of speech and all control of his right side. The stroke had come.

Mrs. Deems quickly called in friends in the hotel, Dr. Deems was helped to bed, a physician was promptly summoned, and everything possible done. But it was all of no avail. He was never to walk or talk naturally again. Thursday morning the Rev. Edward M. Deems arrived from Hornellsville, whence he had fortunately started the evening before, expecting to find his father resting comfortably. Other members of the family promptly arrived, as did also the family physician, Dr. Egbert Le Fevre. Dr. Deems had not lost consciousness, and throughout his eleven months' illness, with the exception of half the first day after the stroke, his mental faculties appeared to be almost as clear as they had ever been.

After a hurried consultation it was decided to move the patient immediately to No. 131 West Ninety-fifth Street, where resided Mr. Marion J. Verdery, Dr. Deems's son-in-law. Accordingly he was dressed and seated in a light, strong, straight-backed chair, in which his son Edward and Dr. Le Fevre bore him carefully to the elevator and thence to a carriage. It was a long drive from Waverly Place (Seventh Street) and Broadway to West Ninety-fifth Street, but the most smoothly paved streets and avenues were followed, and he stood the trip wonderfully well. From time to time he looked out of the carriage windows with a dazed expression, but appeared to be in no pain. Afterward he gave the family to understand that he had no recollection whatever of the journey from the hotel to the house.

Two excellent trained nurses, Mr. Moore and Mr. Olmsted, were secured, one for the day and one for the night. These men were with Dr. Deems most of the time until the end, and he became very much attached to them. At first his condition improved slowly but steadily. A few visitors were permitted to see him each day, and he kept up his cheerfulness wonderfully. He made a few attempts to write with his left hand, but that was soon abandoned as subjecting him to too much mental strain. Then a few of the words in more common use were written plainly on a piece of Bristol-board, in order that he might point to them and thus make known his ideas. But this well-meant effort also proved to be of but little practical use. However, the family and the nurses soon came to understand quite readily his wants and what he was trying to say. He could usually utter the main words in a sentence, leaving the listener to supply the others, always rewarding a quick diviner of his thought with a smile of delight. But it would be difficult to imagine a more pathetic sight than the silent, helpless figure of this man who for sixty years had been distinguished for eloquent speech and energetic action. At first it was apparent that he was engaged in a terrific mental and spiritual battle, but it was soon equally evident that he had won the day. Then patience and cheerfulness were his to the end.

Dr. Deems's many friends came forward nobly and cared for the church and the Institute of Philosophy. His recreations during his illness consisted in seeing his friends and in listening to reading, his wife generally being the reader. He had the newspapers and magazines read to him and went through several works of fiction. But no other reading was permitted to interfere with that of the Word of God and his devotional books. The letters which came to him from sympathizing friends in all parts of the land proved to be to him a source of great comfort. His inability to attend church services was a sore trial to him, and one day, as the family started for the Church of the Strangers, he broke down completely and wept. But he sent messages to the church, and early in the year 1893 established his custom of selecting and sending a verse from the Scriptures to be read from the pulpit of the Church of the Strangers as a message from the absent pastor. One of the last he sent was prophetic: "At evening time it shall be light" (Zech. xiv. 7).

During the first three months of 1893, as has been intimated, Dr. Deems appeared to gain in strength a little, notwithstanding some trouble from indigestion. In February he could, with the aid of the nurse, walk across the room. On February 17th the family, while waiting for the new home in West Seventy-sixth Street into which Mr. Verdery had decided to move, went into a commodious home at No. 517 West End Avenue. March and April were comparatively good months for Dr. Deems. It was while living on West End Avenue that he uttered the complete sentence which came to be known among many of his friends as " Dr. Deems's Easter sermon." Mr. Franklin Putnam, an officer of the Church of the Strangers and a loyal friend, wrote for the "Christian Worker" an account of this interesting episode, and the following extract we are sure will be appreciated by the readers of this memoir:

" You will remember that it was a lovely and charming day throughout, following in after many tedious stormy days; it had a beneficent effect on every one, sick or well. It was about 4 P.M. when I called, and it happened everything was favorable, so that I was ushered into the presence of Dr. Deems at once. Having heard how sick and helpless he had been for four months or more, I naturally expected him to appear as most persons would under such circumstances, very woebegone and broken up. Not so at all; on the contrary, he looked as brave and smiling and cheerful as if nothing at all troubled him. He could not rise, but he put out his left hand and tried to say something, which I interpreted to be his old familiar 'How are you, brother?' Then, with a smile on his face, he pointed out of doors, and I knew he desired to call attention to the beautiful weather. Then he listened very attentively to something I had to say, he making no attempt to reply or say anything, except, perhaps, in monosyllables. He is an excellent listener.

"Sothern, the actor, used to say, 'It's rather difficult for one bird to flock all by himself,' and likewise I soon found it rather difficult to carry on a conversation all by myself. But as soon as I stopped talking and the silence was becoming prolonged, a characteristic trait of Dr. Deems was manifested. How many times I have seen him come to the relief and tide over some embarrassing position or interval for others! On this occasion, as I sat there looking at him, not knowing just what next to say, suddenly there came a merry twinkle in his eye, and he straightened up as best he could and put on a very haughty, proud look, at the same time pointing alternately to his trousers and dressing-robe; but the more I tried the less I seemed to comprehend what he desired me to understand by his pantomime and erratic jumble of sounds and syllables, which seemed to begin where they should leave off, and *vice versa*. At last, in semi-despair, he looked appealingly to 'little mother,' who was present, and she readily interpreted it, 'He desires you to observe how he has come out in new Easter dress,' and explained that the garments were new and that it was the first time he had been dressed since Christmas.

"After that he made several other attempts to say something to me, and his face would light up with the greatest eagerness and anxiety in his effort and determination to overcome the bondage of his infirmity, but in the main they were failures. It was after one of these prolonged efforts, in which the writer and 'little mother,' to whom he invariably turned as his last resort, both failed, although we tried so hard to understand him, that he sank back exhausted by his effort and failure, and such a look of utter helplessness came over him, my emotions were almost beyond my control. I was trying to think of some word of sympathy, some word of cheer that would break the spell; but my heart was too full to utter words, and as I looked at him I saw a solitary tear drop from his half-closed eye. The silence was profound. It seemed to me something not unlike the agony of Jesus when he said, ' Father, if it be possible.'

" It was at this supreme moment that out from the silence came four words, spoken very slowly, very solemnly, but withal very distinct: ' *My—faith—holds—out.*' That was Dr. Deems's Easter sermon. Whatever from my imperfect, weak portrayal it may appear to others, to me it was the grandest, the most glorious, the most impressive sermon of his life."

About the middle of June the family moved to No. 145 West Seventy-sixth Street, where Dr. Deems had every comfort that loving hearts and hands could provide to soothe and sustain him. June 20th was a red-letter day for him and his good wife, for on that date their golden wedding was duly celebrated. Many visitors called at the house and left greetings of love. Early in the day the house became a perfect flower garden, and many beautiful golden gifts expressed the love of friends and relatives. Dr. Deems seemed to be given special strength for the occasion and entered into it with an enthusiasm which was to all a surprise.

In July an effort was made to promote progress in his recovery. Invited to visit Mr. John Inman's home at Stockbridge, Mass., Mr. Cornelius Vanderbilt, whose visits and other kind attentions contributed so much to lessen the trials of Dr. Deems's last days, put his private car at his disposal. Accordingly on July 21st, accompanied by Mrs. Deems, Mrs. Verdery, and a nurse, he went to Stockbridge. So far from the journey on the train injuring the patient, it gave him evident pleasure. But on the second day of his stay in the delightful and hospitable Inman home an internal complication set in, involving high fever and intense pain and endangering his life. Within a few days he was taken home, and after several weeks of extremely careful treatment was restored almost to his former condition, becoming strong enough in

time to take carriage rides and occasionally to take his meals
in the dining-room with the family.

During the fall months Dr. Deems was troubled more and
more by depression, and doubtless was losing vitality. It was
during the first days of November that a fresh internal complication set in, which, although not very painful, refused to
yield to treatment and steadily drained away his strength until,
after a heroic fight, his vitality was at last exhausted.

During the Wednesday night preceding the end Dr. Deems
several times made signs to his nurse by putting his hand up
to his mouth as though in the act of drinking. Was it water
that he wanted? "No." Was it one of his medicines?
"No." Finally the nurse asked him if it was the communion
that he wished. "Yes!" was indicated vigorously and with
smiles and expressions of deep satisfaction. Accordingly,
before breakfast Thursday morning, the family were assembled
in the sick-room around his bed, and Dr. Deems's son Edward
was about to commence the tender service, when his father
had him wait, as he looked around the circle and managed to
say, "Boy?" When the little grandson referred to was found
and seated near his grandfather on the bed, a service of surpassing tenderness and solemnity was held, the dying Christian
joining in here and there with a word in the service that he
could pronounce in the Lord's Prayer, the Gloria, and the
benediction. There was no "scene"; all was done simply,
naturally; but never will the participants forget that communion with one who was so soon to see "the King in his beauty."

Calling his faithful wife to his side early in the afternoon of
the same day, he took her hand and gave her a look in which
was not only recognition, but also unutterable affection, and
then settled back on his couch.

Dr. Arbuthnot wrote to Pope: "A recovery in my case and
at my age is impossible; the kindest wish of my friends is
euthanasia." Ninety-eight years thereafter Lockhart, when

speaking of the dying hours of his father-in-law, Sir Walter Scott, said: "Dr. Watson, having consulted on all things with Mr. Clarkson and his father, resigned the patient to them and returned to London. None of them could have any hope but that of soothing irritation. Recovery was no longer to be thought of, but there might be euthanasia."

When Dr. Deems felt himself beginning to yield to the drowsiness of the last sleep on earth, he by word and sign gave Dr. Le Fevre, his devoted physician, whom he greatly loved, to understand that when he became unconscious it was his wish that no further attempts should be made to keep his body alive a few hours longer, that no hypodermics of stimulants be given, and no nourishment administered. He knew that he was falling asleep in death, that on earth he would awaken nevermore, and, could he have spoken plainly, he would have said simply this: "I know that I am dying; recovery in my case and at my age is impossible; all that mortal skill could do has been done. Let me sleep." He was told it should be as he wished.

Not long after this he passed into sleep, and slept on for many hours; and in that sleep the end came. Just as the clock struck ten on Saturday evening, November 18, 1893, his spirit disengaged itself from his body and returned to God, and one of the most useful, eloquent, lovable, and beloved of men, Charles Force Deems, was dead! Dead? How hard, how impossible, it was and is for those who loved him to realize it!

The tidings of the death of the pastor of the Church of the Strangers spread rapidly through the land, and as they were received doubtless many a tear fell, in both high and low places, at the thought of the passing away of this wise, strong, holy, and lovable man.

The funeral services were held Tuesday noon, November 21st, in his beloved Church of the Strangers, where for nearly a quarter of a century he had with such winning eloquence preached Christ as the Saviour of the world.* For two hours before the services began the body lay in state before his pulpit, and thousands of people of both sexes and all ages and classes looked for the last time upon the face of him whom they so deeply loved. Everything connected with the occasion was marked by a simplicity accordant with his tastes, unless one should take exception to the profusion of flowers which love insisted on offering. In his hand was a beautiful white rose, placed there by one of his children because at Dickinson College, in 1839, he had written in a poem dedicated to the white rose this stanza:

> " Rose of my love! when chilling death
> Shall freeze my heart with his icy breath,
> I would have thee then, companion meet,
> Wrapped in the folds of my winding-sheet."

The church was filled to overflowing with people; many stood out in Mercer Street, and many more turned sadly away, unable to gain entrance. The Rev. Joseph Merlin Hodson, who during most of Dr. Deems's illness, and for some months after his death, served the church as pastor, conducted the services. The faithful church choir sang, among other things, Dr. Deems's hymn, "The light is at the end." The Rev. William T. Sabine, D.D., offered a prayer which seemed inspired, it was so full of rich consolation in Christ Jesus. After a brief but most appropriate and tender address by the Rev. Mr. Hodson, the Rev. James M. Buckley, D.D., preached the sermon, a discourse never to be forgotten by those who heard it, because it was not only a just and eloquent tribute to the noble dead, but also an unspeakable comfort to the living.† The Rev. Amory H. Brad-

* For the details of the funeral, including the addresses, the reader may see the New York daily papers for November 22, 1893; also the " Memorial Number of ' Christian Thought,' " February, 1893, published by W. B. Ketcham, 2 Cooper Union, New York City.
† See Appendix II.

ford, D.D., who had known Dr. Deems long and intimately, and who had been so loyal to the American Institute of Christian Philosophy, pronounced the benediction. Then followed the impressive masonic rites, conducted by Palestine Commandery of Knights Templars. And then, amid the suppressed sobs of his bereft people, the sainted pastor's precious body was borne out of the scene of his earthly labors to be laid to rest in the loving care of him who is able to keep until that day all that we commit to him.*

At the lower end of Staten Island the still thickly wooded and picturesque hills fall abruptly for two thirds their height, and then gradually slope downward to the green meadows which extend to the south shore. On a plateau of this slope stands a large, square, white wooden building, the old Moravian church, venerable with years. On all sides of it rise the marble-covered hills. Immediately around the old church building, beneath evergreens over a century old, lie the "rude forefathers of the hamlet," with only a small square slab of stone laid flatwise over the breast. The prevailing prefix of "Van" leaves no doubt as to their original nationality, and among these is that of the Vanderbilt family, one of whom, Mr. Cornelius Vanderbilt, the commodore, donated at one time fifty acres of land to the cemetery.

Standing upon any one of the higher knolls of this ideal "God's-acre," and looking southward, one obtains an extensive and beautiful view. The little hamlet of New Dorp, with its quaint and scattered farm-houses, including the village post-office and blacksmith's shop, lies at the foot of the knoll. Beyond are the extensive flat lands, which gently slope to the south shore of the island, merging into the blue waters of the lower bay of New York and the silver gray of the broad Atlantic. At the right can be seen a sapphire strip of land known as Sandy Hook, with a stretch of the Jersey coast

* For Memorials of Dr. Deems see Appendix III.

beyond, while at the left there is a full view of Coney Island, with the highlands of Long Island stretching toward Green-wood and the city of Brooklyn.

On the side nearest the sea is a smooth, grassy terrace, in the middle of which is Dr. Deems's family resting-place, a spot chosen by himself. No man could have been less influenced by material considerations than he; yet he took great satisfaction in knowing that here he was to sleep until the Master whom he had served so long and well should bid him arise and be forever with the Lord.

And so, upon that gray autumnal afternoon of Tuesday, November 21, 1893, Charles F. Deems was laid to rest there in sight of the great wide sea,—symbol of the infinite mercy of God,—laid to rest while awaiting the breaking of that resurrection day, the contemplation of the glories of which once, while preaching, led him to break forth in this language of holy rhapsody: "*O morning!* cloudless, tearless, brilliant, balmy, and everlasting! O men, O brothers! bear the weeping. The night is short; the morning comes. Break, O morning! break on the souls that are in the night of sin; and on our graves break, O morning of the everlasting day!"

" IN MEMORIAM

" *To Charles F. Deems*

" Friend of a lifetime! When, long years ago,
  We talked of death as of a legend thing
  That must perforce to others come, and bring
New lessons and new skill wherewith to know
Their meanings,—whether blent of joy or woe,—
  How full of life wert thou! how strong to wring
  Its secrets from the royal streams that spring
In venturous thought or fancy's overflow!
  Ah, couldst thou not a little longer wait
  Thy lagging fellow-traveler on life's road,

Now grown so weary? Thou dost ope the gate
Too soon, that shuts the human path we trode.
Thou taught'st me much of life to live—then why
Couldst thou not stay and teach me how to die?

" The voice we knew so well, whose vibrant tone
The hearts of thousands thrilled;
The voice that challenged us to scorn, disown,
All meaner aims, all selfishness bemoan—
Ah, can a God have willed
That voice like this be stilled?

" The willing feet that trod in lingering pain,
With humble, patient pace,
Through haunts of misery and guilt; that fain
Would follow other wounded feet, whose stain
On earth's paths left their trace—
Have such feet run their race?

" The flashing, subtle intellect, that saw
How fittest to enshrine
Its vivid imagery, was skilled to draw
The lightning thought from heaven to earth by law
Ineffable and fine—
Gone magic so divine?

" The heart that loved all noble love, that knew
Fidelities untold,—
Knew generous sacrifice for love, and drew
From life and death the passion to be true
To God,—can death enfold,
Can heart like this be cold?

"A. M. N."

APPENDIX

I

"Col. iii. 16. The Word of Christ. Embodied in the Holy Scriptures, New Testament. Different ways of using the Word. 1. *Outside*, as a rule for others, or instrument of compression for ourselves. 2. *Inside*. But it may be *poorly*. (1) In the memory, undigested. (2) In partial influence on our lives. But the apostle's injunction is: 1. It should 'keep house'; 2. It should 'keep house richly.' Each Christian an *incarnated gospel*. The doctrines of the gospel. The precepts of Christianity. The promises, all conditioned; conditions fulfilled, promises enjoyed. That will take the world."

II

ADDRESS OF JAMES M. BUCKLEY, D.D., AT THE FUNERAL OF CHARLES F. DEEMS, D.D., TUESDAY, NOVEMBER 21, 1893

After an eloquent account of Christianity's view of life and death, Dr. Buckley proceeded as follows:

"The question of the hour: What was the view of life and death held by him who is silent here for the first time? Did he consider it to be transcendingly important that he should live? Did he wish to die, or did he hold the exact view that Christianity requires—the view enforced and illustrated by Paul? Last Thanksgiving day Dr. Deems, with that bold hand which his friends recognize wherever they see it, wrote the name of a beloved child, and then, 'From her loving father.' The handwriting has outlived the hand, so frail is human life. It is a strange book—'My Septuagint.'

"'The name of this book probably suggested itself to my mind because what it contains has been written since the LXXII. anniversary of my birthday. . . . "How does a man feel at threescore years and ten?" I look into my heart and make the following additional response: I am not conscious of having any of those several symptoms which have generally been supposed to indicate old age, except the one pointed out by Solomon, "They shall be afraid of that which is high." I cannot climb as I once could. Four flights of stairs tire me very much, and I am sensible of a secret wish that all my dear parishioners and friends might live on the first floor. Otherwise, as I write to-day, with the splendor of this beautiful morning streaming into my study and lighting up the life-size portrait of my dear wife, who, by the way, has borne with my manners in this wilderness nine years longer than the Lord endured Israel, I do not feel any lessening of the ability of my body to give me pleasure. Yesterday three meals were eaten with as keen an appetite as the meals I took at college even on foot-ball days. I did more in the week preceding than in any week of my middle life, and last night for seven hours slept a sleep as sweet as that of my childhood. I enjoy beautiful sights—landscapes, lovely women and children, statuary and paintings—as much as I ever did in earlier life. I enjoy boys; I love to see them at play, and when permitted to join them I enter into the plans and purposes of young people with zest.'

"He was serious then, but he becomes more serious.

"'I find myself, I do believe, this day more willing to live and more willing to die than I ever did in any day before. I find myself concerned less with the past and less with the future than I ever was before. I have the abiding conviction that the best of all things is for me to live this day without stop, without haste, with all my power of doing and of enjoying the things which God has given me. I have no intention ever to retire. Often, very, very weary, I think that if a syndicate were to offer me ten millions of dollars to take care of me the rest of my life, provided I would promise never again to speak in public, never again to make an engagement, never again to take an appointment, and to resign now all the offices I hold in church, in school, and in society, I would refuse the ten millions, although I may not have ten months, or even ten days, to live. . . . I sit in my study and talk to my heart and dictate these lines, and feel that I am approaching the experience of the Apostle Paul: "For me to live is Christ, and to die is gain." . . . Being assured of the immortality of my spirit because of my spiritual alliance with him, I have ceased to pray to be delivered from sudden death, which may be a blessing.'

"Five days after having placed the book in the hand of his daughter his own suddenly refused to write. It was the beginning of the end. He then understood the true Christian theory of life, earnestly willing to live, earnestly willing to die, trustfully leaving it to him in whose hands, in the high and holy sense, are the issues of life and death.

"Is a funeral eulogium in harmony with the spirit of Christianity? If it is not, at this moment silence becomes us. Not only is it in harmony with the spirit of Christianity, but that spirit will pardon forgetfulness of the infirmities of those whom we know to have been true to it. Did not the friends of Dorcas assemble and speak of the wondrous work she had done? Did not St. Paul eulogize his friends who had passed away? Are there not many passages in the New Testament which are unqualified eulogiums of the departed? But excess or indiscriminate praise,—to predicate of a person qualities he never possessed, and declare him a model in realms of thought and action which he never penetrated,—this is to degrade the memory of the deceased and to obscure that which the Holy Word characterizes thus: 'The memory of the just is blessed.'

" Dr. Deems was the son and the grandson of a minister of the gospel. The influence of a profession where health and vigor are undisturbed by excess is often seen in descendants to the third and even the tenth generation. He was born with a susceptibility for that kind of excitement without which oratory is impossible. Nature qualified him for peculiar success in any department in which effectiveness depends upon quick response to the changing moods of an audience and upon the adaptive facility which enables one, whatever the grade of intellect to which he speaks, to rise or to sink, not in moral tone, but in exquisite sensitiveness to the lights and shades of thought and expression in simplicity or complexity, according to the reflex influence which every word elicits from the assembly which he addresses. Without the call to the ministry he whose virtues we endeavor to portray this day might have made a lawyer of extraordinary success or a popular orator in the political world. He could lift the hand from the head of the sorrowing boy who wept because he should see his mother's face no more, and place it warm and sympathetic in the hand of the bride on her wedding-day. And quickly as he could turn from one to the other the appropriate word would flow to the lip, the tear to the eye. Those who knew not the man would say, 'This is superficial; such fluctuations of feeling are impossible.' But he lived in the atmosphere of sympathy. He loved every human being; therefore such transitions would ever move as rapidly as his thought, feeling, and sense could correspond to the necessity. He was a scientist—not as an expert, but as a lover and student. He was once professor of natural science in an important college, and succeeded admirably therein. But at the end of one year he said, 'There is not sufficient play for my emotions here. Oftentimes I wish to trace the wonders of God in the natural world and declare that there only a part of the Deity is known, and point to Christ, in whom the whole Deity is known.' ' But,' he said, ' I am not employed for that,' and so he resumed the ministry.

" He was a journalist, but his efforts were all in the realm of morality and patriotism and good things. He would have been out of place upon some papers and magazines; would have embarrassed greatly the management, and would have needed constant supervision. Everything that he did in the department of education was to promote Christian education. He appreciated highly the State. He regarded it as of great importance with respect to the higher education. He had no sympathy with one of his intimate friends who would restrict the education provided by the State to the elements, but placing upon individuals the necessity of gaining the higher education; but he believed that denominational education was essential to supplement the State, because it would be impossible to have a religious institution governed exclusively by the State, and it would be impossible to have a thoroughly effective Christian institution without a denominational center. Therefore he used his influence mightily to induce his friends to contribute largely to the establishment of great religious universities.

" As a lecturer he was unquestionably unique. Almost any good speaker can preach, especially if called unto that vocation. But to be able to preach and to lecture! He could preach as well as he could lecture, and to lecture until the whole assembly burst into peals of laughter or thunders of applause, and yet never utter a word which would in any degree militate against his influence or detract from it if he were to rise and begin a religious service before the same audience—to do that is an astonishing power, and that he possessed. When at his best on the lecture platform, without one word on the subject of religion he moved men in that direction. When from any cause he was less effective in the pulpit than usual there was still a deep undertone of power, which caused men to forget every departure from any particular canon of pulpit rhetoric or pulpit elocution.

"Graduated from an important institution of learning and afterward a professor, he rose triumphant above that formal adherence to the peculiarities or manners of professors, which has ruined so many persons of brilliant talent. The forthgoing of his personality was less obstructed than that of any public man probably in this metropolis. It was a peculiar charm. You felt it in the car, in the counting-room, as really as in the church. He was magnetic, with the magnetism of an honest man's personality coming out at the ends of his fingers, giving the peculiar vibration to his voice, sparkling in his eye. He may speak or be silent, but where he is it comes forth and is felt. Why consume time taken from many cares to say that such a man was a philanthropist? Without that all would have fallen away and he would have been simply one of those cheerful men who go to and fro. His presence would have delighted every one, but it would not have affected any one except as the song of one that singeth well or as the mere sound of a lute across the water in a quiet evening. Fraternity is one of the branches of philanthropy. There can be no fraternity without a philanthropic heart. Men without that may observe the etiquette of fraternity, but the soul is not there.

"He was a reformer who never lost either his head or his heart. Some lose their heads; they will die for a pin as quick as for a post, and all their days fritter away their efforts in attempting the unattainable and in denouncing all who do not attempt it with them. It was not so with him. Others lose their hearts, and they look upon one thing until it assumes proportions of unreal magnitude, and declare that their reform is more important even than the church of God. Not so with him. He loved institutions of different kinds. He had a sympathy with orders, but one of the most splendid passages that ever fell from his lips was this: ' No society, moral or philanthropic, purely of human origin, is to be compared with or substituted for the church of Jesus Christ. Nay,' said he, waxing eloquent, ' the best of them are at the nadir, while the church of the living God, founded by him and built by Jesus Christ, is at the zenith, and ever it will remain.' Yet this day a demonstration will be seen that he, with those noble views of the relation of purely human efforts to the church of Christ, was full of sympathy with the former while giving reverence and supreme devotion only to the latter.

"A peculiar question relating to the Civil War should not be passed unnoticed. He was an ardent Union man. His heart nearly broke when his State decided to secede, but his creed, with respect to his relations to the country, believed as conscientiously as it is possible for a man to believe anything, consisted of three requirements, in this order: his first duty is to his family ; his second duty is to his State ; his third duty is to the federal government. What man is there who observes that nearly every decision of the Supreme Court of the United States has a powerful dissenting minority, so that we expect to see as great men if not greater men than the propounder of an opinion declaring his mistake to be serious, contrary to history, and in its consequences awful, who will yet say that Dr. Deems, after his training, education, and environment, could not conscientiously believe that it was his duty to go with his State? But how went he with his State? To promote cruelty, perfidy, treachery? By no means. He gave his eldest son, and the boy was killed at Gettysburg in 1863. Had our friend been destitute of that spirit of philanthropy which overleaped all bounds, he, like some others, would never have communed with those who directly or indirectly robbed him of his son, his beloved son, his first-born. But no. He could recognize in us what he claimed for himself, and thus, coming in the spirit of fraternity, the spirit of a reunited country, to our city, he began the career which to attempt its description would be to insult the intelligence and the knowledge of those who are here to-day.

" He united the abstract and the concrete in a wonderful manner. Many philosophers are useless in private or public life. They are mere phantoms except in their libraries. Others have no philosophy and waste their days in detail. He was a philosopher in the breadth of his thought, but he promoted and he proposed practical things. He was the founder of the American Institute of Christian Philosophy and the editor of its organ, ' Christian Thought,' until his death, though for some time obliged to avail himself of the aid of a most valuable coadjutor, the Rev. Mr. Devins, who during all his sickness has conferred with him and brought forth the work so that those who read it find in each succeeding number something worthy of careful attention.

" He was without doubt a complacent man. There are those who misunderstand the relation of complacency to piety. They think that it is necessary for a person to declare himself a worm of the dust in order to have a hope in heaven. The artist may receive the congratulations of his friends ; nay, more, he may exhibit his work. The lawyer may be told of his extraordinary addresses at the bar, and it is perfectly proper. The merchant may be praised by a great assembly, who will look upon him as a kind of demigod, and none condemn either him or them. But if a Christian, if a minister, dare to show any complacency, many will say that he is a man of ' like passions ' with the world. And so the apostles declared they were when men undertook to worship them. David was one of the most complacent men that ever lived. They would be unworthy a place in the canon had they not expressed the same complete self-consciousness of his spirit.

"This book begins with a dedication to seventy men departed this life. [His book.] Were I to read these names tears would come to many an eye, for the sons and the grandsons are here. At the thought of a similar day in their experience to that experienced this day by these bereaved children, their attention would be distracted from the occasion of the hour. But it implies a species of complacency for a man to print seventy names of honored men among his friends; yet he earned their friendship by good deeds, kind words. It was right for him to be complacent. But in the depth of his soul he was most humble. Hear this prayer of his, side by side with one of his most complacent utterances:

"'Oh, nail it to thy cross,
  My wretched carnal pride,
Which glories in its rags and dross,
  And knows no wealth beside:
There let it surely die;
  But let my spirit be
Lifted, to sit with thee on high
  And sweet humility.'

"Such complacency is not degrading, but elevating. It is the complacency of Paul, who said when he came to die, 'I am now ready to be offered,' contrasted with the chief of sinners that he called himself all his life, 'and the time of my departure is at hand. There remains for me a crown of righteousness, which the Lord, the righteous judge, shall give me at that day.' Not a crown of humility, but a crown of justice in the economy of grace. So that the cry is, 'Thanks be to God for his unspeakable gift.'

"A long and terrible fight was that in the sick-room. A

man who was never sick, who divided his life into decades after he was sixty, and gave ten years to the need of the American Institute and proposed to give ten years more to a certain subject upon which he conversed with his friends, and then, fancying that he might live longer, said, 'Should I live still longer, I hope to start another enterprise'—this man eleven long months in his sick-room! Still he was the pastor of a church. How did the good man meet his fate?

"There is a tendency on the part of friends to make everything beautiful in the dying Christian. Our power of discernment fails when our friends are so helpless that they cannot speak for themselves, and so it would be suitable to breathe a prayer to almighty God that no exaggeration in the eulogist should here check the flow of respect, admiration, and even veneration.

"His industry never flagged. He had his office desk brought to his home in order that he might work in his accustomed way when he was barely able to sit up. The day before his final attack he sat at his desk arranging his papers and laying out his correspondence for the following day; and much, if not most, of his correspondence was helpful, and scarce any of it ever asked for help—never for himself.

"His appreciative disposition shone out beautifully, always, through his manifold gratitude for the service of those of least kindred to him. No man ever loved his grandchildren more than he. He spoke of them as 'my little host of grandchildren.' Truly he was blessed in them. His physician never left his bedside, so I am informed by those who would not misrepresent, without his blessing him, and he would sometimes, when he could not speak, kiss the hand of his faithful nurse for some act of thoughtful attention.

"His patience never failed. He uttered no word, made no sign of complaint, but in hours of extremest affliction, though his great physical depression often affected the flow of spirits, he said over and over again, 'He doeth all things well.'

"His interest in all things touching the world was keen to the very last. His first inquiry of young men who came to see him was, 'Tell me the news.' His patriotism lost none of its ardor, even during his last sickness. When Congress was convened in extra session he said the day it met, 'Our President! what a responsibility! I pray for him to-day.' His humor was never diminished by either suffering or helplessness. He was unable to speak. It was a great day in that house when he could repeat a whole sentence, and once he was so pleased that he repeated it again and smiled when his family applauded him as though he were receiving the applause of an audience. How pathetic! One day, when it was almost impossible for him to articulate, he made a great effort and said, 'Well, well! I am not on speaking terms with my friends.' Think what being on speaking terms with them had meant for him so many years. Every Sunday but three during his entire sickness he selected and sent to this congregation a scriptural text for their comfort and spiritual upbuilding. His trust in God sustained him to the uttermost. Throughout his sickness his testimony was, 'My faith holds out,' and just before consciousness failed he said, 'At evening time there is light.'

"I almost tremble to say to you that a little while before the last attack he looked at the clock, unable to speak, looked at his son-in-law, who with his wife and their children ministered to him through these months, and significantly shook his head, which was interpreted to mean that he would do well to stay. He looked at her who then responded to that homely but homeful word 'wife.' He gazed so wistfully, and then he looked at his son-in-law so intelligently, and at his daughter so significantly, that they could not but gather his meaning to be, 'Will you take care of her?' They assured him that needed no assurance, and a sweet smile of satisfaction rested upon his face. . . .

"These friends need no commiserating words from me. In the deep sea of their grief that they shall see his face no more they could not bear congratulatory words. He renounced in dying what he would have been so glad to have done for you first. You could smile upon him and read to him and do so much for him. How he longed to be able to do it for you! Let at least this gleam of comfort shine upon you in your dark- ness while you try, perhaps in vain, to behold the light this day of a father's face (yet I would fain hope that you possess the spiritual experience and power which will enable you to count his body among the things that are seen, but his spirit among the things that are not seen, and thus triumph over the afflic- tion of the hour); but as a faint gleam of light remember that you had the privilege of comforting him in the hour and the extremity of death." *

III

MEMORIALS

The breadth of Dr. Deems's sympathies, and the hold on men's respect and affection which he had gained while living, were made evident after his decease not only by the resolutions of various societies and institutions already referred to, but also by the memorial services which were held in different parts of the land and by the erection of the Deems Memorial Chapel.

On the very day of the funeral a service in commemoration of Dr. Deems was conducted in the chapel of the University of North Carolina, at Chapel Hill, when President George T. Winston, at whose suggestion it was held, presided. A memorial service was held in the Church of the Strangers on December 14, 1893, and still another in the auditorium of Prohibition Park, Staten Island, on Sunday afternoon, June 14,

* The above extract is from the " Memorial Number of Christian Thought," February, 1894.

1896. The dedication of the Deems Memorial Chapel occurred at Prohibition Park, Staten Island, on Sunday, May 24, 1896. This beautiful chapel was erected to Dr. Deems's memory by the members of the Prohibition Park Young People's Society of Christian Endeavor.

The most important of the memorial services was that which was held in the Church of the Strangers on December 14, 1893, about one month after Dr. Deems's death. The Rev. Joseph Merlin Hodson, D.D., acting pastor at the time, presided.* After the singing of the hymn "Abide with me," Chancellor MacCracken, of the University of the City of New York, read the Scriptures. Bishop Fowler, of the Methodist Church, then offered prayer. Brief addresses, full of respect, tenderness, and affection for Dr. Deems, were made by the Rev. Drs. Thomas Armitage, of the Baptist Church, and Amory H. Bradford, pastor of the First Congregational Church, Montclair, N. J., successor to Dr. Deems as president of the American Institute of Christian Philosophy, Ex-Mayor Abram S. Hewitt, and Mr. Marion J. Verdery, a son-in-law of Dr. Deems. This deeply interesting service was closed appropriately by the singing of Dr. Deems's comforting and inspiring hymn, "The light is at the end."

* A few months later the Rev. Dr. Hodson became pastor of the Fordham Heights Reformed Dutch Church. After having had their pulpit supplied by various clergymen for over two years, the Church of the Strangers finally gave a hearty call to the Rev. D. Asa Blackburn, pastor of the Westminster Presbyterian Church, Charleston, S. C., to become their pastor. He accepted the call, was installed May 5, 1895, and under his earnest and able ministrations the church is to-day a living, growing power for good in New York City.

Lightning Source UK Ltd.
Milton Keynes UK
UKHW012229110219
337137UK00006B/1213/P